Guide to World Literature

Center for Teaching Library
The Westminster Schools
1424 West Paces Ferry Road, N.W.
Atlanta, Georgia 30327

Guide to World Literature

New Edition

Warren Carrier, Editor
University of Wisconsin—Platteville

Kenneth A. Oliver, Associate Editor
Occidental College, Los Angeles

Based upon the original work
by Robert O'Neal

National Council of Teachers of English
1111 Kenyon Road, Urbana, Illinois 61801

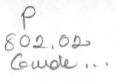

gift — D. Cleghorn 9/86

P
802.02
Guide ...

Grateful acknowledgement is made for permission to reprint the following material: Lyric poetry from *The Prose and Poetry of Henrich Heine,* © Citadel Press, New York, 1969. Lines from the *Rubāiyāt* by Omar Khayyām, © Doubleday Publishing Company. Lines from *Reading Modern Poetry* by Paul Engle and Warren Carrier, © 1955, 1968 by Scott, Foresman and Company. Reprinted by permission. Poetry from *The Interior Landscape, Love Poems from a Classical Tamil Anthology,* translated by A. K. Ramanujan, © Indiana University Press. Cover photo courtesy of the National Aeronautics and Space Administration: Apollo 11 view of the Earth taken by Neil Armstrong, Michael Collins, and Edwin Aldrin, Jr. on July 17, 1969.

Staff Editors: Barbara Davis, Duncan Streeter

Book Design: Tom Kovacs, interior; V. Martin, cover

NCTE Stock Number 19492

It is the policy of NCTE in its journals and other publications to provide a forum for the open discussion of ideas concerning the content and the teaching of English and the language arts. Publicity accorded to any particular point of view does not imply endorsement by the Executive Committee, the Board of Directors, or the membership at large, except in announcements of policy where such endorsement is clearly specified.

Library of Contress Cataloging in Publication Data

National Council of Teachers of English.
   Guide to world literature.

   Bibliography: p.
   Includes index.
   1. Literature—Stories, plots, etc.   2. Literature —Outlines, syllabi, etc.   I. Carrier, Warren Pendleton. II. Oliver, Kenneth A.   III. O'Neal, Robert, 1914– Teachers' guide to world literature for the high school. IV. Title.
PN44.N37 1980   802'.02   80-15093
ISBN 0-8141-1949-2

iv

Contents

Preface

The original edition of the *Teacher's Guide to World Literature* was undertaken as a monumental task by Robert O'Neal and published by the National Council of Teachers of English in 1966. It was intended to encourage reading beyond the traditional English and American texts by making available a useful resource in an area in which few teachers had adequate preparation. The purpose of extending student reading beyond works written in English was obvious: to make students aware of other cultures and at the same time to bring them to understand the universality of the human character and condition. The *Guide* did not provide instant expertise. It did, however, offer, as the title suggests, guidance in what was then a largely unknown field for many.

Today, more than a decade later, world literature in translation is an accepted field of study from high school through college. There can be little doubt that the *Guide* has furnished some impetus in that development.

It became increasingly clear to the Committee on Comparative and World Literature, as it followed the growth of interest in the field, that perspectives on world literature change and that new works appear clamoring for attention; a revision of the *Guide* would be required. Several years ago, therefore, the Committee requested and received permission from the Council to undertake this task.

The new *Guide to World Literature* relies heavily on the pioneer work of Robert O'Neal, retaining, in fact, a substantial number of entries more or less as he wrote them. Some entries have been dropped because the importance of certain writers has diminished or because the works of other writers now appear to have greater salience. The limited section on English and American writers has been eliminated altogether, since these authors are generally taught in British or American literature courses. A substantial number of African and Asian writers have been added because interest in these literatures has grown over the past ten years and because translations have become more available. Finally, the target audience for the *Guide* has been expanded to include college students, especially those in the first two years and those in the community colleges—which also developed substantially during the past decade. Even this expansion, however, cannot alter the fact that the *Guide* is not all-inclusive; certain of the most widely known works have been omitted in favor of lesser known titles.

A significant feature of the original edition which was retained and in some cases expanded is the "comparative comment." The critical stance is similar, with thematic and generic comments as well as historical observations. A bibliography is provided.

A major difference between the first and the revised editions is that the latter was done by committee. It has taken an entire committee to update what Robert O'Neal originally and singlehandedly wrought.

Guide to World Literature

Introduction

The *Guide to World Literature* provides a unique resource for creating a course of literature, suggesting as it does individual works that may be used to extend the limits of textbook anthologies. Its arrangement is alphabetical by author, avoiding national historical progressions and classification by genre, although a separate index by title is provided. The *Guide* suggests a view of literature which looks to the universal experiences reflected in literature. As we move into multi-national economic, ecological, and cultural enterprises and inter-dependencies, it becomes increasingly important for students to recognize national similarities and differences, but above all to recognize our common bond, our common lot. A study of world literature contributes much to an appreciation and understanding of the heritage we share.

"Give me something contemporary, something relevant to my life!" is often the cry of students, yet, Murasaki, the eleventh century Japanese novelist, is applauded in critical circles for his "modernity." Writers of the past can be our contemporaries, for in literature the past is always in the present as well as a part of history. And Murasaki's Shining Prince can be our companion in the twentieth century as he was to the Japanese in the eleventh century. Literature, in brief, frees us from a linear view of time, suggesting as it does other concepts of time—that all exists simultaneously or that time is cyclical.

The Thematic Approach

The thematic approach provides the best opportunity to foster an interest in literature and literary values and a concern for enduring and changing human values. At the same time, the teacher has the opportunity with each new work to raise the student's cultural and historical awareness. The number of themes is endless, of course: love, injustice, oppression, grief, conflict, transience, separation, war. Consider, for example, the theme of oppression. It may be personal oppression, the Korean mother-in-law's treatment of her daughter-in-law, or group oppression, the exploitation of one nation by another, or an interweaving of the two. Such a theme may be explored by selecting, for example, Anne Frank's *The Diary of a Young Girl* (the Nazi occupation of the Netherlands during World War II); Richard Kim's *Lost Names* (the Japanese annexation of Korea in this century); Kartini's *Letters of a Javanese Princess* (the Dutch colonization of Java—now Indonesia). These works have in common young people seeking a personal identity during a period when their countries are dominated by outside powers.

Individual and cultural differences may be explored by examining time. Jay Gatsby in Scott Fitzgerald's *The Great Gatsby* believes he can recapture time, that time can be made to stand still. In contrast, Shingo, the hero in the Japanese work *The Sound of the Mountain* by Yasunari Kawabata, is keenly aware of the passing of time; however, the reader's response to Gatsby and Shingo is similar. The transience of time is explored by the French writer Colette in *My Mother's House* and in *Sido,* by the Japanese writer Murasaki in *The Tale of Genji,* and by the American writer Willa Cather in *Lucy Gayheart.* These three writers in the works mentioned may also be compared for their treatment of the theme of love.

Just as nationality, historical progression, and context are secondary to a thematic approach, so is genre. Indeed, there may be no better way to teach the forms of literature than to introduce several genres which treat the same theme. The discussion of genre in connection with theme provides an excellent opportunity to compare literary effect and to consider why one form may be better suited to a particular content or emotion than another. For example, the theme of war: the eighth-century satire of militarism by the Chinese poet Po Chü-i, "The Old Man with the Broken Arm"; Stephen Crane's novel *The Red Badge of Courage;* the sixteenth-century Vietnamese poems, "On War" by Phung Khac Khoan, "On the War-Scattered Refugees" by Pham Nguyen Du, and "Lament of a Warrior's Wife" by Dang Tran Con, and the twentieth-century Vietnamese poem, "Who Am I?" by Tru Vu; Remarque's novel *All Quiet on the Western Front*—all these view war as an anti-human experience. On the other hand, epics from Greek and Hindi literature and poems from Jamil extol war or at least see military service as a duty. Works from different genres may be selected to reflect the contrasting views and experiences of several cultures and from a number of historical periods.

Close to the theme of war is death, the ultimate human experience. There is the beautiful death of the grandfather in Younghill Kang's *The Grass Roof,* the sorrowing death of the father in Mirok Li's *The Yalu Flows,* the tragic death of the daughter of the Indian poet Nirala, the grief for all transient things in Wen-ti Wei's poem, from the Chinese, "On the Death of His Father." Writers from different times, writing in different languages, choosing different genres to comment on an experience shared by all.

A thematic approach need not—indeed should not—neglect the aesthetics of literature. Within the thematic discussion, literature from different cultures may be analyzed according to principles of form and structure. For example, students may learn that one structure of the novel can be compared to the unwinding of a scroll, plotless but with a unifying aura, a lingering effect, a *yoin,* and that this structure can be found in Japanese fiction from the eleventh century as well as in contemporary fiction. Similarly, students may learn that emotions as large as those expressed in a sonnet or an epic can be expressed in the tightly compressed *haiku.*

Teaching works thematically is perhaps the most challenging of approaches but also the most rewarding for students and teachers. Its advantage is that it—above all other approaches—nourishes *mono no aware,* a Japanese aesthetic and moral principle, which, briefly, means to understand others. A thematic approach to literature, by nourishing *mono no aware,* can, as the Japanese critic Norinaga Motoori wrote in the eighteenth century, "show how weak and foolish men really are and therefore how necessary it is for them to understand, sympathize and help each other." A study of world literature by theme enlarges our aesthetic and emotional sympathies, which, as Walter Pater has told us, is what all great literature should do.

The Generic Approach

The word *genre* comes to us through French from the Latin *GENus, GENERis,* meaning "kind" or "type," and we use it to distinguish literary forms one from another. The basic genres might be identified as epic (long poetic narrative), novel (long prose narrative), drama, and poem. Each of these may be subdivided. A subdivision of epic is the mock epic (Pope's "Rape of the Lock"). Drama includes tragedy and comedy, but also, especially in recent decades, dramatic works which combine qualities of these two or in other ways defy classification. Poetry may be narrative (Browning's poetic mono-logues) or lyric, and these may be further divided. Scott's *Lady of the Lake,* while poetic in form, resembles a novel in scope, and the ballad is a short folk-narrative in verse. The ode (Anacreontic, Keatsian, etc.), the sonnet, the *haiku* are further subdivisions. Prose narratives include many forms: the novel, the saga, and the pastoral are relatively long forms; the novella, the short story, the tale, the fable and the parable are successively shorter, in general. The essay, formal or personal, is yet another prose form.

Genres probably should not be defined with great precision, for the lines between them are often blurred. For instance, a novel, a novella, and a short story can in a general way be distinguished as follows: the novel is a long prose narrative that embraces few to many characters, one or more of whom are thoroughly developed so that we see them in depth, growing or changing. A novel probably will have one or more subplots; in other words, its action is usually complex. A novella is generally shorter and centers on one main character or episode. That character is often developed in considerable depth, and the action is usually simple, that is, within a single plot. The short story typically deals with a single episode; indeed, it is sometimes merely a skillfully developed anecdote. It rarely shows character in depth, though it may, as in de Maupassant's stories, lay bare certain psychological facets of character. In short stories the narrative is frequently a build-up for the conclusion, which may be a surprise ending (as in O. Henry) or a foreseen conclusion that is nevertheless effective (as in Chekhov's "The Kiss"). Other stories may be more subtle and lead simply to a new perception of character or circumstance.

This three-way division of prose narratives is useful at times, but any effort to draw exact lines is unprofitable. Every generic term is a category, a name ready to be applied to any new work that seems appropriate for it, whether in every way or in any way. Thus, because the epic, through such works as the *Iliad,* the *Odyssey,* the *Aeneid,* the *Nibelungenlied,* and the *Ramayana,* has a reputation for presenting a sweeping view of a culture or an era or a people, critics tend to call a novel with any kind of large sweep "an epic." (Perhaps it would be better to speak of such a work as "a novel with epic proportions.")

One of the problems with genre identification is that writers with new vision or with an urge to experiment with form come onto the literary scene rather frequently. Drama was once comfortably divided into tragedy and comedy, labels which have long since proved inadequate. Nevertheless, we can use the understanding of the tragic and the comic which we have acquired through the study of older drama in discussing plays which are both or neither. There are parallel problems with prose narratives. And we may ask similar questions about poetry. Some pieces presented in uneven lines would if written as paragraphs scarcely be suspected of poetic intent. Is poetry to be equated with form? On the other hand, is it possible that form is irrelevant to poetry?

Any notion that leads students to think about how literature works, the effects it achieves and how it achieves them, is useful. When an author selects a genre to work in, choosing one kind of presentation over others, in effect some potentials of the material are enhanced and limited or others removed. What techniques are central to each genre? What techniques are foreclosed by selecting this genre and not that? For example, what does Kafka achieve in "Metamorphosis" that he could not have done in an essay? Or in a play? Is there anything in the story that could not have been done on the stage? Would a play be as effective as a poetic narrative? Why?

Is the movie also a literary genre? When a novel is adapted to film, is change inevitable? Does the reader of a novel have the same relationship to the work as the viewer does to a stage drama or to a movie? Anatole France held that the audience at a theater has a smaller creative role than the reader of a play or of a novel. Is this true?

In short, using genre as a teaching device involves questions about how a given genre works, and that includes questions about how the reader becomes involved. And since involvement of the reader or viewer is a large part of the function of literature, genre is important, even though lines between genres are often blurred.

The Historical and Comparative Approach

"Times change, and we change with them." ("Tempora mutantur, nos et mutamur in illis," Lothair I, German emperor, 795-855.)

"The more it changes, the more it stays the same." ("Plus ça change, plus c'est la même chose." French proverb.)

For the teacher of literature both sayings are true. We see Achilles and Hector with helmet, spear, sword, and shield on the dusty battlefield as representatives of a way of living—and dying—far different from our own. Yet we also recognize in their feelings and values a reflection of ourselves, or of what we would like to be, or of what we recognize in others around us. The external, more or less objective conditions of life; the qualitative human emotions and values; the problems, judgments, decisions, consequences—these are inevitable factors in life and, therefore, in literature. They are not all there is to literature: techniques, texture, nuances—what Sainte-Beuve called the *faculté maîtresse* of the writer, distinguishing personal qualities—are essential. But the conditions, the qualitative elements, the problems, judgments, decisions, and consequences are peculiarly responsive to the cultural environment.

Suppose you had just discovered and read an excitingly good story. The manuscript is obviously not contemporary, but no date is given, no author identified. You don't know whether the story is an original or a translation. How would you go about dating it? Is it classical Greek? Roman? Medieval? Renaissance? Neoclassical? Romantic? Late nineteenth century? Twentieth century? Names might give you a clue. Evidence of the way normal lives were lived would at least eliminate some possibilities, if only in terms of how primitive conditions were; problems, judgments, decisions and consequences would probably help. With enough knowledge of such factors, a moderately accurate date might well be assigned. Alas, we rarely have all the pertinent knowledge.

But reverse the problem. We know the date of a work; now we want to use the story to find out what we can about life in the period represented.

Suppose *Don Quixote* were the only evidence we had of life in Spain in the late sixteenth century. It would come as no surprise that idealists ready to practice their ideals were few and that most people were more concerned with immediate, practical matters. But what was the nature of the ideals? What were the facts and conditions of life for the general citizen? What were the material things with and among which life was lived? Was life more likely to be rural or urban? Were there normal modes of behavior? What kinds of judgments were made? Were the consequences of acts the same as those we would expect today?

Take up a work from another period—say E. T. A. Hoffmann's marvelous Romantic fantasy, "The Golden Flower Pot," in which the student Anselmus falls in love with a blue-eyed snake and copies manuscripts in strange writing for a man who is also a salamander. We again find idealists and realists. Has idealism changed since *Don Quixote?* Has realism changed? Does the urban-rural balance remain the same? Are people's real interests the same? Has the quality of imagination changed? the quality of reason? the relationship between acts or decisions and consequences? the material things with and among which life is lived?

Try the same kind of questioning with Flaubert's *Madame Bovary,* Molière's *Tartuffe,* Melville's *Moby Dick,* and Mark Twain's *Tom Sawyer.*

We must—and do—recognize that every writer is unique; all have their own *faculté maîtresse.* But does this quality negate a writer's value as a representative of an age or lessen the usefulness of looking at the work as a way of understanding a period in history? In the narrowest sense, perhaps; there are few Don Quixotes in this world—none at all, except in imagination. Yet he represents something within each of us, and he represents that human impulse as only a man of the Spanish Renaissance could do. There are few students like Anselmus, yet most of us share some of his qualities. And he and his story could come only from the German Romantic age. For as Anatole France wrote in his *La Vie Littéraire (My Literary Life):*

> The great periods of art . . . were organic. Not everything in them was left to the individual. Man is a small thing, even a great man, when he is alone. We do not adequately recognize that a writer, though he may be very original, borrows more than he invents. The language which he speaks does not belong to him; the form in which he pours his art, be it ode, comedy, tale, was not created by him; he does not possess within himself either his syntax or his prosody. His very thoughts have been breathed into him from all sides. He has received the colors; he has brought to them only the nuances, which indeed, I know, are infinitely precious. Let us be wise enough to recognize: Our works are far from being entirely our own. They grow in us, but their roots are everywhere in the nourishing soil.

Perhaps we might modify France's language and say that every writer inherits a tradition—and the reactions of contemporaries and of the slightly older generation of teachers and writers to that tradition. For times do change and we do change with them, sometimes dramatically, sometimes more gradually. The change from the Hebraic world to the Greek world was dramatic: from a God-centered world to one that focused on humans and the human intellect. The Romans of the centuries immediately before and after Christ emphasized the role of the state and represented yet another sharp change. Christianity moved to combine elements of all three world views, and (after its first dramatic impact) developed gradually throughout the Middle Ages. It is still in the process of change, having proved to be remarkably capable of adaptation to social, political, and cultural factors. The medieval age was marked by Church, Castle, and Cottage—the divine Lord, the earthly lord, and the peasant. It was also the age of three loyalties: to God, to one's overlord, and to one's idealized lady. But these loyalties applied to chivalric figures, not (especially the last one) to the common man. Still another set of unifying ideals existed for the Middle Ages: one God, one state or empire, and one language (Latin).

The Renaissance—"rebirth"—was a natural consequence of the failure of the Middle Ages to achieve a "one-world" ideal. People turned again to their own resources and to local governments and languages. In the Middle Ages they had worked hard to rationalize a preconceived answer. Now they said, in effect: Let us begin with whatever premise we can justify, think logically, clearly, freely, and see where the process takes us. And this new freedom was reflected in art, in philosophy, in literature. Freed from the necessity of accepting the earth as the center of creation, people glimpsed a new view of the universe. Freed from the concept of a unified state, they were ready to accept what the geography of the world had to offer. The Vikings had discovered America too early; the closed-world of the Middle Ages had not been interested. When Columbus discovered it, Europeans were ready to accept and explore it—and growing populations needed its living room and resources. The Renaissance, then, was an age of rapidly developing humanistic interests and, as the Reformation proved, of readiness to let religion grow away from a controlled center toward varied humanistic interests.

This virtual explosion of interests led to fragmentation and to a new need for order. French Neoclassicism, which became the center of a new and closely defined order, was a major response to that need. A closely knit state was formed under the leadership of Richelieu. Academies of notables dictated standards for language (French, of course), the arts, and good taste in general. French Neoclassicism in turn strongly influenced the European Age of Reason, and the human definition became increasingly determined by the rational faculty. The demands of the social structure rose, and the individual declined in importance.

Romanticism came in reaction. Creative genius had never been limited to the rich and powerful. Reason alone had never really been enough, although it had been regarded as the supreme capacity of man. Prior to romanticism the human faculties had been seen as a pyramid, with reason enthroned at the top, served by—and controlling—the emotions, the senses, the imagination and the intuition, which formed the four sides of the pyramid. The romanticists, on the other hand, saw the human faculties as a circle made up of segments representing reason, the emotions, the senses, imagination and intuition. Any one of the five might dominate at a given time. Moreover, variable dominance represented a proper, natural state of affairs. Romanticism was not anti-rational. All of the romanticists used reason and used it well at appropriate times and in appropriate ways. But, as Rousseau, Goethe, E. T. A. Hoffmann, Keats, Pushkin and many others demonstrated, the senses do—and should—dominate at times, as should the imagination or the intuition at others. The ideal was for all faculties to operate simultaneously in whatever balance the situation called for. These two major shifts in perspective—from a social to an individual orientation, from a reason-dominated to a variably balanced, all-faculty orientation—have had a gigantic impact on the modern world, an impact which is still being felt and to which western man is still adjusting. Romanticism might well be called the great revolution of the modern world.

After the first great impact of romanticism came a wide range of literary movements: realism, naturalism, impressionism, symbolism, to name only the most important. Yet equally important was a general trend toward experimentalism. Every age has sought to see the world "as it really is." Every literary movement has been, in its major intent, realistic—an effort to get at the real, the true, the genuine nature of what it means to live this life on this earth. The Age of Reason (the Enlightenment) tried to do it through logic—and through satire which exposed the illogical. Romanticism centered on experience in all of its aspects but emphasized the individual and the internal experience. Realism (the literary movement) accepted much of what romanticists had done but focused on the visible, social picture and—because it was more dramatic and needed correction—on the unhappy, "gutter" aspects of life. Not surprisingly, realists gave more importance to urban life than had the romanticists. The Industrial Revolution, already begun and certainly not yet ended in our day, contributed to this emphasis. Naturalism drew from the growth of science, exploring the effects of heredity and environment while joining the realists in choice of subject matter. Impressionism and symbolism investigated the internal experience: the impressionists emphasized the distinctive way in which individuals meet experience; the symbolists emphasized the nuances of personal experience.

The literary movements mentioned after the Romantic Era and such others as the Pre-Raphaelites in England, the Imagists and Parnassians in France, and the Expressionists in Germany reflected a strong interest in finding new means of capturing the essence of experience. Antoine, for example, established a "free theater" *(théâtre libre)* in Paris in which he presented dramas which he felt had artistic merit but which could not be presented to the traditional theater. Some performances were long (as long as fifteen hours), some were short (as short as about one minute). Subjects that were taboo because of social inhibitions or political views were given a showing. Fantasy, symbolism, dialect were presented. His theater was so successful that a similar one (Die Freie Bühne) opened in Berlin, and several of Ibsen's plays were first presented there. This experimental trend continued into the twentieth century, with writers such as Joyce, Kafka, Gertrude Stein, and e. e. cummings. Thomas Mann and Marcel Proust seem at first glance to be relatively traditional writers, yet their novels explored life in new and penetrating ways. The list of writers could go on with a corresponding range of successful efforts to find new ways of searching the breadth and depth of human experience.

This survey highlights only what one reader of Western literature sees as major touchstones of successive periods and movements. Experts on any one age would add much more, and each would shift the emphasis in some degree. The point is that Anatole France was right: every age is organic, even though within an age all writers have their own *faculté maîtresse.*

In order to present literature as the expression of an age or a movement, it is necessary to have some notion of the organic nature of that age. It is desirable also to introduce several works from that period in order to compare the assumptions of their authors and to discover what each has to say or imply about the lives and experiences each portrays. It is obviously helpful to have some knowledge of history, philosophy, and culture in general, but a fair sense of the quality of an age actually emerges as one reads the literature. Finally, it is particularly useful for a teacher to have a notion of the age which preceded the one being taught. Thus an understanding of the Age of Reason helps us to sense the excitement of new ideas as Romanticism emerges.

It is not my intent to suggest that only the expert in literary history should teach literature in terms of historical perspective. Not even the lifetime student of a single period in the literature of one language comes to know all there is to know about that period. Indeed, it may be absolutely asserted that the scholar who devotes attention so narrowly never acquires the richest knowledge of that particular literature, for literary expression does not grow in a vacuum. The past is present in every age, and movements draw inevitably from contemporary writers in other lands and other languages. "No man is an island"; no movement is an isolated phenomenon. Romanticism, for example, has major roots in France, Germany, and England; to know all three variants is to know any one of them better than would be otherwise possible. American Romanticism drew upon all three and added dimensions from its own new and expanding culture.

But there must be a beginning if there is to be growth. A beginning is made when one reads a single work with even the most naive awareness that it somehow represents an age as well as an author. That first work is enriched when it is compared with a second from the same period. As more works are read and analyzed for ideas, attitudes, and assumptions, the awareness of an age begins and a sense of historical perspective grows. When works from a second age are added and compared with the others, the perspective is enlarged, and both ages take on added richness. One teacher assigning ten or twenty short, easy works can make a valuable beginning, one that makes the next teacher's efforts both easier and more effective. A historical, comparative approach can be, for teacher and students alike, an interesting, even an exciting approach to literature and to an understanding of the developing human consciousness which is, after all, what literature is all about.

Comparative Reviews

Abé, Kobo. THE WOMAN IN THE DUNES (SUNA NO ONNA). 1962. Novel. Japanese.

Author: Kobo Abé (1924–   ) was born in Tokyo and brought up in Manchuria. As a young man, Abé was interested in mathematics and insect collecting. He read Poe, Dostoevski, Nietzsche, Heidegger, Jaspers, and Kafka. In 1951 he received the Akutagawa literary prize and in 1962 the Yomiuri Prize. Teshigahara based an art film on *The Woman in the Dunes,* which was shown at the International Film Festival in Cannes and has received international acclaim as a modern film classic. Kobo Abé is essentially a novelist of the faceless modern person who doubts his own existence or reality. Other works available in English translation include *The Face of Another* and *The Ruined Map.*

Work: The central character is a teacher, a solitary person, alienated from society. He goes on a holiday to collect insects and finds lodging in the home of a woman who lives alone at the bottom of a large sand pit. He gradually perceives that he is trapped in this pit but grows to recognize that life there is no more of a trap than "reality." He thinks:

> It only happened in novels or movies that summer was filled with dazzling sun. What existed in reality were humble, small-town Sundays . . . a man taking his snooze under the political columns of a newspaper, enveloped in gunsmoke . . . canned juices and thermos jugs with magnetized caps . . . boats for hire, fifty cents an hour . . . queue up here . . . roaming beaches with the leaden scum of dead fish . . . and then, at the end, a jam-packed trolley rickety with fatigue.

When the possibility for escape comes, he climbs out of the pit, after establishing that the ladder that has been placed down is not an illusion. Once out, to whom can he tell his story? He climbs back down the ladder into the pit, believing that the ladder will remain and that he is only putting off his escape.

Comparative: This work might be read with Kafka's *The Trial* and Camus's *The Stranger* for comparisons of concepts of freedom and of a man's relationship to society and nature. For a study of alienation in contemporary society, the work could also be compared with *Death in Delhi,* the collection of short stories translated from the Hindi by Gordon Roadarmel.

Achebe, Chinua. THINGS FALL APART. 1958. Novel. Nigerian.

Author: Chinua Achebe (1930–   ) was born in Nigeria and is recognized today as one of Africa's most distinguished educators and writers. He received his education at Government College, Umuahia, and later at University College, Ibadan, where he received a full degree. He has been a producer for the Nigerian Broadcasting Corporation and was the founding editor of the Heinemann African Writers Series. He has been awarded many honors on various occasions and has held both Rockefeller and UNESCO fellowships. He is the author of *No Longer at Ease* (1960), *Arrow of God* (1964), *A Man of the People* (1966), *Chike and the River* (1966), *Beware Soul-Brother and Other Poems* (1971), and *Girls at War* (1972).

Work: Things Fall Apart portrays life in Umuofia, an Ibo village. Through the story of Okonkwo, we observe his people, who believe in the gods of their ancestors and in ancestral worship, who engage in clandestine practices, and who, despite their daily menu of *foofoo* (kola nuts), take pride in physical prowess and dexterity. The wilderness setting among pythons and other wild beasts is appropriate to and even suggestive of the tragic events occurring in the life of Okonkwo, true representative of his tribe. He and his kinsmen are possessed by fears, among them, fear of failure and fear of weakness, and for Okonkwo "the fear of his father's contemptible life and shameful death." Fear permeates the novel and develops a significance similar to that of the chorus in Greek drama.

The story of Okonkwo's failures and successes is typical of the African villager and illustrates the influence of the white Christian missionaries on the Ibo culture. In a traditional wrestling match Okonkwo "throws the Cat," an action which dramatically raises him to an honorable position among his clansmen. Only the beating of one of his wives during Peace Week and his "inadvertent" killing of Ezcudu's sixteen-year-old son are obstacles to his attaining the highest title of achievement. This latter act causes him to be exiled from Umuofia for seven years. On his return, "things fall apart." His clansmen do not welcome him, for "the clan was like a lizard; if it lost its tail it soon grew another." Okonkwo understands the open conflict between his brothers and the white men who had come to bring Christianity, and seeks to avenge himself and the Ibos. He realizes that Christianity is becoming more powerful, while his own gods are diminishing in importance. Embittered, he murders a Christian messenger in revenge against an institution he feels is inhumanly inflicted upon him and his kinsmen. Okonkwo hangs himself, dying as nobly and courageously as he had lived. And, like the Ibo society, he to "falls apart."

Comparative: The theme of insurmountable fear in Achebe's novel may be compared with a similar theme in Richard Wright's *Native Son* and Eugene O'Neill's *Emperor Jones.* Hamlet's return from Wittenberg to find his world out of joint may be compared with Okonkwo's return to Umuofia as "things fall apart." In Shirley Jackson's short story "The Lottery," traditional forces prove too strong for the desperate individual who loses her life in opposition to them—another comparison with Okonkwo's destiny. Finally, as the young men in Turgenev's *Fathers and Sons* fail in their attempt to shape established Russian values into a pattern "nearer to the heart's desire," so does Okonkwo, dealing with tribal value systems, meet with failure.

Aeschylus. AGAMEMNON. 458 B.C. Drama. Greek.

Author: Most biographical information about Aeschylus is legendary, but we do know that he was born in 525 B.C. and took part in the wars between Greece and Persia. He probably fought at Marathon, Salamis, and Plataea. He witnessed the rise of Athens as the center of Greek civilization and played a major role in the development of Greek drama by making moral conflicts the subjects of his dramas. By adding a second actor and reducing the size and role of the chorus, he greatly increased the possibilities for dramatic action and characterization. He was also innovative in developing costume and stage design. Aeschylus wrote approximately ninety plays, of which seven survive, including the only extant trilogy, the *Oresteia.* He died in Sicily in 456 B.C.

Work: This first play of the *Oresteia* presents the return from Troy of Agamemnon, leader of the Greek armies, with his mistress, Cassandra, and their murder at the hands of his wife, Clytemnestra, and her lover, Aegisthus. Thus the play begins in the middle of the chain of murder and retribution that comprises the myth of the House of Atreus. Clytemnestra and Aegisthus both have a moral obligation, according to the primitive law of retribution and inherited blood-guilt, to commit these acts: Clytemnestra to avenge the death of her daughter Iphigenia and Aegisthus to avenge the murder of his father and brothers by Agamemnon's father, Atreus. According to the same code, however, their actions call for further vengeance to be wreaked in future generations, and the images of webs and nets suggest that all the characters are entangled in an inescapable trap. *Agamemnon,* then, portrays a barbaric pattern of inherited guilt that takes vengeance upon the innocent as well as the guilty and continues to demand further vengeance. The play forces us to ask how such a primitive system of justice may be remedied and how blind submission to Fate can be avoided. This question is answered in the remaining plays of the trilogy, *The Libation Bearers* and *The Eumenides,* which insist that only by assuming personal responsibility for their actions and by subjecting the demands of Fate to a more humane principle can the characters free themselves from the web which entangles them.

Comparative: The complete story of the *Oresteia* appears frequently in literature, although most treatments of the myth begin after Agamemnon's murder and focus on the conflicts within Clytemnestra's children, Electra and Orestes, the subject of the second play in the trilogy, *The Libation Bearers.* Seneca's *Agamemnon,* Alfieri's *Agamennone,* and the first part of

Eugene O'Neill's *Mourning Becomes Electra* do present the Agamemnon story. O'Neill, however, replaces Fate with Freudian psychology (which is for him just as inescapable) and updates the story to the American Civil War. There is also a brief retelling of the story in Homer's *Odyssey*, and the events leading up to this tragedy are treated in his *Iliad*, in Virgil's *Aeneid*, and in Seneca's *Thyestes*.

Aeschylus. THE LIBATION BEARERS (CHOEPHOROE). 458 B.C. Drama.
    Greek.

Author: See *Agamemnon*.

Work: This is the second part of the *Oresteia* trilogy and tells the story of the revenge of Agamemnon's children, Orestes and Electra, on Clytemnestra, their mother, and Aegisthus. As in *Agamemnon*, the play is concerned with the evolution from a primitive concept of justice and blind fate to a more civilized belief in personal responsibility for one's actions and in justice tempered by mercy.

Both Clytemnestra and Aegisthus could argue that according to primitive law they were guiltless for Agamemnon's death. But as the chorus here and in *Agamemnon* reminds us, the primitive code of justice demands further vengeance, and under such a system there can be no end to bloodletting. Thus the strong-willed Clytemnestra of the first play has become a woman terrified by dreams of guilt and retribution, and both she and Aegisthus are relieved when a messenger brings them news that Orestes is dead. But the messenger is Orestes himself, who has returned, ordered by the god Apollo, to avenge his father's murder, even though he knows he must thereby become his mother's murderer. This dilemma is clearly presented when Orestes reveals his identity to his mother before killing her, a dramatic scene which would have been impossible before Aeschylus introduced the second actor to Greek drama. Immediately after killing his father's murderers, Orestes learns that even though his actions were ordered by Apollo, he is now guilty of a personal sin which must be expiated. The play ends as the Furies, demanding vengeance for Clytemnestra's murder, rise up to pursue Orestes.

Comparative: Although Aeschylus, following Homer's *Odyssey*, concentrates on the vengeance of Orestes, he presents us with a complex moral dilemma not found in the earlier work, where the focus was on Orestes as the dutiful son avenging his father's murder. Whereas both of these versions concentrate on the son, it is the character of Electra which has held the greater fascination for other writers, developing what Sigmund Freud was to call the Electra complex. The rather innocent girl in Aeschylus becomes a far more capable, bitter, and implacable protagonist in *Electra* by Sophocles, which also presents a far more despicable Clytemnestra and Aegisthus. Euripides, in his *Electra,* is far more sympathetic to Clytemnestra and portrays an Electra whose desire for vengeance borders on the pathological. This aspect of her character has been further developed by numerous authors. In Mérimée's *Colomba* the heroine is as implacable as the Electra of Sophocles but so manipulative and vengeful as to remind us of the Electra of Euripides. Eugene O'Neill, in *Mourning Becomes Electra,* illuminates her character with Freudian psychology, but his Electra seems more Euripidean than Sophoclean, at least until the end of his trilogy. Giraudoux's *Electra* looks back to the implacable heroine of Sophocles and is again the symbol of pure, if cold, justice. In *The Flies,* Sartre portrays her as a courageous figure of justice but retains some of the humanity and sympathetic quality of the young girl in Aeschylus. Richard Strauss's opera *Elektra,* a powerful retelling of the story by Hugo von Hoffmannsthal, is based on Sophocles but incorporates many of the Freudian overtones found in O'Neill.

The story of a young man caught in the dilemma of avenging his father's death by murdering his mother is also the story of Shakespeare's *Hamlet.*

Aeschylus. EUMENIDES. 458 B.C. Drama. Greek.

Author: See *Agamemnon.*

Work: This is the final play of the *Oresteia* and the conclusion of the myth of the House of Atreus. Orestes has come to the temple of Apollo at Delphi, pursued by the Furies, primitive spirits who represent the ancient *lex talionis,* blood demanding blood. Under this law, guilt need not be personal since it may be inherited from an ancestor, and there can be no end to killing. The ghost of Clytemnestra demands that the Furies pursue their ancient function, which is older than the laws of the new, more civilized Olympian deities. Apollo, however, supports Orestes, and a trial is held before Athena, the goddess of wisdom. The Furies argue that their system guarantees law and order through fear of justice and retribution. Orestes argues that his act was ordered by Apollo with the sanction of Zeus and was justified by his father's murder; more importantly, he has atoned for his crime and no further vengeance is necessary. Athena casts a tie-breaking vote in favor of Orestes. The Furies, offended by the loss of their ancient rights, threaten dire consequences, but are placated by being granted the new role of benevolent goddesses *(Eumenides).* Thus concludes Aeschylus's argument that the rule of the younger, more civilized gods of intellect and order must supplant the primitive forces of blind fate and vengeance. Guilt in the trilogy is personal rather than inherited and must be atoned for personally. Justice, tempered by reason and compassion, is the concern of the whole society in a civilized state and cannot be left to fate or primitive ideas of vengeance.

Comparative: Few of the writers who have developed this story are interested in Orestes after his murder of Clytemnestra. Two exceptions are O'Neill in *Mourning Becomes Electra* and Sartre in *The Flies.* O'Neill, like Aeschylus, insists that guilt must be expiated through suffering, although for him this is more clearly the result of psychological forces. Sartre portrays the Olympian deities, represented by Zeus, Aegisthus, and the Furies (religion, the state, and conscience), as allied in tyranny and insists that one must oppose the guilt assigned by a tyrannical political and religious system and obey an inner moral law, the mark of individual freedom. This conflict between guilt imposed by a system and responsibility to an inner law is the theme of Sophocles' *Antigone* (where inner law and divine law coincide and oppose political law), Kafka's *The Trial,* and Camus's *The Stranger.*

Alain-Fournier (Henri-Alban Fournier). THE WANDERER (LE GRAND MEAULNES). 1912. Novel. French.

Author: Alain-Fournier was born in La Chapelle-d'Angillon in 1886. He was killed at age 28 in World War I. He left no other writing besides letters and fragments.

Work: Young Seurel tells the story of Meaulnes, who comes to his parents' boarding school and one day, in an unauthorized absence, loses his way and finds himself at a betrothal festival in a decayed castle in a winter woods. Almost all the guests are children, and the atmosphere is fairylike. Here Meaulnes falls in love with the daughter of the castle, Yvonne. When the festival ends tragically, Meaulnes is transported back to the school, where he realizes that he has no idea where he has been. The story becomes the saga of the two schoolboys who try to rediscover the way to the lost domain, of their eventual success, of the marriage of Meaulnes and Yvonne, of the tragic crosscurrents of another love affair—that of Yvonne's brother and his betrothed— of Yvonne's death, and of Meaulnes's revelation of himself. He is an eternal searcher, a wanderer after beauty and mystery who cannot end his quest.

All this takes place in a fairytale world that allegorically represents the human struggle after ideal beauty and suggests the slight grasp of it that one is allowed to enjoy.

Comparative: Parallels to this portrayal of young love may be found in George Meredith's *The Ordeal of Richard Feverel* (Chapter 18, "Ferdinand and Miranda") and in Giraudoux's *Ondine,* with its fairytale quality. The closest parallel in plot, characters, and the motif of the search is found in Eugène Fromentin's *Dominique.* The idealism of the characters compares with that in Goethe's *The Sorrows of Young Werther.* Other pictures of French school life are in Pagnol's *Topaze,* in Anatole France's *My Friend's Book,* and in Colette's *Claudine at School.* A parallel to the first part of *The Wanderer* can be found in "The Sleeping Beauty," a fairy tale in prose, verse, or ballet music. The theme bears close resemblance to Gerstäcker's *Germelshausen,* which also has a supernatural quality. The quest motif also appears in Joyce's *A Portrait of the Artist as a Young Man.*

Alegría, Ciro. THE GOLDEN SERPENT (LA SERPIENTE DE ORO). 1935. Novel. Peruvian.

Author: Alegría (1909-1967) was raised on the banks of the Marañón River of which he writes. He studied under the poet César Vallejo. In 1934 he was exiled to Chile for taking part in the movement against Trujillo. He lived in the United States for eight years and taught at the University of Puerto Rico in later years.

Work: The novel is laid in Peru's wild mountainous regions where a great river brings both life and death to the Cholos. Though the "hero" of the novel is the river, a series of half-connected stories merges with its course, rising with its floods and falling in times of peace. The love story of Arturo and Lucindas, who flee the wrath of the constabulary after a village fiesta with the help of Arturo's brother Roge, is delightfully and tensely told. So is the tale of how Roge loses his life in a desperate voyage on a balsa raft down the river rapids. Most of the little stories are tragic, like the story of Don Osvaldo, a mining engineer who comes from the capital in his shiny new mountain clothes and boots and gradually learns to understand the people and share their ways, even to the chewing of coca leaves. Just as he learns to understand the Marañón River—the golden serpent of the novel's title—he is bitten by a yellow snake and dies. The simple people of the uplands who fight unwillingly with the law are epitomized in the character of Riero, an outlaw by the accident of circumstances.

The novel is not tightly plotted. It moves like the day-to-day living of the Cholos themselves and the wandering of the river. It is lively. The violence and peace of both the river and its people fill the pages.

Comparative: This novel is structured much like Ivo Andrič's *The Bridge on the Drina* and, though geographically worlds apart, has a similar effect. In locale, it compares interestingly with W. H. Hudson's *Green Mansions* and contrasts with Thornton Wilder's *The Bridge of San Luis Rey;* indeed, the city sophistication of Wilder's characters seems like the reverse side of the Peruvian mirror. For another tale of a violent river on which mankind depends, see Pearl Buck's novella *Old Demon River.*

Andreyev, Leonid Nikolaevich. THE SEVEN WHO WERE HANGED (RASS-KAZ O SEMI POVESHENNYKH). 1909. Novella. Russian.

Author: Andreyev (1871–1919) was born into a middle-class family in Orel, educated in the public schools, and trained as a lawyer at the University of St. Petersburg. Highly neurotic, he made several suicide attempts and after failing at careers in law, painting, and journalism turned to writing. His first story was published in 1898, and he rapidly became a bestselling author. Although criticized by the intellectuals for the melodramatic and pseudo-profound quality of his work, he remained a popular favorite. Many of his plays and stories reflect a concern with morbid psychology and the ultimate problems of existence, and generally Andreyev's pessimistic views prevail. A supporter of the social revolutionaries and the 1908 rebellion, he became increasingly conservative and opposed the Bolshevik Revolution of 1917, which he viewed as a threat to civilization. He died in poverty in exile in Finland.

Work: The Seven Who Were Hanged is probably Andreyev's best story, although it too succumbs to the pseudoprofundity and mysticism for which he has been criticized. Its sympathetic treatment of the condemned and its strong opposition to capital punishment, however, lift it from the commonplace.

The novella portrays the thoughts of seven men and women condemned to death. Five are young revolutionaries, one is a confessed murderer, and the seventh is a poor peasant who has murdered his master. The reader learns the thoughts of these prisoners as they await execution and confront the meanings of their lives and deaths. Among the revolutionaries, Werner, the girl Musya, and, to some extent, Sergei can rationalize their deaths as required by the cause in which they believe, although each has moments of doubt. Andreyev's real sympathies, however, rest with the ignorant Yanson and Tsiganok, neither of whom has the intelligence to make any sense of his own death. This is particularly true in the case of the peasant Yanson, who is incapable of seeing even a causal relation between his crime and his execution.

The last to die is the revolutionary Tanya Kovalchuk, who laments that she must die alone. Her cry perhaps embodies Andreyev's belief in the ultimate meaninglessness of life. Even the hope symbolized by the spring dawn which ends the novella is crushed as a remnant belonging to one of the revolutionaries is trampled into the mud.

Comparative: Andreyev's obsession with the meaning of life in the context of unpredictable and unavoidable death links him with Tolstoi, although Tolstoi's view never lapses into the horror which Andreyev emphasizes. Andreyev's contention that man's rationality does not provide answers to life's ultimate questions is similar to that of Dostoevski. These themes have been treated by numerous modern existential authors, for example Camus, Sartre, Kafka, and Hesse.

The criminal has often been depicted as being isolated within and by society. In some cases, such as Koestler's *Darkness at Noon* or Solzhenitsyn's *One Day in the Life of Ivan Denisovich,* this theme of isolation is used primarily for political criticism, but in works such as Dostoevski's *Notes from Underground,* Camus's *The Stranger,* Sartre's *The Wall,* or Kafka's *The Trial,* ones isolation from peers is seen as part of the human condition rather than the result of living within a particular political state.

Malraux's *Man's Fate* also portrays the mind of a revolutionary who dies without achieving anything except certain realizations about the human condition.

Anouilh, Jean. ANTIGONE. 1944. Drama. French.

Author: Anouilh, a prolific dramatist, writes for both stage and film. Born in 1910 at Bordeaux of a musical mother and a tailor father, he studied law and found work in an advertising agency; eventually he drifted into stage life and found his place.

Work: The story of this one-act tragedy follows Sophocles, but the philosophical statement and dramaturgy are different. The characters are allowed to express emotions more fully than they were in the Greek drama, and nobility is shown to be not always noble. Like Cocteau, Anouilh sees tragedy as a machine which must inexorably run down once it has been wound: "When your name is Antigone there is only one part you can play; and she will have to play hers through to the end." Antigone is allowed to appeal to the audience's sympathy in such statements as: "I'm just a little young still for what I have to go through." To allow for such emotional betrayals, Anouilh provides his heroine with a nurse-confidante in the manner of the seventeenth century. To take the responsibility for the tragic action away from Fate, Tiresias is absent, and Creon, as a modern figure, must make his own decisions; he does not repent, as does the Sophoclean Creon, but allows events to run their course. He is driven by the duties of kingship and by loyalty to the state (as he warns himself in warning Oedipus) and insists on the loneliness of his position. Antigone's beloved brothers are shown to be "a pair of blackguards," not worth her effort and sacrifice. Thus the heroine, who would prefer to remain a child, is seen as willful in her opposition to Creon's orders. Because of the youthful and passionate nature of her rebellion, Antigone reminds one of Giraudoux's Isabel or his Ondine.

Comparative: Anouilh's use of the chorus may be compared to that of Thornton Wilder in *Our Town.* The views which Anouilh expresses through the chorus about the purpose of tragedy and the nature of the tragic character may be read in relation to those of Arthur Miller in his preface to *A View from the Bridge.*

Anouilh, Jean. BECKET, OR THE HONOR OF GOD (BECKET, OU L'HON-
    NEUR DE DIEU). 1959. Drama. French.

Author: See *Antigone.*

Work: In this four-act tragedy, the roistering young Henry II has one friend he trusts as he sets about the large business of reconciling his Norman loyalties and the duties of citizenship he owes his Saxon underdogs. This friend is Thomas à Becket, a neat, smart, personable young man who can feel loyalty but never love. In the campaign against France, Henry, beset with the need of both income and suzerainty from the Catholic kingdom-within-his-kingdom, suddenly makes Becket the Archbishop of Canterbury—this even though Becket is of Saxon ancestry, and this even though Henry's four powerful but stupid barons are Becket's savage enemies. Once he is archbishop, entrusted with the "honor of God," Becket is surprised to find that he must in conscience oppose the policies and desires of his friend and king. Henry cannot tolerate this opposition. Becket flees to France and enjoys the political protection of King Louis. Becket next goes to Rome to ask the Pope to relieve him of his archbishopric so that he may fulfill his life as Henry's loyal subject. The Pope, playing politics, delivers him again to France. There Henry and Becket have a memorable meeting in which they try to reconcile their differences, memorable because of the signs of friendship that almost destroy the political maneuvering. But reconciliation fails. Henry is torn between his love for Becket and his responsibility to forge a strong kingdom. Becket must be sacrificed. Alone before the altar of Canterbury, Becket is attacked by the four barons and falls under their swords. The play begins, actually, as Henry undergoes penance at the tomb of Thomas, and the drama is a series of personal flashbacks and elaborately effective lap-dissolves.

    The reader likes everyone in this play: King Louis for his ironic and intelligent grasp of political necessities, Henry for his blunt honesty and his sureness in calling things by their proper if indelicate names, Becket for his unswerving devotion to what he assumes to be his duty. We are captive to the sway of large, opposing emotions, even in the reading of the play.

Comparative: Creon is caught in a similar dilemma in Anouilh's *Antigone* and that of Sophocles. Elizabeth the Queen is likewise torn between justice and necessity in Schiller's *Mary Stuart.* A comparative study can also be made with T. S. Eliot's *Murder in the Cathedral.* Finally, it is worth mentioning that the pilgrims of Chaucer's *Canterbury Tales* are en route to Becket's tomb.

Anouilh's choice of subject matter in *Becket* reflects a revival of interest in classic tragedy (as in Miller's *A View from the Bridge*); at the same time, however, he relies on all the cinematic devices of modern stagecraft. (See similar techniques in Miller's *Death of a Salesman.*)

Anouilh, Jean. THE LARK (L'ALOUETTE). 1953. Drama. French.

Author: See *Antigone.*

Work: The Lark is a two-act tragedy on the trial and martyrdom of Joan of Arc. Joan is being tried in a courtroom, where sudden fades and dissolves remove her to the past where she hears voices or quarrels with her father or runs after Beaudricourt to secure her horse—only to be caught up short by the officer of the court. Pleading her defense, Ladvenu and Cauchon are foils to the Inquisitor, who would condemn her for espousing too noble a vision of humanity. Warwick, her British enemy, reluctantly learns to admire Joan and to dislike the duty that requires him to demand her punishment. Anouilh adds a sardonic note at the play's end as Joan re-enacts "her happiest day," the day of Charles's coronation; but Joan smiles about it, dismissing the coronation as secondary to the salvation of her country.

The Lark is an interesting example of "antitheater," for in it drama becomes not the illusion of reality, but the destruction of that illusion, just as the play within *Hamlet* is known to be only a play while the exterior drama is treated as "real." Through this device Anouilh adds whimsy and drollery to serious moments in *The Lark.*

Comparative: This combination of the whimsical and the serious may also be found in Anouilh's *Antigone* and in his *Becket,* in Wilder's *The Skin of Our Teeth,* and in the whimsical philosophical remarks of Giraudoux's young girls. Shaw, in his *Saint Joan,* also relies on whimsy, but he handles his material in a straightforward chronology and provides the illusion generally expected in theater. The result is more dignified and tragic than Anouilh's version, though it is interesting to note in both plays the effective balance between tragedy and humor.

Modern playwrights seem to be drawn to history for the subjects of their tragedies: see Anouilh's *Becket,* T. S. Eliot's *Murder in the Cathedral,* and Maxwell Anderson's *Mary of Scotland.* For a contrast between the modern and classical approach to tragedy, compare one of the Anouilh tragedies to Shiller's *Mary Stuart.* The Inquisitor may be compared to his counterpart in "The Legend of the Grand Inquisitor" from Dostoevski's *The Brothers Karamazov.*

Anwar, Chairil. THE COMPLETE POETRY AND PROSE OF CHAIRIL ANWAR. Translated by Burton Raffel. State University of New York Press, Albany, 1970. Poetry. Indonesian.

Author: Chairil Anwar was born July 26, 1922, in Medan, Sumatra, when Indonesia was the Dutch East Indies. That modern Indonesian poetry—in its most contemporary context—began with him is a claim he himself would probably not have made or felt justified in making. He died April 28, 1949, with only some seventy poems to his credit. A product of the conflict inherent in a culture dominated first by the Dutch and then by the Japanese, Anwar wrote poetry that is fiercely independent in spirit and nationality.

Work: Chairil Anwar's poetry is lean, intense, almost ferocious. There were things to be said and Anwar was the sayer. That he died young lends a special poignancy to his poems.

Comparative: Anwar belongs in the study of contemporary world poetry. See, for example, *The Contemporary World Poets* edited by Donald Junkins. Also see for comparison the Indonesian W. S. Rendra: *Ballads and Blues,* poems translated from the Indonesian by Burton Raffel, Harry Aveling, and Derwent May.

Aristophanes. THE BIRDS (ORNITHES). 414 B.C. Drama. Greek.

Author: Aristophanes (ca. 450-385 B.C.) was born of a wealthy family and began to write at an early age, but little is known of his life. Though he seems not to have held public office, he was obviously keenly interested in politics, contemporary literature, and philosophy. He opposed the Peloponnesian War (431-404 B.C.) and blamed it on Athenian policies. The earliest of his comedies (*The Acharnians,* 425 B.C.) attacked Athens' war party, and in it a citizen, Dikaipolis, makes his private peace. *The Knights* (424 B.C.), the first play Aristophanes produced under his own name, attacks the demagogue Cleon, who had prosecuted Aristophanes for his earlier criticism. *The Wasps* (422 B.C.) satirizes the Athenian love of lawsuits and features a chorus of waspish old men. In *Peace* (421 B.C.) a farmer riding a dung beetle rescues Peace who has been buried. *Lysistrata* (411 B.C.) concerns a sex strike which succeeds in ending the war. In *Thesmophoriazusae* ("Ladies' Day at the Festival of Demeter," 411 B.C.), the women of Athens try Euripides for slandering their sex. In *Plutus* (388 B.C.), his last extant comedy, the god of wealth, when he is cured of his blindness, enriches the virtuous and condemns the wicked to poverty.

Aristophanes is the only surviving author of Old Comedy, and even in his own time he was revered for his perfect mastery of language and his use of every imaginable comic device. Fantastic costumes abounded, especially in the choruses. Old Comedy was frankly ribald—in costume, in situation, and in language.

Work: Peithetairos and Euelpides, two elderly citizens dissatisfied with life in Athens, seek a better place to live. They are guided by a crow and a jackdaw to the king of the birds, Epops, a hoopoe. Peithetairos proposes that the birds build a kingdom, a city between earth and sky, thereby making themselves masters of both by intercepting the smoke from mortal offerings to the gods. After initial hostility from the fabulously costumed chorus of birds, who believe humans to be their worst enemy, the birds enthusiastically concur. A long choral ode on the advantages of being a bird follows, and the new state, Cloudcuckooland, is proclaimed. Various frauds and civic nuisances who want to move into this new utopia are unmasked and driven off. The rainbow goddess, Iris, is arrested for crossing the border without a visa. Prometheus, hidden by an umbrella from the watchful eye of Zeus, comes to offer help. The Olympians quarrel with foreign gods. Poseidon arrives with Heracles and a foreign god (who speaks no Greek) to arrange terms for peace. Peithetairos demands the sceptre of Zeus and the hand of his young companion Basileia ("Sovereignty"). The comedy concludes with a splendid wedding feast as the bird chorus sings the wedding hymn. The costumes of birds and gods in this comedy are unparalleled in their zany splendor.

Comparative: Only Shakespeare has rivaled the lyric quality of Aristophanes as well as some of his baser puns. The winged Peithetairos is at once admirably heroic in his desire to transcend the obvious limitations of Athenian society and knavish, even crude, as, for example, when he observes that the nightingale has certain nonmusical attributes. In his ingenuity, Peithetairos may be compared to other Aristophanic heroes; later comic characters, like Molière's Sganarelle in *The Doctor in Spite of Himself* and the perennial wily servant, share his quick intelligence and his ability to transcend the limitations of the existing world.

As social criticism, Molière's *Bourgeois Gentleman* demonstrates a comparably elaborate situation and resolution. The concluding ritual marriage in *The Birds* might be likened to the quadruple marriage that ends Shakespeare's *As You Like It.* Cloudcuckooland, the world's most fanciful utopia, bears some resemblance to the would-be academy established in Shakespeare's *Love's Labors Lost.*

In general, Aristophanes used brilliantly comic devices which have been borrowed for over two thousand years and still work in vaudeville, television, and the theater. Laurel and Hardy and the Marx brothers relied on similar stock devices: disguise, pratfalls, parody, nonsense, satire. The comic imagination of Aristophanes was simply prodigious; no other writer has ever so completely moulded our impossible world into new forms to celebrate.

Aristophanes. THE FROGS (BATRACHOI). 405 B.C. Drama. Greek.

Author: See *The Birds.*

Work: This play was performed, it must be recalled, in the theater of Dionysus at the base of the Acropolis. Dionysus, god of wine and revelry as well as the patron of drama, finds that no good tragedies are being written; he misses Euripides so much that he determines to descend to Hades to retrieve him. Donning the disguise (club and lion skin) of Heracles, who had made the descent before, over his traditional saffron robe, Dionysus sets off with his slave Xanthias and a donkey.

After a series of ludicrous adventures, including an encounter with the chorus of frogs, they arrive at the palace of Hades, where a contest is about to occur between Aeschylus, present occupant of the Chair of Tragic Drama, and Euripides, who has challenged his right to it. Pluto has arranged a poetic contest to settle the issue and appoints Dionysus judge; in return for this service Dionysus may take the winner back to Athens. Aeschylus and Euripides attack one another in a long and hilarious debate. A gigantic pair of scales is brought in, and lines from their tragedies are weighed in its pans. Though Dionysus had made the journey to bring back Euripides, he now chooses Aeschylus instead.

As Aeschylus leaves, he requests that Sophocles (too much the gentleman to have participated in all this) be installed in the Chair of Tragic Drama and Euripides forever excluded. At a farewell banquet, Pluto sends Aeschylus off with various death-dealing gifts for specific prominent Athenians.

Comparative: Disguise is a traditional device of comedy, and a Greek audience would be aware of the ability of the gods to disguise themselves successfully by every imaginable metamorphosis, though they had not yet observed the disguise of Dionysus in the *Bacchae* of Euripides, since that play was not produced until after the death of its author. The bumbling attempt of Dionysus at disguise in *The Frogs* is a deliberate reduction of the god to a figure of fun, and his disguise proves as ineffectual as the hiding of Falstaff in *The Merry Wives of Windsor.* Aristophanes has Euripides himself dress up to escape detection in *Thesmophoriazusae;* Athena's helmet is used to fake pregnancy by one woman in *Lysistrata.* Numerous Shakespearian heroines disguise themselves for one purpose or another. The list is endless.

Because Roman and later Renaissance comedy descended from Greek New Comedy, there has never again been such outright parody of living and well-known figures as Aristophanes regularly committed, in *The Clouds,* for example, with Socrates but with Aeschylus and Euripides as well. In tone and underlying assumption, however, it may be enlightening to compare Aristophanes in one way and another with modern European dramatists like Ionesco, Max Frisch, and even Alfred Jarry. Salvador Dali and the Surrealists could be examined for yet another zany modern equivalent of this ancient, brilliant comic imagination.

Aristophanes. LYSISTRATA. 411 B.C. Drama. Greek.

Author: See *The Birds.*

Work: Lysistrata is a spirited comedy that evokes laughter today, even though much of its humor is made up of inside jokes that require knowledge of people and events of the times to understand. The play was first performed in 411 B.C. in Athens. The story line is straight and uncomplicated, beginning with the fact that Athens has been at war with Sparta for twenty years. Everyone is tired of the war; and, since the men have been unable to win it or stop it, Lysistrata shares her scheme with the ladies of Athens and Sparta. They will deny sexual favors to their husbands until the men end the war. (It must be noted that not all the ladies approve of the strategy.) The play is largely given over to attempts by the men to get inside the Acropolis, where the women have gathered. The various ploys and deceits fail until the sex-starved men concede to the women, resulting in the end of the war.

Comparative: Shakespeare's *The Taming of the Shrew* is another classic presentation of the war between men and women. *The Tub,* an anonymous fifteenth-century French farce, also pits man against wife.

Armah, Ayi Kwei. THE BEAUTIFUL ONES ARE NOT YET BORN. 1968. Novel. Ghanaian.

Author: Ayi Kwei Armah was born in 1939 in Ghana, educated in Ghana and also at Harvard and Columbia Universities, and currently lives in the United States. He has worked as an editor, translator, script writer, and teacher of

English. The protagonists of his novels are alienated men who must face a thoroughly dehumanized society; thus his work joins the mainstream of Western fiction. His other published novels include: *Fragments* (1970), which mirrors important events in Armah's own life and is concerned with the stifled artist, particularly the writer, in contemporary Africa, and *Why Are We So Blest* (1971).

Work: The novel describes the social ills of Ghana during the 1960s. Though the country has been granted independence from Great Britain, it is unable to cope with the responsibility that accompanies freedom. Ghanaians are exploited by the white power structure, a structure which is supposedly designed to raise their standard of living but which, in reality, only further dupes and disillusions an already desperate people.

The Gold Coast is the setting against which "the man," a typical Ghanaian, is portrayed. Although he holds the position of Recorder at the Railway Administration Office, "the man," his cynical wife Oyo, and their children are among the many hopeless indigents of Accra and the Gold Coast. Anxious for an improved life-style, Oyo is annoyed by the ineptness of her husband which prevents him from receiving the bribes that would provide material comforts. They cultivate the friendship of a Party man, Koomson, and his highbrow wife, Estella. On the occasion of a party at Koomson's elegant home, "the man" and Oyo become truly aware of their modest living standards as they observe the expensive furnishings, clothes, and food. Here is the beauty for which Oyo and her husband struggle, but he is nothing—a *chichidodo.*

As the novel progresses, the reader meets "the teacher," who attempts to enlighten as he relates the myth of Plato's cave, and Sister Manaan, who occasionally gives the youths weed to smoke to provide temporary relief from their sordid state.

Conflict and turmoil in politics bring the destruction of Nkrumah's government, and the Party Socialists, including Koomson, are either arrested or driven out of town. "The man" helps Koomson to escape through his night-soil hole, a humiliating experience for such a man. Then, as "the man" is en route home, he sees the bus driver slip money to a policeman enabling Koomson to escape imminent arrest. The back of the bus bears this inscription: The Beautiful Ones Are Not Yet Born.

Comparative: The theme of this novel may best be discussed in connection with "the teacher's" retelling of the myth of Plato's cave: Men tend to stand apart and disappoint themselves when, in reality, they are free to choose what they want. In the end they enslave themselves. Only man can free himself.

In its disillusioned and desperate tone, largely effected by the writer's use of black and white symbols, this novel may be compared to *Native Son* by Richard Wright. In its portrayal of character, it is reminiscent of *Things Fall Apart* by Chinua Achebe, especially the characterization of Okonkwo. In its presentation of problems common to all people, it may be compared to Solzhenitsyn's *Matryona's House.*

Asturias, Miguel Ángel. **EL SEÑOR PRESIDENTE.** 1946. Novel. Guatemalan.

Author: Miguel Ángel Asturias (1899-1974) won the Nobel Prize in 1967, the second Latin American to do so. Born in Guatemala City, the son of a Supreme Court judge and importer, he earned a Doctor of Law degree in 1923 at the Universidad de San Carlos de Guatemala and went to study at the Sorbonne. From 1923 to 1933, he traveled off and on in Europe, in Latin America, and in the Middle East before returning home to become a journalist and broadcaster. In 1942 he was elected to the National Congress of Guatemala, going on to a career in the diplomatic service in 1945, which took him to posts in Mexico, Argentina, France, and El Salvador. Asturias lost his citizenship in 1954 because of his leftist leanings and in the late 1950s became a correspondent to a Caracas newspaper and advisor to publishers. For a time he lived in Genoa, Italy. Returning to Guatemala in 1966, he received full restoration of his citizenship and served as Ambassador to France until his death.

Besides *El Señor Presidente,* the trilogy by Asturias beginning with *Viento Fuerte (Strong Wind),* 1950, and continuing with *El Papa Verde (The Green Pope),* 1954, and *Los Ojos de Los Enterrados (The Eyes of the Interred),* 1960, has been gaining readership in the United States. This trilogy considers the issue of United States economic and political pressures in Central America through the story of the United Fruit Company.

Work: El Señor Presidente is based on the dictatorship of Estrada Cabrera of Guatemala, although the novel gives no clue to its date or locale except for a printed wedding announcement alluding to the time sequence. The dictator of the story stays in power by means of utter cruelty and barbarism. He allows no one grounds for hope and keeps his subjects at bay through constant punishment.

He uses the murder of one of his hatchet men to get at his political rival, General Canales, by having a group of beggars beaten until they will swear that Canales carried out the murder.

To further his scheme against General Canales, the President-dictator uses his friend Miguel Angel Face as a decoy to bring about the General's death. Angel Face, who is in love with the General's daughter, betrays the President and gets the General safely to the frontier. Because El Señor Presidente maintains a police state in a corrupt society, he is able through playing favorites to maintain his reign of terror.

Comparative: Because of his involvement with dream sequences, myth, and propaganda, Asturias is frequently compared with the men from whom he learned some of his techniques—Tristana Tzara, André Breton, and Robert Desnos.

AUCASSIN AND NICOLETTE. 13th Century. Fable. French.

Author: Unknown.

Work: Aucassin and Nicolette is the work of a troubadour of Provence, a region encompassing part of southern France and northwestern Italy. It is a *chante-fable,* a prose story interspersed with poems or songs, and it is one of the finest short literary products of the Middle Ages. It is a simple love story (but not adulterous love as in the courtly romances) based on the traditional loyalties of the Age of Knighthood—loyalty to God, to one's overlord (in this case, to one's father), and to one's lady. But it is a story which brings those loyalties into question; indeed, Aucassin rejects them all.

Aucassin loves Nicolette, not as an idealized lady to be served by noble deeds but as a woman to be lived with, even if this means refusing to do those noble works. He refuses to fight the enemy which is invading his father's country because his father will not countenance his love of Nicolette, a Saracen slave who has been reared a Christian by her adoptive father. Aucassin enters the battle only when his father promises to let him meet Nicolette. But the promise is rescinded and the lovers are separately imprisoned. Aucassin is urged to abandon his love so that he may go to heaven when he dies, but he responds, "to Paradise go only . . . old priests, the old cripples and maimed ones . . . and those who . . . are dressed in tattered rags . . . and dying of hunger and thirst. . . . I have nothing to do with them. But to Hell I wish indeed to go, for to Hell go the handsome clerics, and the fine knights who have died in the tourneys . . . and . . . the fair and courteous ladies who have two or three lovers . . . and the harpers and jongleurs, and the kings of the world. With them do I wish to go—provided that I have Nicolette, my very sweet love, with me."

The lovers escape, are united, travel, and are separated again. It is discovered that Nicolette is a Saracen princess. Disguised as a minstrel, she returns to Provence and is reunited with Aucassin.

Embedded in this delightful story is a serious questioning of established traditions. The stratified life of the Middle Ages is beginning to crumble.

Comparative: There is a quality to this story which suggests *The Thousand and One Nights* and *The Decameron.* Certainly there would be a fine comparison, both in the themes of love and loyalty and in the manner of telling a love story, with any of the various versions of Tristan and Isolt. The conflicts surrounding love and loyalty are best and most searchingly treated in the *Nibelungenlied.* In Chaucer's *Canterbury Tales,* the Wife of Bath gives us quite another view of love and offers interesting contrasts.

Azuela, Mariano. THE UNDERDOGS (LOS DE ABAJO). 1915. Novel. Mexican.

Author: Azuela (1873-1952) studied medicine in Guadalajara, Mexico, and practiced in his native state, like Chekhov, among the very poor. He early began writing for recreation. In his youth he supported the uprising of the liberal revolutionary Francisco Madero and later won a place in his government. After the overthrow and death of Madero, Azuela joined Pancho Villa's army as a doctor and learned about war first hand. After their defeat, he escaped to El Paso, Texas, where he wrote his best known novel of the Revolution, *The Underdogs.*

Work: The novel is a grim, realistic picture of the Mexican Revolution as it was to the common soldier. Demetrio leaves his wife and family when government soldiers enter his pueblo; looking back from the mountains, he sees his home burning in the night. He becomes the leader of a brawling group of revolutionaries who are more often hungry and without ammunition than brave or noble. They endure minor and major skirmishes; men of his group are hanged and shot. He and his men burn and destroy and get drunk. They talk about war in terms of food, of women, and of remembered incidents of the pueblo life they have left behind them. There is no fanatic idealism or stirring patriotism. They fight because they have started to fight, and they keep on fighting as a stone keeps falling and rolling when it is dropped into a canyon (also a theme in Malraux's *Man's Fate).* A young idealist, the educated Cervantes, joins them, and it is he who pilots the crude, brave, sincere Demetrio into a position of authority with the revolutionary army. The novel ends as casually and as inconclusively as it begins.

Comparative: In its recounting of the often haphazard, discouraging, and trivial experiences of a little group of hungry revolutionaries, this book brings us closer to an understanding of man's true condition in time of war than do Remarque's *All Quiet on the Western Front,* Hemingway's *For Whom the Bell Tolls,* or Crane's *The Red Badge of Courage.* Its view of the role of the common soldier in creating a victory or defeat is close to Tolstoi's view in *War and Peace:* the man who shouts "Hurrah!" may lead an army to victory, just as the man who screams "We are defeated!" may singlehandedly bring an army to ruin. Its depiction of the nature of combat reminds us of Julien

Sorel accidentally wandering onto the battlefield of Waterloo in Stendhal's *The Red and the Black*.

Balzac, Honoré de. **EUGÉNIE GRANDET**. 1833. Novel. French.

Author: Balzac (1799-1850) was born and educated in sunny Touraine but left for Paris to study law. He quickly gave up this career, installed himself in an attic, and determined to devote himself to literature. For a time he was an editor and publisher, but financial misfortune, often resulting from his mania for speculation, dogged him the rest of his days. He is famous for his realistic powers of observation and is considered a precursor of the school of realism. His projected *La Comédie humaine*, though unfinished, contains ninety-five novels and stories with interrelated characters, over two thousand in all.

Work: The novel tells the story of a miser, Grandet, and his daughter, Eugénie, who is sacrificed to the love of money both by her father and her fiancé. Life in the Grandet household with Eugénie, her parents, and the servant girl consists of uneventful toil, thin fare, and discussions about crops and finance until Eugénie's cousin Charles arrives from Paris. His father has gone bankrupt, and Charles has been entrusted to Grandet, his uncle. He and Eugénie fall in love.

To help Charles make his fortune in the Indies, Eugénie gives him the hoard of gold birthday coins that her father has awarded her over the years. It is her first act of daring. After Charles has gone, her second act of daring is to confess her "crime" to her miserly father. She is made a bread-and-water prisoner in her own household; her mother, distressed by shock, sickens and dies. Charles gets rich but does not write to Eugénie.

Balzac impressively reveals the slow, uneventful trickle of time while Eugénie waits. A secondary plot develops as Grandet tangles with Paris merchants to redeem his brother's bankruptcy with profit for himself. Charles returns to France and has an opportunity to marry into nobility if he settles honourably with his father's creditors. Eugénie, now an heiress after her father's death, receives the news bitterly but in a final act of love pays off the debts of her uncle so that Charles may make this rich marriage.

This novel is one of the "Provincial Scenes" in *La Comédie humaine*. Along with *Le Père Goriot* it is one of his best and shows his great attention to the details of scene, which assume almost characterlike proportions in his novels.

Comparative: Flaubert's *A Simple Heart* and *Eugénie Grandet* are similar in setting, and the servant girls are similar in characterization. But Flaubert selects details while Balzac floods us in them; Flaubert avoids comment while Balzac chats to us about morals and events. Each author bases time sequences on insignificant happenings but moves the story ahead straight-forwardly. The picture of the proud aristocracy and the bourgeoisie is similar in each work. The stock figure of the French miser is also found in Molière's comedy, *The Miser*. Finally, Eugénie revolts against her cloistered life some-what as Adela does in García Lorca's *The House of Bernarda Alba,* or, for that matter, as Nora does in Ibsen's *A Doll's House.*

Balzac, Honoré de. LE PÈRE GORIOT. 1834. Novel. French.

Author: See *Eugénie Grandet.*

Work: The novel examines a father's love, pathological and beyond restraint, for two selfish daughters. Old Goriot, a retired grain dealer, lives in a cheap boarding house, the Maison Vauquer, having given all his funds to the pleasure of his two daughters, Delphine and Anastasie, who have made brilliant but unhappy society marriages. We see Goriot depriving himself of every resource, even his sentimental keepsakes, to satisfy the demands of his daughters.

Eventually wrung dry, sick and old, Goriot dies, attended only by Rastig-nac, a young boarder in the Maison Vauquer, and Bianchon, a medical stu-dent. Goriot calls for his daughters in his death throes, but they are unable to come because of the crises they have reached in their marriages and social lives.

Vautrin, one of the Vauquer boarders, is especially interesting because he is an underworld character whose viciousness, as Balzac describes it, becomes warmer and more human than the behavior of so-called respectable society.

This realist novel is perhaps the best example of the method by which Balzac undertook to create *La Comédie humaine,* a complete study of eigh-teenth century society. He was tremendously successful at bringing his char-acters to life, individuals yet reflections of the period when the bourgeois were struggling to take over society and the aristocrats were fighting back with dwindling financial resources and prestige.

Comparative: King Lear is the standard comparison with *Le Père Goriot,* for Goneril and Regan remind us in some ways of Delphine and Anastasie, and Lear parallels Goriot. For studies of children who can do no wrong in the eyes of their parents, see Arthur Miller's *Death of a Salesman,* and Émile Zola's *Earth.* For a study of the degeneracy of the European social system at this time and for a treatment of the middle-class social climber, see Maupas-sant's *Bel-Ami.* Rastignac as a young man on the rise resembles Maupassant's hero in *Bel-Ami* or the hero in Pushkin's "The Queen of Spades."

Banerji, Bibhutibhushan. PATHER PANCHALI (SONG OF THE ROAD).
    1928. Novel. Bengali.

Author: Bibhutibhushan Banerji was born in 1894 north of Calcutta and died
in 1950. He took his B.A. at Ripon College in Calcutta and became a teacher.
He was later appointed inspector to the Society for the Protection of Cattle
and still later became a clerk in an estate office. He returned to teaching,
however, and continued to teach for the rest of his life. He is credited with
fifty published works—seventeen are novels of which this work is the most
famous due primarily to the film version by Satyajit Ray. Banerji is considered one of the greatest Bengali writers of the twentieth century.

Work: The contemporary setting for many an Indian novel is the village,
where most Indians do indeed live. The urban novel is rare. But *Pather
Panchali* is not just another "village novel"; neither does it focus on grinding
poverty as so many Indian novels do or present the idealized village as Tagore
had done. The two main characters are children, Opu and his sister Durga.
The story is about them; the reader sees through their eyes and comes to
know the world and the people in it as they know them. The structure of the
novel is deeply rooted in the *panchalis,* a chanted form of storytelling—
episode by episode. As the children travel down the road, not knowing what
is beyond the next bend, we see the village, the family, and the natural
surroundings through their experience and emotions.

Comparative: This novel might be read in conjunction with literature of
adolescence by American writers—particularly as a counter to the introspec-
tion and concern over personal problems that we consider typical of adolescents. A comparison of this novel, especially its characterization of the
children, with Younghill Kang's *The Grass Roof* and Mirok Li's *The Yalu
Flows,* two Korean novels, would emphasize human universalities as well as
the differences among cultures. For yet another treatment of adolescent
children, see Alberto Moravia's *Two Adolescents.*

Baudelaire, Charles. FLOWERS OF EVIL (LES FLEURS DU MAL). 1857.
    Poems. French.

Author: Baudelaire (1821-1867) was born and died in Paris. The only son of
an elderly man who died when Charles was seven, he was subjected to a stern
military stepfather. He was frequently poor and in debt, though his mother
finally settled a small income on him. A "Bohemian," he enjoyed shocking
the bourgeoisie. His writing began with art criticism, and he was the first
French critic to recognize the musical talent of Richard Wagner. As a translator, he was largely responsible for the popularity of Edgar Allan Poe in

France. *Les Fleurs du mal* first appeared—with several sensual poems ex-purgated by the authorities—in 1857. Variously called Romantic, Parnassian, and Decadent, Baudelaire is in many ways the first modern urban poet.

Work: Morbid, sensual, urbane, Baudelaire's poems, addressed in classical poetic forms to the "Hypocrite reader— You— My twin— My brother," deal with subject matter ranging from corpses and swans to voyages to imaginary lands, from prostitutes and cold rain in the city to escape into an aesthetic beyond. His poem "Correspondences" contributed to poetic theory the concept of synesthesia: impressions received by one sense organ are the symbolic and aesthetic equivalents of those received by other sense organs. For example, "Some aromas are . . . sweet as the sound of hautboys, meadow-green. . . ." Baudelaire saw Nature as a living temple of symbols that look back at the poet with friendly eyes.

In a characteristic romantic poem, "The Albatross," he sees the poet at home in flight of fancy but awkward and mocked in ordinary life:

> The Poet is like that Prince of clouds
> Who frequents the storm, the archer mocks;
> Exiles aground in sporting crowds,
> His giant wings will not let him walk.

A more sensational poem, "The Metamorphosis of the Vampire," begins with a sensuous woman "twisting and turning like a snake on coals" and ends with the same woman revealed as a diseased creature who has "sucked the marrow from my bones." Finally:

> There trembled a confusion of old bones
> Which squeaked in turning like a weathervane,
> Or like a signboard on an iron pole
> Swung by the wind through the long winter nights.

The evocation of the lover's extreme emotions from seduction to revulsed aftermath to wintry meaninglessness is powerful and illustrates Baudelaire's attempt to break through conventional subject matter and attitudes in poetry.

A typical urban poem is "Spleen LXXV": Paris in January, as the cold rain "spills mortality in the fog of the slums." He describes his thin and mangy cat shivering, the soul of an old poet wandering the gutter, and concludes gloomily:

> The great bell groans, the smoking coals
> Accompany the rheumy clock in falsetto
> While in a worn pack of cards that reeks of perfumes
> Ominous memento from a dropsical old dame
> The handsome Jack of Hearts and the Queen of Spades
> Chat nastily of their defunct amours.

Baudelaire's poetry speaks of a spiritually damned world, of a morally bankrupt society, of corrupted love, of beauty haunted by melancholy.

Comparative: For a comparison with an earlier French poet who combines
the traditional with an urban sense of reality, see François Villon. The Baude-
lairian obsession with the morbid and his desire to create effect find comparisons in the work of Edgar Allan Poe. For a similar fascination with decadence,
see Swinburne. For the long-range thematic influence of Baudelaire on
modern poetry, consider the poems of T. S. Eliot.

Beaumarchais, Pierre-Augustin Caron de. THE BARBER OF SEVILLE (LE
BARBIER DE SÉVILLE). 1775. Drama. French.

Author: Born the son of a watchmaker, Pierre Caron (1732-1799) took the
title of Beaumarchais from a small property held by his first wife. He won
Madame de Pompadour's favor by gifts of miniature timepieces and became
her attendant and finally her instructor in the harp. He advanced rapidly at
court and even became a French secret agent for a time. During the American
Revolution, he served the cause of France by outfitting expeditionary ships.
In a life crowded with incident, Beaumarchais wrote this comedy and *The
Marriage of Figaro.* At the time of the French Revolution, he was discredited
by the new government and spent years in exile, returning to Paris to die.

Work: The Barber of Seville is an Italianate farce in four acts. It relies on
stock characters in familiar situations—a heroine who is the captive of her
elderly guardian and a lover who relies on disguise and surreptitious meetings
—but something new was added by Beaumarchais in the character of Figaro,
the barber-surgeon. The Comte Almaviva, a young Spanish grandee, falls in
love with Rosine, jealously guarded by the old Bartholo, who wishes to marry
her. Aided and abetted by his friend Figaro, Almaviva under the name of
Lindor makes several entries into Bartholo's house and arranges an elopement
with Rosine. But as things turn out, Figaro and Almaviva, entering Rosine's
quarters at night, find a notary waiting to marry her and Bartholo and prompt-
ly use this handy resource to unite Rosine and Almaviva.

   Figaro walked on the stage fourteen years before the French Revolution
and one year before the American one. He is a new sort of man, the product
of the reexaminations of society by Rousseau and Voltaire: a commoner,
clever and intelligent, who is intimate with, even contemptuous of, the
nobility as he defeats the hereditary privileges of law and order which had
always belonged to the rich. The French court was delighted with the wit of
the play, unaware that this same revolutionary philosophy would soon be
their downfall. This drama is the source of Rossini's opera of the same title.

Comparative: Molière's *The Precious Damsels* has a weak forerunner of
Figaro called Mascarille; and, as in Molière's earlier play, *The School for
Wives,* Beaumarchais also takes the side of the young lover against the rich,
old suitor. A study could be made of other works that helped to prepare

revolutionary philosophy, sometimes innocently and sometimes more directly —Tom Paine's *Common Sense,* Harriet Beecher Stowe's *Uncle Tom's Cabin,* and Marx and Engels's *Communist Manifesto.* Another intriguing theme is the cloistered rearing of European girls, here and in Molière's plays; echoes may be found even in the twentieth century in García Lorca's *The House of Bernarda Alba. The Marriage of Figaro,* a sequel to *The Barber of Seville,* is equally delightful.

Beaumarchais, Pierre-Augustin Caron de. THE MARRIAGE OF FIGARO (LE MARIAGE DE FIGARO). 1781. Drama. French.

Author: See *The Barber of Seville.*

Work: In this three-act comedy, a sequel to *The Barber of Seville,* the plot is complicated by impersonations, masquerades, and mistaken identities. The page, Cherubino, precociously in love with every woman he sees, is involved in most of the lively incidents; however, the main story line continues that of *The Barber of Seville.* Figaro, Almaviva's valet, is preparing to marry saucy and charming Suzanne, in spite of an earlier promise to marry the elderly Marcelline, a promise he had made when he borrowed money from her. Almaviva, who has by now grown tired of his countess, Rosine, intends to exercise his seigneurial privileges by enjoying Suzanne's favors. The plots and counterplots evolve as Figaro, the countess, and Suzanne plan to outwit Almaviva and to expose him for what he is—an old lecher. In the final development, Almaviva makes an evening assignation in the garden with Suzanne, but it is, of course, the countess herself who shows up, wearing Suzanne's gown. Figaro, believing his love has betrayed him, is about to do violence to the Count. Figaro's dilemma with Marcelline is resolved when it turns out that he is in reality her son who had been stolen at birth. All problems eliminated in wonderfully witty scenes, Figaro and Suzanne marry joyfully.

In the third act, Figaro speaks out against the nobility: "Because you are a great lord, you think yourself a genius; you had only to be born, that's all; . . . but I, the devil!" A long monologue against hereditary privilege and in support of the rights of the ordinary man follows. Beaumarchais was speaking for the spirit of his time, and his words foreshadow the revolution that was soon to come.

Comparative: The situation of the lovers and their overlord is similar to that in Lope de Vega's *Fuenteovejuna* and in his *Paribáñez* and resembles that in Molière's *The School for Wives* and in Moratín's *The Maiden's Consent. The Marriage of Figaro* is at least in part a comedy of manners like those of Wilde, Shaw, Sheridan, and Goldsmith, and it relies on bright, sparkling dialogue as do these dramas. But there is nothing quite like the Beaumarchais sparkle lavished on the witty, ingenious Figaro. Mozart's opera of the same title has also been popular.

Cherubino might be considered a nascent Don Juan; see Molière's *Don Juan* and the comparisons suggested there. He is also an ironic echo of Almaviva as we first saw him in *The Barber of Seville*.

Beckett, Samuel. WAITING FOR GODOT (EN ATTENDANT GODOT). 1952. Drama. French.

Author: Beckett was born in Dublin in 1906, took degrees at Trinity College there, and studied and taught in Paris. He wrote several collections of poetry and stories in English, but after 1947 wrote mostly in French, his adopted language. Other works include *Molloy* (1951), *Malone Dies* (1952), and *Krapp's Last Tape* (1960).

Work: This play, an example of mid-century disillusionment and futility, and of their antitheses—persistent hope and habit—has enjoyed worldwide stage popularity and translation. To an extent, the drama is anti-theater.

Beside one small tree in the center of the stage, two tramps, Estragon and Vladimir, wait for Godot. They talk, they argue, they play childish games, they pull off their boots and put them on again (evening and morning), they eat carrots or black radishes under the tree which is bare or suddenly has leaves (passage of seasons). Pozzo, leading his servant Lucky in on a rope, moralizes while Lucky farcically entertains the three. Pozzo and Lucky leave. When they reappear in Act II, Pozzo is now blind, and Lucky leads him (passage of years). Estragon and Vladimir discuss suicide as an alternative to waiting and receive several messages from a boy regarding why Godot is again delayed. They go on waiting, repeating the same stage business as before.

Comparative: As allegory, the play compares with Wilder's *The Skin of Our Teeth.* See also Sartre's "The Wall" and Camus's *The Stranger*. The character of Pozzo and his victimization of Lucky is matched insidiously by Mario and the magician in Thomas Mann's story and may be considered to be a comment on the "human condition" (see Malraux's *Man's Fate*). In the general character of "new theater" and "anti-theater," Beckett's plays resemble Ionesco's, and all of them spring partly from Chekhov's innovations. Gogol's Akaki in "The Overcoat" perhaps introduces to literature such lost and despairing "little men" as Pozzo and Lucky.

Bédier, Joseph, ed. THE ROMANCE OF TRISTAN AND ISEULT. 13th Century. Tale. French.

Author: Joseph Bédier (1864-1938) was a medievalist and literary historian who, among his numerous publications, collected and made consecutive various legends.

Work: This courtly romance, retold and modernized by Bédier, is filled with the life of the Middle Ages, with love, adventure, superstition, heroics; it is, of course, the story of the star-crossed lovers which became the subject of Wagner's opera, *Tristan and Isolde.*

Tristan, serving his liege King Mark of Cornwall, fights and kills the giant Morholt of Ireland, Iseult's uncle. Unaware of this connection, Iseult herself cures Tristan of the wound he gained in this battle. By magic, a bird brings one of Iseult's golden hairs to King Mark, who falls in love with her. Tristan, now recovered, is sent to bring her in marriage to Mark. On the sea, bound for Cornwall, Tristan and Iseult unwittingly drink a love potion which had been prepared for Mark and Iseult and are immediately enthralled by love for one another: "drinking Passion and Joy most sharp, and Anguish without end, and Death."

The story now focuses on Tristan and Iseult, torn between their consuming love and their pledged loyalty to Mark. As they are desperately thrown together and hopelessly torn apart, the story becomes a tragedy which, after Tristan's exile and despairing marriage to another Iseult, the Iseult of the White Hands, reunites the two lovers in death.

This tale has become part of the Arthurian legends and appears in numerous retellings.

Comparative: The theme of the star-crossed lovers is found in Shakespeare's *Romeo and Juliet* and in Keller's *A Village Romeo and Juliet.* For similar motifs (such as the lovers living in a hut in the forest) on courtly love and life in the Middle Ages, see *Aucassin and Nicolette.* For a sardonic parody on both the original material and on Wagner's opera by the same title, see Thomas Mann's novella *Tristan.* Conrad's *Victory,* a similar story of a noble character, separated and aloof, tricked into fatal action by love, is relevant; particularly interesting here is the comparison of Schomberg, the gossipy and malevolent man in Conrad's story, with Gorvenal and his calumnious henchmen in the story of Tristan and Iseult. Malory's *Le Morte d'Arthur* has parallels in the love of Guenever and Lancelot, with Arthur taking the place of King Mark. Also in the Malory collection will be found parts of other versions of the Tristan and Iseult legends.

This work has had such a large influence on literature that it is impossible to list all of the retellings.

Boccaccio, Giovanni. THE DECAMERON (IL DECAMERONE). 1353.
    Stories. Italian.

Author: Giovanni Boccaccio (1313-1375) is widely believed to have been born in Paris. He, himself, promoted that myth. Instead, he was probably born in Certaldo, Italy, the illegitimate son of a Florentine merchant. He was trained for commerce in Florence and was expected to become a merchant.

He had no natural inclination for business, however, and moved to Naples, where he fell in with a group of learned men and enjoyed the court life of that city. An important turning point in his life occurred when he fell in love with a lady of the court, Maria d'Aquino. This love made him a poet. Maria, to whom he gave the pseudonym *Fiametta* (Little Flame), was both inspiration for and subject of much of his poetry. It was at her importuning that he wrote a novel in prose, *Il Filocolo*.

Among his poetic works are *Il Filostrato, Teseida,* and the *Roman de Troie.* These works are not widely read, for Boccaccio's genius does not lie in poetry and epic but in his strong narrative ability. Boccaccio spent his later years in Florence, where he wrote *The Decameron,* his most admired work. There is irony in the appraisal of history, for Boccaccio believed that the works he wrote in Latin, which he also wrote in Florence, would be those that would make him famous.

Work: The work opens as seven women and three men flee the plague (1348) in Florence. To pass the time, they agree that every day each will tell a story based on a new theme. By the time the plague has run its course, each has told ten stories, the hundred stories that make up *The Decameron.* Part of the brilliance of the work lies in the narrative framework that surrounds the story and provides the occasion for the tales. The stories are further graced by Boccaccio's lucidity and strong sense of story. *The Decameron* served as a veritable mine for later authors, who borrowed stories from it for their own use.

Comparative: Compare Chaucer's *Canterbury Tales* and other series of tales similar to *The Decameron* in subject and arrangement: *The Thousand and One Nights,* Marguerite de Navarre's *The Heptameron,* Balzac's *Droll Stories,* and the Indian beast fables, *The Panchatantra.* Comparisons to Boccaccio's sharp description of the plague may be found in Manzoni's *The Betrothed,* Defoe's *A Journal of the Plague Year,* Pepys's *Diary,* Giono's *The Horseman on the Roof,* and Camus's *The Plague.*

Böll, Heinrich. GROUP PORTRAIT WITH LADY (GRUPPENBILD MIT DAME). 1971. Novel. German.

Author: Heinrich Böll (1917–   ) was awarded the Nobel Prize for Literature in 1972. His citation reads: "for his writing, which through the combination of a broad perspective on his time and a sensitive skill in characterization has contributed to a renewal of German literature." Most of Böll's short stories and novels deal with World War II and its aftermath in Germany. Strongly anti-war, he shows the effect of war and defeat on the German people.

Although he does not overtly moralize, his examination of the human conscience and his concern with the tragedy of war make his works profoundly moral. Böll, who is the president of International P.E.N., an association of authors, donated a portion of his Nobel Prize money to help authors who are political prisoners. Other works include *Billiards at Half-Past Nine* (1961), *The Clown* (1965), *Absent without Leave* (1965), *Eighteen Stories* (1966), *Irish Journal* (1967), *End of a Mission* (1968), *Children Are Civilians Too* (1970), and *Adam and the Train* (1970).

Work: Using a multiple point-of-view, Böll presents the biography of a fictional character, Leni Pfeiffer, the lady of the title. The interviews through which this multiple point-of-view is created are conducted by an "author," who refers to himself as the Au. and who is himself a major character in the novel. Although Böll augments his portrait of Leni with objective descriptions and "official" documents, her personality and her previous life are drawn almost entirely from the Au.'s interviews with approximately sixty characters, who reveal as much of themselves as they do of Leni. Indeed, Leni herself assumes both human and mythical aspects.

Married and almost immediately widowed at the outbreak of World War II, Leni has an illegitimate child by a Russian prisoner-of-war. At the end of the novel, despite her age, she is again pregnant, this time by a Turk who has been one of her lodgers. Böll uses her story as a vehicle for satiric thrusts at German militarism and human hypocrisy, but he also presents brilliant, often sympathetic vignettes of many of his characters. Among the most memorable of these are Sister Rahel, probably an unrecognized saint; Boris Lvovich, Leni's Russian lover; Margret Schlomer, Leni's amoral best friend; Leni herself; and the Au., who emerges as a clearly delineated and likable character in his own right.

The multiple point-of-view, the galley of characters who constitute the "group portrait," and the adventures of Leni more than suggest that the huge canvas of this novel has allegorical elements. Gilbert Highet has suggested that Leni possibly represents Germany or at least symbolizes one aspect of the country—its people destroyed by the war, briefly attracted to Russia and the ideals of Communism, and finally taken over by invaders.

Comparative: In its use of a multiple point-of-view, this novel may be compared with Faulkner's *The Sound and the Fury* or *As I Lay Dying,* although in Böll's novel the multiple point-of-view is filtered through the consciousness of the Au. and is, therefore, colored by his reactions to people and events. In its anti-war aspects it may be compared with Crane's *The Red Badge of Courage,* Remarque's *All Quiet on the Western Front,* or Solzhenitsyn's *One Day in the Life of Ivan Denisovich.* In its wry and satirical presentation of life in modern Germany, it is best compared with Grass's *The Tin Drum.* As a portrait of a heroine remarkable for her fortitude, it lends itself to comparison with Henry James's *Portrait of a Lady.*

THE BOOK OF SONGS (SHIH-CHING). Translated by Arthur Waley. Grove Press, 1960. Also **THE CONFUCIAN ODES.** Translated by Ezra Pound. New Direction Paperbacks, 1959. Chou period (111–256 B.C.) Poetry. Chinese.

Author: These songs from North China, dating from approximately 800 to 600 B.C. and comprising the oldest collection of Chinese poetry, are considered one of the Confucian classics. Tradition says that during the Chou dynasty, the king sent out officials to listen to the songs sung in the countryside so that he might get the "soundings of the people," whether they suffered and complained or were satisfied with their rulers. Some of these "soundings" made their way into the Classic of Poetry, or the Odes. Confucius was attributed to have said, "Why don't you study the Odes? The Odes will arouse you, give you food for thought, teach you how to make friends, show you the way of resentment, bring you near to being useful to your parents and sovereign, and help you remember the names of many birds, animals, plants, and trees."

Work: The songs, on such themes as courtship and marriage, warriors and war, agriculture, feasting, music and dancing, hunting, and friendship, are essentially in ballad form.

The two translations cited above might well be used together in presenting this work. Waley provides a useful introduction, and his translations carry the greater authority for accuracy. His notes expand the context of the poems, though most of them require no special background. Pound's translations, however, are required reading for the study of Chinese literature, for the study of contemporary poetry, and for the study of the relationship between the poetic sensibility of the Confucian period and that of contemporary America. Pound's language makes the scalp tingle, and his translations "sing," thus coming closer to what these poems were—songs. In 1915, T. S. Eliot observed that Pound was the "inventor of Chinese poetry for our time." While each generation must have its own translators, Pound has created a modern classic that cannot be displaced, even by a new generation of translators whose work is based on sound scholarship.

Comparative: To compare forms, images, and themes such as love and separation, see *The Interior Landscape: Love Poems from a Classical Tamil Anthology* translated by A. K. Ramanujan, and *In Praise of Krishna* translated by Edward C. Dimock, Jr. with Denise Levertov. For a study of the songs in their Chinese literary context see *Chinese Literature, an Anthology from the Earliest Times to the Present Day* edited by William McNaughton.

Borges, Jorge Luis. A PERSONAL ANTHOLOGY. 1967. Stories, poetry, and essays. Argentinian.

Author: Jorge Luis Borges (1899–   ), intellectual, fantasizer, aesthete, comes from an old-line, closely knit criollo family of Buenos Aires. His father, author, jurist, and student of languages, possessed an outstanding English library, and the young Borges read extensively from it and was educated by an English tutor.

The family's stay in Geneva, Switzerland, prior to World War I and until 1918, further encouraged Borges's international tastes, allowing him the opportunity to learn French, to study German, and to embrace Schopenhauer, a distinct influence on his writings. From 1919 to 1921 Borges traveled in Spain, took up residence in Seville and Madrid, and studied the Ultraístas, Dadaists, and Surrealists.

Back in his beloved Buenos Aires in 1921, the shy, reserved, very private author published major collections of his poetry in 1923, 1925, and 1929. Worldwide acclaim greeted Borges after the appearance of his fiction collections: *The Garden of the Forking Paths* (1941), *Ficciones* (1944), now considered his most important single work and a book which won for him the Argentine Writers' Association Prize, and *El Aleph* (1949). Usually apolitical, Borges opposed the Perón dictatorship (1946-1955) and, as a result, lost his library post in Buenos Aires. Following Perón's fall, however, he was named director of the Argentine National Library as well as Professor of English and North American Literature at the University of Buenos Aires.

Despite the rapid deterioration of his eyesight in the 1950s, Borges continued to write and has achieved great fame, winning his country's National Prize for Literature in 1956 as well as the Paris International Editors Prize in 1961. He has lectured at Harvard and at the Universities of Texas and Oklahoma.

Borges has produced verse, essays, stories, sketches, and screenplays; his fame rests mainly on short pieces collected from the several genres. He has translated Gide, Kafka, Faulkner, and Virginia Woolf.

Work: The anthology contains a total of forty-eight pieces—essays, short stories, sketches, and parables—and is the work upon which Borges wishes to stake his reputation. The selections are arranged according to their "sympathies and differences." For the most part, the pieces are impressionistic, offering little or no plot line or characterization. Always his concerns are with the philosophical, the aesthetic, the ritual, the puzzle, the epiphany. The pieces make suitable reading for only the most advanced students because Borges demands that the reader meet the level of his encyclopedic mind with its inventory of arcane and disparate bits of information from various cultures.

In "Death and Compass," the chief symbols are the labyrinths—which, along with leopards, roses, daggers, and books, frequent his works. The hero, Erik Lonnrot, learns that no matter how clever his reasoning, life does not fit his conclusions. He is doomed to repeat his mistakes until his next life, when he is promised a labyrinth made of a single straight line, "invisible and everlasting."

"The Aleph," the title of one of the more notable stories, is the place where "all the places of the world are found, seen from every angle." In search of the memory of the dead Beatriz, Borges, narrator and hero, is briefly imprisoned in a cellar by his host, whereupon he discovers the aleph that pictures for him all the images of past reality and imagination.

From "The Secret Miracle" we learn that the poet must create his work because it "prevents the spectators from forgetting unreality, which is the necessary condition of art."

The poems, for the most part, repeat the same ideas—"I am one with all mankind," "I am history repeating itself."

Comparative: In narrative stance, theme, and symbol Borges frequently mirrors Poe. At times his sense of the unreal is one with Kafka's; his image patterns may be compared with those of Mallarmé.

Bownas, Geoffrey, and Anthony Thwaite, eds. and trans. THE PENGUIN BOOK OF JAPANESE VERSE. Penguin Books, 1964. Poetry. Japanese.

Author: The poets represented in this anthology range from anonymous folk poets of the eighth century to established contemporary poets, and all major periods and schools of Japanese poetry are included. There are emperors and empresses, princes and princesses, government officials, frontier guards, court ladies, priests, and samurai. Most Americans will not recognize the famous *haiku* writers included here: Bashō, Buson, and Issa.

Work: What Wordsworth declared in 1800, that "poetry is the spontaneous overflow of powerful feelings," the Japanese have known from the beginning of their long poetic tradition. For them, poetry is the language of emotion and feeling, the tongue in which people speak at times of intense joy, pain, longing, or indignation. That is not to say that there is no intellectual poetry in Japan but that the Japanese poets tend to tell us what they feel more than what they think.

The introduction to this work surveys the language of the Japanese poets, the forms *(tanka, haiku, renga, and senryū),* and the subjects (the feelings evoked by love, by separation, by falling blossom, by the autumn moon, by old age and death). Probably no poetry is more accessible, or more familiar with the truest feelings and emotions of the individual.

Comparative: Most forms of Japanese poetry are very brief, but they are full of suggestion, reverberation, and allusion and thereby require reflection. It is wise, therefore, to ponder long the poems in this collection before comparing them with other works.

For those who wish to begin only with *haiku,* see *An Introduction to Haiku: An Anthology of Poems and Poets from Bashō to Shiki,* with translations and commentary by Harold G. Henderson. Read carefully the definition of *haiku* there and in this work, since it is a form frequently misunderstood and consequently poorly interpreted and imitated. Although the *haiku* can be an excellent introduction to the reading and writing of poetry, it is not simply a seventeen-syllable poem. For *haiku* within a prose context, see *The Year of My Life* by Issa Kobayashi.

For other titles of Japanese poetry and literature, see The Asian Literature Bibliography Series, *A Guide to Japanese Poetry* by J. Thomas Rimen and Robert E. Morrell, *A Guide to Japanese Prose* by A. H. Marks and Barry D. Bort, and *A Guide to Japanese Drama* by Leonard C. Pronko; also recommended is *Ten Thousand Leaves: Love Poems from the Manyoshu,* an illustrated edition of poems from the oldest Japanese anthologies translated by Harold Wright. For comparisons with other cultures in the East Asian tradition see *Sunflower Splendor: Three Thousand Years of Chinese Poetry,* edited by Wu-Chi Liu and Irving Yucheng Lo, *1000 Years of Vietnamese Poetry* and *The Bamboo Grove: An Introduction to Sijo,* edited and translated by Richard Rutt. For a comparison with other brief forms, including imagery and subject matter, see *The Interior Landscape: Love Poems from a Classical Tamil Anthology,* translated by A. K. Ramanujan, and the *Ghazals of Ghalib,* edited by Aijaz Ahmad. For a comparison of images with American and British poets see *The Imagist Poem,* edited by William Pratt.

For more recent developments in Japanese poetry see *Post-War Japanese Poetry,* edited and translated by Harry and Lynn Guest and Shōzō Kajima.

Brecht, Bertolt. MOTHER COURAGE AND HER CHILDREN (MUTTER COURAGE UND IHRE KINDER). 1941. Drama. German.

Author: Bertolt Brecht (1898-1956), born into a bourgeois family in Augsburg, revolted against middle-class morality and after World War II lived in East Germany. In his youth, during the last days of World War I, he served as a medical orderly in the German army. After the war he became a playwright and drama critic. For the rest of his life he earned his living as an author. With Hitler's rise to power, he left Germany in 1933 and spent fourteen years of exile in Switzerland, Denmark, Finland, and the United States (1941-1947). After appearing before the House Un-American Activities Committee on October 30, 1947, he returned to Europe and several months later settled in East Berlin. Although proficient in several literary genres, he earned his greatest fame as a dramatist. His best-known plays are *The Threepenny Opera* (in collaboration with Kurt Weill), *Mother Courage and Her Children, The Life of Galileo, The Good Woman of Setzuan,* and *The Caucasian Chalk Circle.*

Work: Although *Mother Courage* is set in seventeenth-century Germany during the Thirty Years War (1618-1648), in idiom, situation, and characterization the play could be about any modern war. Its leading character, Mother

Courage, herself explains that she received her nickname because she drove like a madwoman through the bombardment of Riga, not for patriotic reasons, but because in her cart she had fifty loaves of bread that were going moldy. This explanation is the key to her character: she is concerned primarily with her business, a canteen wagon from which she sells goods to warring armies. It makes very little difference to her whether she sells to one side or the other—just so she stays in business.

The play follows Mother Courage for twelve years, as one by one she loses her three children. Her elder son enlists for money and is deemed a hero when he kills peasants to get their cattle; later, during a brief armistice, he does the same thing and is shot as a criminal. Her younger son becomes an army paymaster and is killed when he refuses to reveal to the enemy where he has concealed the regimental cashbox. Her only daughter, a mute, is killed by the enemy because, unable to shout a warning, she has climbed to a rooftop and is beating a drum loudly to warn the villagers of a surprise attack. At the opening of the play Mother Courage's wagon is pulled by her two sons while she and her daughter ride in it. At the end of the play, the indomitable Mother Courage has harnessed herself to it in order to follow the war.

From its opening lines this is clearly an anti-war play. However, Brecht has another target: the bourgeois desire for money represented in the actions of Mother Courage and of many of those around her. Mother Courage is herself an enigma. Though Brecht claimed that she was a negative character, a profiteer, audiences tend to be moved by her sheer will to survive and her indomitable spirit.

Comparative: The play may be compared with Brecht's anti-war poetry, notably "To Posterity" and "General, That Tank," found in *Modern German Poetry* edited and translated by Michael Hamburger and Christopher Middleton. Büchner's *Woyzek,* though quite differently set up and developed, is comparable in its attitude toward war. *Mother Courage* also lends itself to comparison with a number of anti-war novels, notably Stephen Crane's *Red Badge of Courage,* Erich Maria Remarque's *All Quiet on the Western Front,* and Anatoly Kuznetsov's *Babi-Yar.* As an indomitable woman, Mother Courage herself may be compared with a whole spectrum of heroines, beginning with the Medea of Euripides and continuing through the centuries to Leni in Heinrich Böll's *Group Portrait with Lady.* Finally, there is something of Shakespeare's Falstaff in Mother Courage's amoral attitude toward life and war.

Brecht, Bertolt. THE THREEPENNY OPERA (DIE DREIGROSCHENOPER), in collaboration with the composer Kurt Weill. 1929. Drama. German.

Author: See *Mother Courage and Her Children.*

Work: Brecht has generally preserved Gay's plot, and *The Threepenny Opera* is fairly considered to be an adaptation of *The Beggar's Opera.* The action is set in Victorian London.

Macheath, captain of a syndicate of thieves and cutthroats, "marries" Polly Peachum, only daughter of Jonathan Jeremiah Peachum, outfitter of phony prosthetics for beggars and "cripples" and himself captain of an underworld kingdom of these subjects. A hilarious wedding takes place in a barn which has been converted into a palace with stolen furnishings of London's great salons. Hating to lose his daughter and mistrusting Macheath, Peacham arranges for his betrayal to the police. The sheriff of London, Tiger Brown, turns out to be Macheath's old army buddy, who does his best to help Macheath escape.

Mack refuses to alter his habits, however, and continues his weekly visits to his harlot "wives," who sell him to the constables through Peachum's bribery. His kind "wife" Lucky helps him to escape, and he turns over his business to Polly. Once more Mack reverts to custom and visits the girls. This time he is arrested while the great Coronation goes on outside the prison. Sentenced to be hanged, he is saved at the last moment by a sudden pardon, plus ennoblement, which arrives by courier (Tiger Brown) from the Gracious Queen. We presume that Mack and Polly live happily ever after.

Interspersed in the action are delightful light verse ballads, ballades, and catches. Each scene is preceded by a gloss as if the work were an eighteenth-century novel instead of a twentieth-century drama. Signs come down from the proscenium, illustrated charts contribute to the ballads—all highly amusing and unexpected even in the reading.

This chant-comedie has been enormously successful in Europe and the United States. Its success stems from the popularity of Weill's music ("Mack the Knife" is a song that America knows well) as well as from Brecht's sardonic but hopeful view of life.

Comparative: Comparisons may be found in the "Court of Miracles" from Hugo's *Notre Dame de Paris,* in Stevenson's short story about François Villon titled "A Lodging for the Night," and in Cervantes's "Rinconete and Cortadillo" from his collection of twelve *Exemplary Novels.* There are also echoes from Villon's poetry and biblical quotations used seriously and in mockery. The wedding in *The Marriage of Figaro* by Beaumarchais is comparable with the wedding of Mack and Polly.

Bulgakov, Mikhail Afansievich. THE MASTER AND MARGARITA (MASTER I MARGARITA). 1928-1940, pub. 1966-1967. Novel. Russian.

Author: Mikhail Bulgakov (1891-1940), after a brief medical career, turned to literature. Although he accepted the revolution, he refused to write in the prescribed socialist realist style, a refusal which brought him into conflict with the authorities. Like Chekhov, Bulgakov was more concerned with the impotent upper classes than with the rising "new man." His first novel, *The White Guard* (1925), was produced by the Moscow Art Theater as *The Days of the Turbins* (1926) and was banned after a few performances. A series of short satires, published as *Deviltry* (1925), led authorities to brand him as an enemy and "internal émigré." By 1930, his works were barred from publication, though he was allowed to work as a literary consultant for the theater until his death. During these years he continued to write satirical attacks on the Stalinist regime, and many of these works, including *The Heart of a Dog* (1925), *Black Snow* (1936-1939), and *The Master and Margarita* (1928-1940), have recently been published in expurgated form in the Soviet Union.

Work: This novel intricately weaves together two stories, one of which is an account by a character in the novel of Christ's confrontation with Pilate. Numerous clues connect the two stories, and both make the same point—the point made by all of Bulgakov's works: "the greatest crime is cowardice."

The Christ story is a philosophical attack on cowardice supposedly written by the Master (an author confined to an asylum near Moscow) and retold in segments by various characters in the novel. The tale centers on Pilate's desire to save Yeshua (Jesus) and his final capitulation to political necessity. Bulgakov (for whom the Master is a thinly disguised double) seems to be attacking the authorities for permitting many would-be saviors and benefactors to be exiled or condemned because it is expedient. In this respect it is interesting to note that Bulgakov's works have been highly praised by Pasternak and Solzhenitsyn.

The "realistic" level of the novel is a raucous, fantastic tale of Stalinist Moscow. The devil and his assistants, including a gigantic cat who is a deadshot with a pistol, appear as a magic act at a Moscow theater and in the course of their adventures reveal the situation in socialist Russia. The story becomes a vehicle for Bulgakov's attack on the housing situation (one of the characters is named Bezdomny—literally "without a house"), political corruption, literary censorship, and many other failures of the revolution. Like his Goethean counterpart, this devil does much good in his exposure of corruption and in his liberation of the Master, who is returned to Margarita in exchange for a pact to serve the devil. The Master, however, is granted not salvation but merely rest, for like Pilate he has capitulated to the authorities.

Comparative: The most immediate thematic comparison is to be made with the Faust stories, most notably Goethe's. Bulgakov's use of satire follows that of a long line of Russian writers, most notably Gogol, Ilf, and Petrov. The more serious side of the novel's attack on Stalinist Russia suggests comparison with Solzhenitsyn's novels. Other interesting treatments of the Christ story include Anatole France's short story, "The Procurator of Judea," and "The Legend of the Grand Inquisitor" from Dostoevski's *The Brothers Karamazov.*

Calderón (Pedro Calderón de la Barca). LIFE IS A DREAM (LA VIDA ES SUEÑO). 1635. Drama. Spanish.

Author: Calderón (1600-1681) was a soldier, priest, and author, like his contemporary Lope de Vega, but he was a more rigid writer and chose universal themes instead of the nationalistic ones that Vega favored. *The Prodigious Magician* (1637) is well known for its statement of the Faust theme.

Work: This three-act tragicomedy is a parable on the illusion of reality and the reality of illusion. Prince Sigismundo has been kept captive all his life because prophecy stated that he would overthrow the king (his father) and become a prime force of evil released on the world. The king decides to test the truth of the prophecy and has Sigismundo drugged and brought to court. When Sigismundo awakens, he behaves wildly and attempts murder and rape. He is returned to his dungeon and told that those experiences were no more than a dream. However, the evil that he is convinced he has done, even in a dream, so works upon him that when he is released by a political coup, he is reformed and can control his passions. Having conquered himself rather than his father, Sigismundo is ceded the crown.

Comparative: Pirandello offers another dramatic expression of this theme in *Six Characters in Search of an Author,* and Richter examines the idea in a modern novel, *The Waters of Kronos.* Kafka, in *Metamorphosis* and *The Trial,* twists the theme into nightmare. Thurber's "The Secret Life of Walter Mitty" turns Calderón's theme into pathetic comedy. The idea of a dream changing a man's character (in the case of Calderón's drama, "dream" would have to be put in quotes) is an old one: Jacob and his vision of the heavenly ladder, Joseph interpreting the dreams of other Potiphar's prisoners, the dreams of Aeneas that direct his actions, and so on. Sigismundo's confusion between reality and dream is the material for Cervantes in *Don Quixote* and for many other authors down through modern literature—Beckett's *Malone Dies,* for example. Much of "fairy tale" literature also raises the question of where reality ends and fantasy begins. Gerstäcker's *Germelshausen* (from which the musical play *Brigadoon* came) is a fine example.

Camus, Albert. THE STRANGER (L'ÉTRANGER). 1942. Novel. French.

Author: Camus, born in Algeria in 1913 and killed in an auto accident near Paris in 1960, studied philosophy, was a newspaper reporter and editor for a Paris publishing house, edited the underground newspaper *Combat* during the German occupation of France, and was awarded the Nobel Prize in 1957. He wrote novels, stories, essays, and plays.

Work: This existentialist novel deals with the problem of the self in relationship to individual freedom, society, and nature. Meursault reacts to events, both in society and in nature, in a seemingly natural way; that is, he does not act according to the patterns of his society but in a purely personal and socially indifferent way. Thus he appears casual and even callous at his mother's death; he is willing to marry or not marry his girl friend when she suggests marriage; his friends choose him, he does not choose them. In seeming reaction to the overwhelming heat as well as to what he thought was the flash of a knife in an Arab's hand, Meursault shoots an Arab who is sitting in the cool shade of a rock. When he is placed on trial, he does not respond to the threat to his life in the usual way; he does not repent of his crime, but is unhappy over the loss of his freedom. His social and moral indifference, even more than his crime, weighs against him in the minds of the officials who try him; and, indeed, he is condemned to die as much for his lack of conformity to social patterns as for murder. In his cell, waiting for death, he opens his heart to the "benign indifference of the universe" for the first time and begins to understand what freedom signifies.

Comparative: The theme of freedom and the self in this book contrasts with the theme of Gide's *The Immoralist.* Michel of *The Immoralist* sought individual freedom by breaking from his socially created self, but Meursault has his freedom taken from him because he is so honestly himself that he seems to behave with inhuman indifference. Gide's protagonist seeks his almost-animal, instinctive self through alienation from society and from his former self; Camus's hero begins in an almost animal-like, unaware alienation and is forced to understand his paradoxical dilemma: an apparently hypocritical society which will destroy him for being alienated from it, and an indifferent universe to which he has responded naturally but which retaliates by depriving him his freedom. See also similar themes in Dostoevski's *Notes from Underground* and Mann's *Death in Venice.*

Camus, Albert. THE PLAGUE (LA PESTE). 1947. Novel. French.

Author: See *The Stranger.*

Work: The novel is laid in Oran, Algeria, but the plague is allegorical and can be read in reference to France's moral degeneration and to the Nazi occupation during World War II. All in all, *The Plague* is a serious, reflective, fascinating study of humanity in a state of siege, the moral determinants and the outcomes.

In remarkable passages the rapid assault of pestilence is described as it invades a provincial, self-satisfied town. The narrator, through his own comments and through the observations of conscientious Dr. Rieux and Jean

Tarrou, the diarist, pictures the rise of the epidemic. A gallery of memorable characters adds significance to the principal observations: Cottard, an outsider in society and a petty racketeer who attempts suicide, who later tries to become a friend to everyone, and who at last goes down fighting the police in a burst of insanity; Grand, a would-be author whose nicety never allows him to go beyond the first sentence of his projected opus; Rambert, a journalist who accidentally enters Oran and makes one involved attempt to escape before deciding to settle in and endure this common misfortune of humanity; and Father Paneloux, the voice of Christian conscience expressing God's judgment. There is also the nameless old man who spits at cats, his actions symptomatic of human quirks and persistence. Even the story of Meursault *(The Stranger)* is mentioned in the city of Oran.

The allegorical element of this work ("the whole town was running a temperature") refers to the spiritual turpitude of France and contemporary society; the buboes of the plague, for instance, are labeled "stigmata." Endurance, the first state of France after the collapse, finally turns to panic and lawlessness. But through the events of this common suffering the narrator observes: "No longer were there individual destinies; only a collective destiny, made of plague and the emotions shared by all."

Tarrou dies. Dr. Rieux's wife, sent off to a sanitarium before the outbreak of the plague, also dies. The people, once the pestilence is ended, return to being what they were before, "and this was at once their strength and their innocence."

Comparative: Rieux, like Rivière in Saint-Exupéry's *Night Flight,* fights unflinchingly a losing battle. The general situation of humanity faced with an emergency that brings out its innate quality and capacity is that of Tolstoi's *Master and Man* and Dinesen's "The Deluge at Norderney." An amusing analogue to Grand, who is unable to write beyond the initial sentence of his masterwork, is Dickens' Mr. Dick in *David Copperfield.* Among other French works with thinly disguised political and propagandistic references written during the occupation is Anouilh's *Antigone.*

Catullus, Gaius Valerius. THE POEMS OF CATULLUS. Translated by Peter Whigham. Penguin, 1969. Also **ODI ET AMO: THE COMPLETE POETRY OF CATULLUS.** Roy Swanson. Bobbs Merrill, 1959. 1st Century B.C. Poems. Roman.

Author: Catullus, the greatest Latin lyric poet, was born in Verona about 84 B.C. and died in his thirtieth year, having become the dominant figure among the New Poets *(neoterici)* of the Rome of Cicero, Pompey, and Caesar. We know little of his affluent family, but we do know that Catullus was devoted to a brother. Catullus came to Rome in his youth; he owned two villas—one in Tibur (Tivoli) and one in Sirmio (on Lake Garda)—but lived mainly in Rome where he met the woman celebrated in his "Poems to Lesbia" cycle. This great love of his life, whom he met in his early twenties, seems to have been the beautiful but notorious Clodia Metelli, wife of the consul Q. Metellus Celer and sister of Cicero's arch-enemy, Publius Clodius. She apparently found him a charming but passing attraction, and the content of his poems ranges from rapturous early love to disillusion at her unfaithfulness and finally to hatred. Catullus apparently accompanied Gaius Memmius to the Near East while the latter was governor of Bithynia; during this voyage he probably wrote the famous lament, "Ave atque vale," for his brother whose tomb near Troy he visited.

Work: Of his poems, over a hundred have survived. These are divided into three groups according to length: Poems 1-60 are short pieces of great metrical variety; 61-68 are the longest (61 being a lovely epithalamium or wedding song); 69-116 are short elegies (the longest being 26 lines) and epigrams. The poems were not published by Catullus himself but by a later editor. All but Poem 62 come from a single manuscript discovered in 1311 near Verona.

Catullus was master of all varieties of verse. He belonged to a group of deliberate innovators, though Sappho was the model for his most passionate poems (see especially Poem 51, a direct translation). His range is remarkable; he could change abruptly in mood from delicacy to obscenity, from pathos to sneer, from ecstatic love to contempt. His distinctive quality stems from the immediacy and vitality of his verse in which the realism of tone and detail serve to heighten the grandeur of theme.

Catullus satirized Caesar and others and wrote invective against rivals, but he is best known for the love poems to Lesbia.

Comparative: The influence of Catullus pervades European poetry. Virgil's "Complaint of Dido" in the *Aeneid* is modeled on the poignant lament of Ariadne in Poem 64. Sir Philip Sidney wrote the first formal epithalamium in English in 1580, which marks the beginning of the influence of Catullus on this form in England. Poem 5, the popular "Vivamus mea Lesbia" ("Let us live and love, my Lesbia") can be directly compared to Ben Jonson's "To Celia" (1605) and Marvell's "To His Coy Mistress" (1646), since Catullus's poem served as model. Shakespeare's Sonnet 93 and John Donne's "The Extasie" deal with the same material.

Cellini, Benvenuto. THE LIFE OF BENVENUTO CELLINI (LA VITA DE BENVENUTO CELLINI). Completed in 1562; published in 1728. Autobiography. Italian.

Author: Benvenuto Cellini (1500-1571), whose autobiography remained unpublished until one hundred and fifty-seven years after his death, was one of the great artists of all time. Goldsmith, silversmith, and sculptor, he was a proud, contentious man who quarreled fiercely with his patrons as well as with his rivals. Early in life he apprenticed himself to a goldsmith in his native town, Florence. At sixteen he was producing works of art and was already in serious trouble with the authorities for engaging in a duel. After exile in Siena and a period of wandering in Italy, he was eligible to return to Florence, which he did. But he was soon in trouble again and fled to Rome. There he was so admired as a goldsmith by the rich and powerful that he had more commissions than he could meet. Soon in trouble again, this time for killing a rival goldsmith, he fled to Naples. When he returned to Rome, he was imprisoned, tried to escape, and was finally pardoned by a powerful Cardinal. Back in Florence, he was soon in prison again, this time on charges of immorality. His brawling, sprawling life was filled with quarrels with men of low and high rank, with duels, with romantic episodes and adventure—and always he worked at his art. The saltcellar that he made for Francis I, a gold and silver masterpiece of baroque ornamentation, is regarded by some critics as one of the most beautiful works of art ever produced.

Work: The Life of Benvenuto Cellini offers a vivid picture of life during the sixteenth century and, filled with exaggeration and boastfulness as it is, reveals a boisterous, colorful personality. It is a book which documents how petty Cellini could be as a person and how noble he was as an artist. He shows himself a braggart, a namedropper, a liar, and a murderer. At the same time, he is energetic, creative, and daring. Some of the episodes in his autobiography are so well known that even people who have not read the book are familiar with them: Cellini's calling up of the devil at midnight in the Coliseum, his casting of the famous statue of Perseus though he was near death with illness, his dramatic release from prison through the intervention of a Cardinal who held that an artist of Cellini's ability could not be expected to meet the moral standards of common men. The *Life* projects a man of heroic proportions and reveals an age unique in its zest.

Comparative: An insight into the politics of Cellini's time can be gained by reading Machiavelli. Cellini sets a precedent for the notion that artists should receive special allowances, an idea that flowered again during the Romantic period. Dumas, in the *Three Musketeers,* offers comparable romantic adventures, and Aristophanes and Petronius may be used for their views of the raucous lives of poets and artists of other periods. In 1837 Berlioz based an opera on Cellini's autobiography.

Cervantes, Miguel de. DON QUIXOTE. 1615. Novel. Spanish.

Author: Cervantes (1547-1616) was born the son of a poor Spanish surgeon. He saw action in Italy and took part in the sea battle of Lepanto (1571), where he lost the use of his left hand. Along with his brother, he was later

captured by the Turks and taken into slavery in Algiers. After several unsuccessful escape attempts, he returned to Madrid and began to write plays.
He worked for a time as a quartermaster for the navy and was called to
account for deficits in his bookkeeping. Finally, he retired to a writing career,
and the first part of *Don Quixote* appeared in 1605. The book was an immediate success, but Cervantes realized little money from it. Philip is reputed to
have said when he saw a student from the palace balcony in fits of laughter,
"that man is either crazy or he is reading *Don Quixote.*"

Work: One of the world's truly great novels, *Don Quixote* is sometimes said
to have begun the genre as we understand it—the exploration of the interior
life. The novel bridges the medieval period and our own, for Sancho and
Quixote embody the twin desires of all humanity.

The story is probably known to everyone. The mind of the elderly Don
has become unhinged from reading too many romances, but at the same time
Quixote perceives evil in the world and the need for a knight-errant to attack
it. Refurbishing the rusty armor in his attic and engaging the stout little
Sancho Panza as his mule-mounted squire, the Don sets out to free the world
of its troubles. He sees windmills as giants, frees a miserable gang of cutthroats, and adopts as his liege lady a scullery girl. Finally, a friendly student
named Carasco dresses in armor, defeats the poor tired Don, and orders him
to retire honorably from knight-errantry.

Insanity does not entirely characterize Quixote's condition, for a real
awareness of the dangers to the world exists in the Don's cloudy mind.
Sancho, the hard-headed practical man, wavers between doubts about the
Don's madness and the sanctity of his purpose, but finally comes to share,
at least partially, his master's ideals. The problems in *Don Quixote* center on
the difficulty of recognizing what is real and what is imagined, what is good
and what is evil. The Don's joust with the world is thus comic and tragic.

Comparative: A summary of *Amadís,* the novel whose chivalric and ridiculous
excesses inspired Cervantes to write *Don Quixote,* might be read as well as
selections from the fantastic adventures in Malory's *Le Morte d'Arthur.*
Ridiculous aspects of outworn chivalry appear in White's *The Once and
Future King* and in Twain's *A Connecticut Yankee in King Arthur's Court.*
Comparisons may also be made with picaresque novels such as Quevedo's
Lazarillo de Tormes. Celestina by Fernando De Rojas is valuable for period
information.

The contrast between the practical Sancho and the heroic Don is echoed
in Shaw's *Arms and the Man.* Another statement of the theme "What is real?"
is found in Calderón's *Life Is a Dream.* Flaubert's *Madame Bovary* demonstrates the effects of romantic reading as a preparation for living in a
realistic world. But finally, there is no adequate comparison, for *Don Quixote*
stands alone and supreme.

Chateaubriand, François-René de. **ATALA** (1801) and **RENÉ** (1802). Novels. French.

Author: The Vicomte de Chateaubriand (1768-1848) was commissioned in 1791 to go to America to explore for the Northwest Passage. He spent five months in the New World and was fascinated with the Indians ("children of nature"). The two sketches cited above were intended for a long work of prose and poetry, *Les Natchez,* and were written in the same romantic strain as Bernardin de Saint-Pierre's *Paul and Virginia.* Chateaubriand's political career began with the downfall of Napoleon, and he became a minister at Ghent for Louis XVIII and then ambassador to England.

Work: In these two romances of love and mysticism in the New World, we find aspects of the then new attitude called romanticism.

In *Atala,* the old Indian Chactas tells his life story to his adopted European son, René. Chactas and his people had been defeated by the Muskogees, and Chactas goes as a refugee to Saint Augustine, where he is reared by the Spaniard Lopez. But Chactas wearies of civilized life and refuses to embrace Christianity. He returns to the wilds and is captured by the Muskogees and condemned to burn. The lovely Atala, a chieftain's daughter and a Christian convert, frees him and goes away with him. They meet a hermit in the wilderness who converts Chactas. Atala, Chactas learns, is only half Indian, for her real father was Lopez. In Chactas's absence Atala poisons herself because she had vowed on her mother's deathbed never to love a man. Chactas and the hermit come back in time to join their tears with hers, and Atala dies, forgiving and forgiven.

In *René,* the European tells his history. Like Chateaubriand himself, René grew up in solitude with only a sister as a close companion. René's father has died, and the old estate passes to a brother. René and Amelia, his sister, are cast out on the world. They set up a modest home together, but in grief at the miseries of the world René is driven to wander over the face of Europe. Finally he and Amelia rejoin and for a brief time know happiness again, but Amelia then renounces the world and flees to a convent. René is not allowed to see her, but he is present as she takes her vows and hears her murmur under her mourning veil: "Merciful God, let me never rise from this deathbed, and lavish upon my brother all Thy blessings, who has never shared my guilty passion." René flees in grief to the New World to find in the life of the simple savage the natural religion which Europe has lost.

Romantic motifs in *René* include self-pity, long contemplations amid the rugged solitudes of nature and the mossy ruins of Gothic castles, the mystical languors and trappings of religion, and the longing for the faraway (America and its Indians, in this case). Symptoms such as these gave rise to a diagnosis of one aspect of the romantic age: *mal de René.*

These are the novel fragments that France wept over in the early 1880s. Chateaubriand created characters of excessive nobility, swept them with impossible passions, and set them in a wild Eden which was still obedient to God's first laws. The American student will enjoy the inaccuracies of Chateaubriand's lush descriptions—palm trees in Kentucky and crocodiles along the Mississippi—and the quaint customs of the Muskogees and the Seminoles he reports.

Comparative: Atala's story has some points of contact with Hudson's *Green Mansions.* René's story is the material of a Gothic romance; see Horace Walpole's *The Castle of Otranto* for something of the atmosphere. Another example of romanticism in bloom is Goethe's *The Sorrows of Young Werther;* indeed, "Wertherism" and *mal de René* are terms for similar symptoms.

Chatterjee, Bankim-Chandra. KRISHNAKANTA'S WILL (KRSNAKĀNTER UIL). 1878. Novel. Bengali.

Author: Chatterjee (1838-1894), son of a rural tax-collector, belonged to an orthodox Brahmin family. He received a modern education and was one of the first to take his degree at Calcutta University. He held office in the Indian Civil Service for thirty years. He had a good knowledge of English and English literature and wrote at first in English. He is often considered the father of the Indian novel and is credited with introducing the historical novel into Bengali literature. His themes reflect the patriotism of the time and the effort to revive the former glory of India.

Work: Govindalal is married to Bhramar when she is eight, and they live in the house of his uncle, Krishnakanta. Bhramar is dark-skinned and not pretty. One day Govindalal sees the widow Rohini going to the pool for water; he is attracted to her, and she falls in love with him. (Concurrent with this story is the involvement of Rohini with Haralal, Krishnakanta's eldest son, who tries by a forged will to acquire property of his father that should go to Govindalal.)

Rohini confesses her love to Govindalal. He wishes to send her away to avoid trouble, but she goes with her story to Bhramar. The jealous wife asks Rohini to drown herself in the pool. Rohini ties a pitcher around her neck and almost succeeds in drowning. Govindalal, seeing her body in the water, rescues her and falls in love. Krishnakanta changes his will to cut Govindalal off without a rupee, and Govindalal and Rohini run off together.

Govindalal is gone for seven years, during which time Bhramar shows herself to be ever-loving and faithful while Rohini ties Govindalal to herself with every measure of deceit. The seven years end with Govindalal's recognition of how Rohini has used him, and he commands her to commit suicide. Govindalal is tried for murder but acquitted through bribery. He returns to his native village in time for Bhramar's death. In the epilogue, Govindalal disappears, reappearing twelve years later as a monk doing penance and paying honor to Bhramar's memory.

Motivations are sometimes vague in this novel, and the behavior of the characters may appear childish to Westerners. The author interposes himself as a poetic commentator at some annoying times, but the story and the storytelling are in the Indian tradition.

Comparative: For other views of the Indian wife see the Savitri episode in the *Mahabharata,* the *Ramayana,* Kalidasa's version of the story of Shakuntala, also from the *Mahabharata,* and the twentieth-century novel *Binodini* by Rabindranath Tagore. Tagore's short stories, poems, and plays also introduce Indian life in twentieth century terms. Western literature centering on women includes Solzhenitsyn's short story *Matryona's House,* Maupassant's novel *A Woman's Life,* and Shakespeare's *The Merchant of Venice.* Kipling's *Kim* and Markandaya's *Nectar in a Sieve* offer other views of India.

Chekhov, Anton Pavlovich. **THE CHERRY ORCHARD (VISHNOVYI SAD).** 1904. Drama. Russian.

Author: Chekhov (1860-1904) was born in Taganrog into a family of former serfs and small shopkeepers. In 1879 he went to Moscow to study medicine. He earned his degree in 1884, but had already begun writing comic sketches to put himself through school and shortly after graduation turned to writing. He shifted from a purely comic to a more realistic depiction of life and character, perhaps as a result of his medical studies or of his own poor health. His greatest stories often depict the difficult and primitive life of the villagers among whom he practiced. He began writing dramas, and *The Seagull* (1896), initially a failure, became a major triumph when performed in 1898 at the Moscow Art Theater under the direction of Stanislavski. It was followed by *Uncle Vanya* (1897), *Three Sisters* (1901), and *The Cherry Orchard* (1904). In 1901 Chekhov married the actress Olga Knipper of the Moscow Art Theater and in his last years he was a close friend of Stanislavski, Tolstoi, and Gorki. He died in Germany of tuberculosis at the age of 44.

Work: The Cherry Orchard is typical of Chekhov's dramas which do not emphasize a great hero or a dramatic moment but tend to simplify plot in order to concentrate on character, atmosphere, and the depiction of life as it was lived in Russia before the revolution. Chekhov saw the life of the Russian aristocracy as stagnant and drab, having outlived its usefulness and clinging to the romantic dreams of a dead past.

The impoverished Madame Ranevskaya, whom Chekhov saw as "a comic old woman," is typical of her class as she tries vainly to cling to her old estate and its cherry orchard. Lopakhin's plan to chop down the orchard and rent out the land for summer cottages for the rising middle class is repulsive to her, but the old social order cannot maintain itself and must not be allowed to stand in the way of progress. All of Russia, explains the perennial student Trofimov, is a cherry orchard which must be cleared for the people. The aristocrats and those who believe in them, like the former serf Firs, must stand aside for the new order. At the close of the play, the cherry orchard is sold to Lopakhin; as Firs dies, alone on stage, the sound of an ax felling a tree is heard.

Chekhov's concern with character-revealing details is at least as great as his interest in plot, and Lopakhin's announcement of his purchase of the estate is dramatically no more important than any of the daily events and frustrations of the characters. Chekhov was more interested in portraying than in judging his characters, who, finally, are all worthy of our sympathy. The close of the play is at least as tragic as it is optimistic and elicits regret as well as hope.

Comparative: The theme of a sterile old order yielding to a new, particularly apparent in Russian literature before the revolution, appears as early as Pushkin's *Eugene Onegin* and continues in Turgenev's *Fathers and Sons,* in which the forward-looking Bazarov has much in common with Chekhov's Trofimov. That theme is also present in the novels of Dostoevski, Pasternak, and Sholokhov. Outside Russia, accounts of the passing of the old aristocracy and the rise of the new middle class may be found in Balzac's *Le Père Goriot,* Lampedusa's *The Leopard,* and Mann's *Buddenbrooks.* Stylistic comparisons, however, are at least as interesting as thematic comparisons, for Chekhov was primarily interested in psychology and atmosphere rather than plot. Chekhov has been a major influence in twentieth-century theater and has much in common with playwrights such as Ibsen, O'Neill, and Tennessee Williams.

Chekhov, Anton Pavlovich. SELECTED STORIES. 1884-1904. Stories. Russian.

Author: See *The Cherry Orchard.*

Work: Chekhov began writing humorous sketches to support himself while still a medical student. For the most part, these are short (he once said he never spent more than twenty-four hours on any one of them), impressionistic, and comic pictures of Russian life on all social levels. Many are relatively simple anecdotes, such as the tale of the wily peasant in "He Understood"; but the best of them hints at the degradation and stagnation which was to become the major theme of his later work. Despite their humor, the bullying of the simple maid in "The Nincompoop" and the adulterous affair of "Ninochka" indicate Chekhov's growing concern with the darker side of existence.

Although his stories became increasingly serious and dealt with many of the crises facing pre-revolutionary Russia, Chekhov steadfastly refused to take sides or to pass overt moral judgments on his characters; and he insisted that art remain objective. If his stories portray a brutalized and degraded society, it is not a condemnation so much as a statement of fact. Chekhov demanded "truth, unconditional and honest," in art; he did not propagandize. But despite his efforts to remain uninvolved, he was deeply disturbed by what he saw in his society, and a sense of moral outrage is evident if not explicit. "A Dreary Story" (1889) depicts an old professor reviewing his life and realizing that he has lived without purpose and without providing solutions to the problems facing society.

Following his return from a visit to a prison island, Chekhov increasingly committed himself to social, though not political, reform, and his stories reflect his horror at his surroundings. His most famous tale, "Ward Six" (1892), describes the life of Dr. Ragin, the head of a hospital, who finds that the only man capable of intellectual discussion in the backwoods town is deemed insane and has become an inmate in a mental ward. Ragin becomes aware of the insanity and filth around him and is himself eventually locked in the ward, where he dies as a result of the brutality of the supposedly sane people. Lenin particularly praised this tale.

Chekhov turned his attention in late stories to depicting the life of whole classes as realistically as possible. His long story "Peasants" (1897) is an uncompromising look at rural life without the sentimentality that obscured similar treatments by other authors. It is a life of cold, hunger, meanness, and stupidity, where boredom is broken only by a fire or a visit from an unsympathetic tax collector.

Chekhov's approximately 600 stories provide a complete gallery of portraits of every type of individual. The pictures are alternately humorous and tragic, depressing and uplifting, but they are always accurately and objectively drawn.

Comparative: Chekhov was influenced by French naturalism and Russian realism, and many of his best stories can profitably be compared with others in these traditions. In his depiction of the harsh realities of lower-class life in "Peasants" and elsewhere he reminds us of Zola, for example in *Germinal.* Tolstoi and Turgenev also portrayed peasant life, although usually more sentimentally. In some of the earlier stories, in "He Understood," for example, the wily peasant reminds us of similar figures in Gogol—Ossip in *The Inspector General* and Chichikov in *Dead Souls.* Many of Chekhov's little people are reminiscent of Gogol; "The Death of a Government Clerk" and "The Nincompoop" have main characters who are descendants of Gogol's Akaki Akakievich.

The reminiscences of the spiritually bankrupt professor in "A Dreary Story" is similar to Tolstoi's "The Death of Ivan Ilyich," which, however, ends on a more positive note.

Chekhov is always more concerned with character than with plot; he observes his characters in a given situation and describes accurately and in detail how they respond, and through their actions he reveals their essential natures. In this he and Maupassant are forerunners of the modern short story, and writers such as Katherine Mansfield and Sherwood Anderson are their literary heirs.

Clark, John Pepper. THE SONG OF A GOAT. 1961. Drama. Nigerian.

Author: John Pepper Clark may well be, according to critics of African literature in English, not only the best African poet but one of the major contemporary poets writing in English today. Born in 1935 in Kiagbodo, Nigeria, Clark was educated at Warr Government College, Ughelli (1948-1954), and the University of Ibadan, where he received his B.A. with honors in 1960. He was awarded the Parvin Fellowship (1962-1963) at Princeton University, where he studied for a year. Later he wrote *America, Their America* in which he severely criticized American customs and values. He was a research fellow at the Institute of African Studies, University of Ibadan, 1961-1962 and 1963-1964, and since that time has been a lecturer in the Department of English at the University of Lagos.

Among his published works are: *Three Plays: Song of a Goat, The Masquerade, The Raft* (1964), a play *Ozidi* (1966), and poems (1956-1964) entitled *A Reed in the Tide* (1965). He is also the author, director, and producer of a documentary film *The Ghost Town,* sponsored by Ibadan University and the Ford Foundation.

Work: The Song of a Goat, a play in four "movements," is written in a clear, simple style with only seven characters. It explores, as does much of modern African drama, various taboos as well as the relationship between the living and their dead ancestors. *The Song of a Goat* reflects the bewildering, natural phenomena that surround the traditional African who is curious about Death and Sleep and who is in search of answers about the nature of humanity, whom he often finds to be hypocritical.

Didactic in tone, the play is informational to those interested in studying the mores of Africans. Ebiere, wife of Zifa, is troubled by her apparent sterility after the birth of a son. She goes to Masseur—family doctor, confessor, and oracle—to determine what can be done to make her fertile again. Masseur advises her to have a talk with both families, at which time Zifa may propose "to make you over to another in his family." After Ebiere leaves, Zifa comes in to talk with Masseur, who tells him he has allowed "fertile/ Ground made over to you to run fallow/ with elephant grass." Admittedly, Zifa is embarrassed but he is not willing for Tonya, his younger brother, to share his bed. He hopes to regain his potency even though Masseur warns him that one can ill afford to drift with the tide "because the tide always turns back on one."

The "Second Movement" presents the "song of the goat" which only Orukorere, Zifa's half-possessed aunt, hears. She sounds the alarm, usually suggestive of death, a fire, or some other evil occurrence, but no one takes her seriously, for she has "double-vision" and is perhaps mad. As Orukorere "sings of souls tied down with ropes," the reader recognizes that this alarming episode foreshadows the tragedy that later befalls the house of Zifa.

In the "Third Movement" Tonya and Ebiere become more intimate. When Tonya reprimands Ebiere for her bitterness about life, she hisses, and Tonya is astonished to hear such a sound coming from a "happy wife." Here we have a reversal of roles—Ebiere seduces Tonya—and as they spend their passions, the cock crows, another ill omen.

Thus it is that in the "Final Movement" Zifa, shocked and degraded by Tonya's intimacy with Ebiere, turns on him after the sacrificial ceremony and orders him to put the goat's head—horns, ears and all—into the pot, which breaks. Tonya realizes that he is trapped, for one does not break the sacrificial pot. He runs into a room and locks the door. Orukorere cries out to the neighbors to come, Ebiere faints, and Tonya uses his loincloth to hang himself. Zifa breaks the door down and enters only to find Tonya already dead. Sorrowfully, Zifa concedes defeat. Tonya performed as a man where Zifa was powerless and took his own life before Zifa could reach him. Zifa mourns, torn with despair and remorse. The "Final Movement" ends as the neighbors leave and Orukorere dashes the oil lamp to the ground in desperate recognition that the light in the compound has gone out.

Comparative: In theme and portrayal of a hero, *The Song of a Goat* is reminiscent of Swift's *Gulliver's Travels* and Goethe's *Faust*. Traditional African tenets regarding sacrificial offerings and the fall of human kind as operative forces have their parallels in the Old Testament.

Cocteau, Jean. THE HUMAN VOICE (LA VOIX HUMAINE). 1930. Drama. French.

Author: Cocteau (1891–1963), born of a family of Parisian lawyers, was educated at the Lycée Condorcet and early distinguished himself for his high spirits and originality. Artist, poet, playwright, and film director, he was an innovator in each medium and associated with leaders in many fields, including Picasso, Stravinsky, and Diaghilev.

Work: A rather ordinary, unimaginative woman talks to her lover over the telephone. With emotion and sincerity she recalls the beginning of their love affair, discusses its break-up, promises to deliver the love letters she has saved, tries to decide the ownership of their dog, chronicles her ineffectual attempt at suicide, and pleads for reconciliation beneath a gallant pretence of calm. Little else occurs in this small tragicomedy. It is effective because of the tension and sense of concealment she brings to the shabby affair. It is also effective because of what the listener imagines is said on the other end of the line while she listens and is silent.

The staging must be imagined carefully: there is high drama in the solitary actress seated in the soft dusk of a boudoir with the glaring white light of the bathroom at stage rear forming a visible contrast—something like the underplayed emotional tone of the drama.

Comparative: A literary descendant of Browning's dramatic monologue or of the conventional stage soliloquy or aside, Cocteau's play may also be compared to Strindberg's *The Stronger,* in which, though two women are on stage, only one speaks, gradually revealing all that has occurred before the present action.

Cocteau, Jean. THE INFERNAL MACHINE (LA MACHINE INFERNALE).
   1934. Drama. French.

Author: See *The Human Voice.*

Work: This modern version of *Oedipus Rex* demonstrates the enduring vitality of the Sophoclean tragedy. Oedipus is born under a curse: he will kill his father and marry his mother. His parents, Laius and Jocasta, put him out in a pasture to die. Rescued, the baby Oedipus is taken to the court of Polybus, where he is reared as that king's son. Learning of the prophecy, Oedipus flees his "home," making his way to Thebes. On his way, he meets and kills his natural father, unaware of who he is. He then marries Jocasta and begets children by her. When knowledge of the terrible sins of incest and patricide is realized by him, Oedipus destroys his sight and condemns himself to exile. Jocasta hangs herself.

Comparative: Cocteau's play relies on expressionistic stage techniques, but the French playwright has not tampered much with the basic plot of Sophocles. He has made the troubles more subjective and immediate by adding certain intimate scenes that classical tragedy would not have permitted. For example, in a bedroom scene, Cocteau shows Oedipus and his mother-wife, Jocasta, alone for the first time with their mutual but unrecognized nightmares. Again, at the end of the drama, Jocasta is allowed to emerge from her role as wife to assume tenderly the role of mother as she leads the blinded Oedipus safely from the palace and down the stairs. Tiresias, the harsh soothsayer in Sophocles, is here a sympathetic character, filled with admiration for the final redemptive act of Oedipus in putting out his sight, becoming a king indeed. Several of these innovations increase the chilling certainty of the tragedy, at least to modern audiences used to cinematic close-ups and more sentiment than classical drama ordinarily allows. Cocteau has also emphasized one dimension of tragedy by conceiving of it as a tightly wound machine which everyone is powerless to stop until the action is completed. The application of this concept is also apparent in Saint-Exupéry's *Night Flight* and in Anouilh's *Antigone.* This last, since it concerns the sons and daughters of Oedipus, is an appropriate sequel to the Oedipus play.

Self-destruction through ignorance, at least in part, touches the plot of *Hippolytus* by Euripides and that of the parable told to David after he has taken Bathsheba from Uriah the Hittite.

Cocteau, Jean. THE HOLY TERRORS (LES ENFANTS TERRIBLES). 1929. Novel. French.

Author: See *The Human Voice.*

Work: Les Enfants terribles is the story of young friends whose association continues into adulthood. Paul, injured by a snowball and rescued by his friend Gerard, remains out of school for months, cared for by his sister, Elizabeth, since their mother is ill and dies shortly after the accident. Gerard becomes a close member of the trio which develops its own secret language and excludes the outside world. When Agathe enters this closed world, she and Paul become lovers. Elizabeth, unconsciously jealous of Agathe, marries a rich American who dies in an auto accident on their wedding night. The group then moves into the young widow's house to continue their childish and cabalistic relationship. Elizabeth is increasingly drawn toward her brother and succeeds in breaking up his relationship with Agathe. Paul takes poison. Elizabeth shoots herself, believing that in death her brother will be exclusively hers.

The novel was made into a movie directed by Cocteau himself in 1945 and is now considered a classic.

Comparative: For another treatment of warped adolescent behavior, see Thomas Mann's "The Blood of the Walsung's." Mann's "Disorder and Early Sorrow" presents still another unusual brother-sister pair.

Colette, Sidonie Gabrielle. GIGI. 1944. Novel. French.

Author: Colette (1873-1954) was reared in Burgundy under the strong influence of her mother, who molded her love for country things. She married

Monsieur Willy (the music critic Henri Gauthier-Villars) at twenty and began her career as a captive writer, producing the Claudine series. After Willy had been shaken off, Colette entered music hall life, married two more times, and became a successful novelist and even the proprietor of a beauty salon. During the First World War she converted her husband's estate into a hospital and was for her services made Chevalier of the Legion d'Honneur. In 1945 she was elected to the Goncourt Academy, the only woman to receive that honor. When she died, the entire city of Paris went into mourning.

Colette has a unique position in contemporary French letters: she writes of children and pets and of people who cannot possibly be allegorical or symbolic, and she freely mixes autobiography into her fiction; thus she is an anachronism in the self-conscious and skeptical arena of modern European fiction.

Work: The novel is set in Paris in the early part of the twentieth century and is perhaps the most brilliant showpiece of Colette's charm, sympathy, and wit. Gilberte (Gigi) is being reared by Mme Alvarez, her grandmother, and by Aunt Alicia, as the family's more marketable possession. In this *demi-monde* where "instead of marry 'at once' it sometimes happens that we marry 'at last'," Gigi is being carefully trained in the graces that will make for a rich if dubious alliance. Alicia teaches Gigi how to eat ortolans properly, how to attack a lobster, and how to recognize fine jewels, while Mme Alvarez trains her to handle her skirts and come right home after school. A rich old friend of the family, "Uncle" Gaston, who has liked Gigi for her childishness and her companionship over a game of piquet, suddenly begins to notice her as a woman. Gaston makes the traditional offer to the family, and the alliance is accepted by everyone but Gigi. She breaks the glittering family tradition by refusing anything but marriage—and she gets it.

Comparative: The *demi-monde* is seldom treated in any way but sordidly, condescendingly, or sensationally (see Maupassant's *Bel-Ami*), and no adequate comparison exists for this light Gallic trifle. Mann's *Confessions of Felix Krull, Confidence Man* approaches the irregular life with good humor but with greater indignity. Colette's work and Maugham's *Of Human Bondage* look at the same class in the same historical era.

Corneille, Pierre. LE CID. 1636. Drama. French.

Author: Corneille, born in 1606, studied law before turning to playwriting. After a few unsuccessful comedies, he wrote *Le Cid*. In this play, the internal drama of human emotions begins to take the place of external stage commotion. Richelieu esteemed *Le Cid* so highly that he pensioned the author for life; however, the growing popularity of Racine darkened Corneille's days with jealousy until his death in 1684.

Work: This neoclassical drama is filled with swordplay, rival factions, and high-strung emotional conflict. Rodrique, son of Don Diègue, and Chimène, daughter of Count Gomès, are happily in love until Gomès is led to insult the Don. Since Diègue is old, he calls on his son to avenge him; Rodrique kills Gomès, knowing that he has forfeited Chimène's hand by defending his father's honor—even though paradoxically he has increased Chimène's respect for him. In this period of French literature, honor is regarded as the highest emotion, more powerful than love. Chimène now must ask the king for her lover's life, lamenting: "Alas, how cruel the thought./ How cruel the prosecution I am forced to./ I must demand his life, yet fear to take it./ If he dies, I shall die, yet I must slay him."

But all turns out well in this seemingly hopeless situation. Rodrique defeats two Moorish kings, wins his ruler's forgiveness, and then defeats the knight who volunteered to kill him to redeem Chimène's family honor. The Spanish king commands the lovers to end their quarrel, since both have demonstrated nobility.

Comparative: For the historical background to Corneille's play, see the Spanish national epic, *Poem of the Cid.* For other expressions of the theme of chivalric honor, consider the epic *Song of Roland,* Rostand's *Cyrano de Bergerac,* and Chikamatsu's *The Battles of Coxinga.* The theme of the star-crossed lovers is of course found in Shakespeare's *Romeo and Juliet* and Keller's *A Village Romeo and Juliet.* This play also provides a useful vehicle for teaching the unities of time, place, and action.

Cortázar, Julio. HOPSCOTCH (RAYUELA). 1963. Novel. Argentinian.

Author: Julio Cortázar, a bold experimenter with novelistic form, was born in Brussels in 1914 of Argentinian parents and grew up in Argentina, which he left in 1951 because of his opposition to the regime of Juan Perón. He now lives in Paris.

Cortázar was educated at the Teachers College of Buenos Aires, graduating in 1936, followed by a year of study at the University there. He taught for a while in a province school. In 1944 he took a position at the University of Cuyo in Mendoza. Since 1946 he has been employed as a free-lance translator, translating French and English into Spanish; he now works four months a year in this capacity with UNESCO. He has translated works of Poe, Gide, de la Mare, Chesterton, and Jean Giorno into Spanish.

Other well-known works are a collection of stories entitled *Bestiario (Bestiary),* 1951; a novel *Los Premios (The Winners),* 1960; and a collection of stories published in the United States as *Blow-Up and Other Stories* (1968). Antonioni loosely based his film *Blow-Up* on the title story of that collection.

Work: Hopscotch is Cortázar's masterpiece and has been called Latin America's first great novel. Part philosophical manifesto, part demonstration against traditional literary form and language, part spiritual pilgrimage, *Hopscotch* is perhaps best described as an anti-novel. The book can be read in two ways. The first fifty-six chapters are to be read in sequence; then the reader may hopscotch about according to a plan drawn up by the author that involves reading fifty-six chapters twice and one chapter four times. In the alternative sequence, for example, the first ten chapters are those numbered 73, 1, 2, 116, 3, 84, 4, 71, 5, and 81. Cortázar explains that he is "trying to break the habits of readers—not just for the sake of breaking them, but to make the reader free."

Hopscotch is about a search by Horacio Oliveira, an Argentinian, for an integrated self. A man of middle years, Oliveira has moved to Paris, where he lives the life of an unattached expatriate. His mistress is called La Maga, and the friends who surround him are referred to as the Club. His friends seem to have formed personalities, ambitions, drives, but Oliveira wishes to live for the present moment, so he floats through life, dealing with the immediate pieces but never realizing the whole. There are many conversations involving the Club; there are love scenes; there is much improvisation. The humor runs from hard-bitten to ironic to stinging, as Cortázar displays his mastery of word-play, parody, fantasy, obscenity, and farce. He alludes to foreign literatures and even American and European jazz musicians and composers.

Comparative: The pyrotechnics of the book and the nature of the quest make *Hopscotch* comparable to James Joyce's *Ulysses.* Because of his inventive technique, Cortázar has also been likened to Laurence Sterne, and Proust. His immediate influence, of course, is Borges, and his fantasy has certainly felt the effects of Poe.

Dante (Dante Alighieri). THE DIVINE COMEDY (LA DIVINA COMMEDIA).
Written between 1306 and 1321. Epic poem. Italian.

Author: Dante Alighieri (1265-1321) was born and educated in Florence. He early distinguished himself as a poet and became an important figure in local politics. Because of political intrigue against him, he was banished from Florence in 1302 and never saw that city again. He was protected by several Italian cities and princes and made his final home in Ravenna.

Work: The Divine Comedy is a long narrative poem in three parts: Hell, Purgatory, and Heaven. Dante travels through these three regions, meeting various real and mythological personages, many of whom want to tell their sad or happy stories to him. In the process Dante creates an allegory of life on earth that is lavish in its imagery. He also offers the reader his ideas on theology, mythology, philosophy, astronomy, politics, ethics, esthetics, morality, and various other aspects of human knowledge. Though *The Divine Comedy* is generally lofty in purpose and elevated in tone, Dante cunningly relegates for the most part his enemies to Hell and his personal heroes to Heaven. By the time Dante has ended the trip, he has examined the nature of faith and plumbed the depths of humanity.

It should be noted that the term *commedia,* as Dante used it, means a poem written in a tone between that of noble tragedy and popular elegy, and that the appelation *divina* was added later by admirers.

The book is a vision, the autobiography of a soul, and superb poetry. It is also significant for its intense intellectual insights and has been regarded as the most inventive book ever written by a single author. Of further importance, *The Divine Comedy* was written in the Tuscan dialect at a time when there was no standard Italian language, and the book had such widespread impact that it was largely responsible for causing the Tuscan dialect to be adopted as the standard Italian language. It holds particular interest, too, because its dramatic imagery effectively created a new concept of Hell, Purgatory, and Heaven, because it may well be the finest love poem ever written (Beatrice, whom Dante loves, is enthroned high in heaven), and because it raises questions about the meaning of life which are as pertinent today as when Dante wrote.

Comparative: While the poem is unique, Bunyan's *Pilgrim's Progress* treads some of the same ground, with the allegorical Pilgrim making a journey to the Celestial City. Milton's *Paradise Lost* and *Paradise Regained* provide some interesting contrasts and comparisons, especially in their use of a religious cosmology and in the sweep of ideas. As an epic, *The Divine Comedy* can be compared with Homer's *Iliad,* or Virgil's *Aeneid* (which also has a descent into the lower world), and with other religiously and ethically oriented works of epic proportion, such as the *Ramayana.*

Dostoevski, Fyodor Mikhailovich. **CRIME AND PUNISHMENT (PRESTU-PLENIYE I NAKAZANIYE).** 1866. Novel. Russian.

Author: Dostoevski (1821-1881) was born in Moscow and raised in a severe and religiously orthodox household, where he gained a thorough familiarity with the Bible. At seventeen he was sent to the College of Military Engineering in St. Petersburg and there read widely in Shakespeare, Schiller, Dickens, Balzac, Gogol, Pushkin, and Sand. Shortly after his graduation his father was brutally murdered by serfs on his estate. Dostoevski resigned his commission, which he never wanted, to devote himself to writing.

His first novel, *Poor Folk* (1846), was a success. He became a member of a group of liberal "westernizers" and joined a radical group which may have plotted to kill Czar Nicholas I. The group was arrested in 1849 and its members condemned to death. Dostoevski was actually standing before the firing squad when his sentence was commuted to hard labor in Siberia and service in the army. During his exile he underwent a spiritual and political conversion and became an extreme Slavophile.

In 1859 he returned to St. Petersburg, where he suffered from severe poverty for the next decade, the result of numerous dependents as well as gambling debts. He was forced to write under extreme pressure and in 1866 produced *The Gambler* (partially based on his own experiences) and *Crime and Punishment*. These were followed by *The Idiot* (1868-1869), *The Possessed* (1871-1872), also called *The Devils,* and *The Brothers Karamazov* (1879-1880), which finally brought him moderate fame and income. He intended this as a prelude to another novel, the hero of which would have been Alyosha, the youngest Karamazov brother.

Work: Dostoevski's story revolves around the murder of an old pawn-broker by the student Raskolnikov, an intellectual who murders not out of passion but as the result of a theory that the extraordinary—for example Napoleon—are not bound by the law of the common person. Raskolnikov considers himself above the common law, but after committing the act he is tortured by self-doubt. He feels no remorse, at least not until the end of the novel, but his nervous attacks, nightmares, fainting fits, and fears of discovery prove that he is not the man he thought he was, that he cannot escape the nonintellectual side of human life from which he had argued that the exceptional man should be free.

Dostoevski is not interested in external events of plot so much as in the psychology of his characters. Thus the events of the story—chance meetings, surprising revelations of secrets, the introduction of minor characters or extraneous events—allow him to develop the psychology of his central figures. The story of the Marmeladov family, for example, in addition to providing the background for the pure and angelic Sonya who will eventually lead Raskolnikov back to God, is designed to give the reader a more complete picture of Raskolnikov, to exhibit a side of him which he himself has discounted. It is precisely the realization of this nonrational side of the murderer which allows the police examiner Porfiri Petrovich to work so effectively on Raskolnikov's fears. Porfiri does not use the details of the crime to bring Raskolnikov to justice, for Raskolnikov has effectively prevented conviction by tangible evidence. But Porfiri is a psychological detective, whose materials are gathered from just that aspect which Raskolnikov had sought to deny.

The conclusion of *Crime and Punishment,* with Raskolnikov's conversion and the promise of future happiness with Sonya, is an affirmation of the complexity of human kind and the ultimate sterility of any purely intellectual system of principles. Reason is incapable of providing us with solutions to the problems of human existence; only faith and purity, as evidenced in

Sonya, are capable of giving us the strength to face the suffering which is the necessary condition of human life.

Comparative: In the superficial structure of his plots, with their melodrama and sensationalism, and, more importantly, in his realistic and sympathetic descriptions of contemporary life, particularly of the lower classes, Dostoevski's novels often remind the reader of their great predecessors—the works of Dickens, Balzac, Hugo, and Gogol. As Dostoevski himself said of his generation of realistic writers: "We have all come out of Gogol's *Overcoat.*" But Dostoevski's greatest achievements lie not in plot or external description but in his in-depth study of human psychology, the internal world of his characters. On a superficial level, Dostoevski's treatment of the criminal mind belongs to the tradition of Poe's "The Tell-Tale Heart" and Pushkin's "The Queen of Spades," and it in turn engendered other, similar works. But, more importantly, this psychological depiction of character led to the development of the stream-of-consciousness technique in writers such as Joyce, Proust, Kafka, and Woolf.

Of equal importance is the influence of Dostoevski on novelists, philosophers, and poets who saw in Raskolnikov the embodiment of the modern man, whose actions are based upon theories of which he cannot be certain. Raskolnikov in this respect is much like Gide's Michel *(The Immoralist)*, Kafka's Joseph K. *(The Trial)*, and Camus's Meursault *(The Stranger)* and, along with his spiritual brother, the Underground Man, is seen as the father of a long line of existential heroes.

**Dostoevski, Fyodor Mikhailovich. THE LEGEND OF THE GRAND INQUISI-
TOR (LEGENDA O VELIKOM INKVIZITORE).** 1880. Chapter from
the novel *The Brothers Karamazov (Brat'ya Karamazovy).* Russian.

Author: See *Crime and Punishment.*

Work: In Book V of *The Brothers Karamazov,* entitled "Pro and Contra," Ivan Karamazov tells his brother Alyosha the story of a poem he has written. This story of Christ's return to earth during the Spanish Inquisition, his arrest by the Grand Inquisitor, and the Inquisitor's long monologue defending his actions, forms the core of the novel and, by extension, of Dostoevski's work as a whole.

Ivan, the intellectual atheist who tells the tale, clearly sides with the Grand Inquisitor. According to the Inquisitor, Christ's refusal to provide the people with bread, to prove His own divinity, and to provide an authority to follow in worldly matters was founded on a mistaken belief in the dignity of humanity and desire for freedom of the will. On the contrary, claims the Inquisitor, people willingly sacrifice their free will in exchange for bread and religious and secular authority; indeed, they prefer to be led like sheep rather than to make decisions in the absence of rational certainty. The Church therefore provides the authority all seek and in the name of rational humanism or socialism makes life bearable.

Ivan makes it clear that the Inquisitor is not an evil man bent on personal gain. In his own way he is saintly and motivated by a sincere desire to provide everyone with a solution to doubt. But the essential questions cannot be resolved by reason and intellectual argument. For Dostoevski, only acceptance and faith provide a solution. It is significant, then, that only the Inquisitor speaks in Ivan's story and that Christ merely kisses the Inquisitor and silently disappears. The chapter ends as Alyosha, the religious brother, imitates Christ's action and kisses Ivan goodbye.

Comparative: Dostoevski intended Ivan's story to be contrasted with the biblical story of Christ's temptation in the desert (Matthew 4:1-11), a story also treated by Kazantzakis in *The Last Temptation of Christ.* All three accounts present the essential conflict between faith and reason, a conflict which forms the central theme of many modern writers and philosophers, including, but not limited to, Kierkegaard, Nietzsche, Rilke, Kafka, Sartre, and Camus. Not all these writers, of course, agree with Dostoevski that patient suffering is the solution of the human dilemma. Works such as Kafka's *The Castle* or Camus's *The Plague* suggest the necessity for a continual struggle for knowledge, even in the face of certain defeat.

Anouilh's *The Lark* also presents the conflict between a religious figure who views humanity as essentially noble and worthy of Christ's gift of freedom of choice and a Grand Inquisitor who attacks this noble view.

Finally, "The Legend of the Grand Inquisitor" is a summation of themes Dostoevski used elsewhere. Ivan Karamazov's attempt to deny all but the rational element of human existence is similar to Raskolnikov's intellectual pride in *Crime and Punishment,* and it is this view which the Underground Man so viciously ridicules.

Dostoevski, Fyodor Mikhailovich. NOTES FROM UNDERGROUND (ZAPISKI IZ PODPOL'YA). 1864. Novella. Russian.

Author: See *Crime and Punishment.*

Work: This short novel sounds a new note in Dostoevski's work and, according to many critics, in modern literature as a whole. It is often considered the first existential novel, and Dostoevski calls his protagonist an "anti-hero," a man directly in conflict with established theories concerning society. As suggested by the title, the protagonist is a man whom society considers in some sense a criminal, but it must be emphasized that it is he himself who defines the underground and who has chosen to separate himself from his fellows.

The first part of the novel is an exposition of the Underground Man's philosophy, or rather, in a modern twist, his rejection of all philosophical systems which society accepts, particularly the rational humanism of the utopian socialists. In what may be considered a direct attack on the socialist propaganda of Chernyshevski's *What Is to Be Done?* (1864), the Underground Man attacks his audience's faith in the ability of reason to build the utopian paradise on earth. All rational systems, he explains, overlook our essential irrationality. They seek to make us into machines which operate by mechanical laws. In so doing, they would deprive us of free will, the essential element of human life. Thus, the Underground Man upholds our right to act contrary to what reason would dictate to be in our own best interest, to do things harmful and stupid in the name of free will and in the hope that two plus two will not always equal four.

The second part of the novel relates three episodes in the life of the Underground Man, each of which demonstrates his vengeful nature, his pettiness, his maliciousness, and his ultimate despair. Clearly, if his honesty has revealed a true aspect of human nature, it has not provided him with an acceptable alternative to the pettiness of life against which he rebels. We are torn between reason and will or passion, and the only solution lies in a religious submission to suffering, in the life of the meek and penitent, as exemplified in this work by the prostitute Liza.

Comparative: Dostoevski's later novels are largely expansions of the themes touched on here. Raskolnikov in *Crime and Punishment* is also a critic of society who is torn between the demands of reason and of will. The solution through suffering is pointed out to him by Sonya, another saintly prostitute. *The Brothers Karamazov,* Dostoevski's last novel, again portrays this essential conflict, with each of its main characters representing one part of human nature. Ivan Karamazov's story of the Grand Inquisitor also contrasts the free will Christ offered to humanity with the obedience demanded by the Inquisitor to the rational system of the Catholic Church.

Existentialist writers and philosophers have much in common with Dostoevski. Nietzsche admitted that he learned much from the Underground Man, and the heroes of both Camus and Sartre similarly reject the view of humanity as essentially rational. These three authors, like Dostoevski, reject optimistic schemes built upon faith in human reason, although they also reject his alternative of suffering and religious submission.

Dumas, Alexandre, père. THE COUNT OF MONTE-CRISTO (LE COMTE DE MONTE-CRISTO). 1844. Novel. French.

Author: Dumas (1802-1870), the son of a famous octoroon general under Napoleon, lived a full and riotous life, always in debt and writing his way out. Relying on a "fiction factory" wherein many collaborators ground out research and incidents as raw material, he produced over three hundred swash-buckling narratives and dozens of well-plotted but violent dramas. His novels often appeared first as newspaper serials. Dumas built a castle named Monte Cristo, which he lost through debt, and produced a son, Alexandre Dumas *fils,* who became a prime mover in the French realist movement and who was the author of *Camille,* the story used in Verdi's *La Traviata.*

Work: This pseudohistorical novel begins with an imaginary conspiracy to rescue Napoleon from exile. Edmond Dantès, a young seaman on his way home to marry Mercédès, stops at Napoleon's island to exchange letters of whose contents he is ignorant. He is accused of conspiracy by three false friends and imprisoned in the Chateau d'If for fourteen years. Here he makes the acquaintance of another prisoner, the Abbé Faria, who reveals to him the secret of a huge treasure hidden on the island of Monte-Cristo and who by his death gives Edmond the opportunity for a thrilling escape. Once free, Dantès becomes the "Count of Monte-Cristo," enormously powerful and rich, and filled with superhuman knowledge of the world, of magic, weapons, and the secret vices and fears of all peoples. He returns to life to find his father dead and Mercédès married to one of his enemies.

The larger part of the novel recounts how Edmond gets even with his enemies by cleverly setting in motion complicated schemes involving many people, but his real vengeance is gained by the way he plays on greed, jealousy, and other human weaknesses. Dozens of subplots are in development simultaneously, and the book is crowded with impossible coincidences made less noticeable because of the fast pace of the storytelling.

Comparative: The Count of Monte-Cristo may be used to invest European history with glamor, to serve as part of a study of the historical novel after the pattern of Sir Walter Scott, and to illustrate the "factory" production of collaborative novels.

This adventure novel may be compared with other works of Dumas, especially *The Three Musketeers* and its sequels, or with the works of Haggard *(She)* and Verne *(20,000 Leagues Under the Sea).* The theme of the return for purposes of vengeance may also be explored in Silone's *The Secret of Luca* and Dürrenmatt's *The Visit.*

Dumas, Alexandre, père. THE THREE MUSKETEERS (LES TROIS MOUS-QUETAIRES). 1844. Novel. French.

Author: See *The Count of Monte-Cristo.*

Work: A novel of high adventure laid in seventeenth-century France, *The Three Musketeers* is not to be regarded as a serious historical study; however, the manners, the human relationships, and in general the code of behavior do reflect the period in which Richelieu governed France.

Young D'Artagnan, who comes from Gascony to Paris to make his fortune by wit and arms, enters into a splendid "All for one—one for all!" alliance with Athos, Porthos, and Aramis and is off on the trail of adventure. Anne of Austria, Queen of France, is having a dangerous affair with the Duke of Buckingham, and Cardinal Richelieu seeks to catch her in it. The four heroes save her honor by a dash to Britain to bring back the diamond studs which she gave to Buckingham as a love pledge. D'Artagnan and Athos are also involved in trouble with a she-demon named Lady de Winter, one of the Cardinal's agents. Many sword fights later this woman is executed, the queen is saved, France is secure, and our heroic four disappear, intent on further adventure.

The novel is filled with humor, lovemaking, duels, and intrigues in dark alleys and in convents at midnight; it never ceases to move briskly. Sequels include *Twenty Years Later, Louise de la Vallière,* and *Le Vicomte de Brage-lonne.*

Comparison: For pure adventure, *The Count of Monte-Cristo,* also by Dumas, works well; for a view of the period, Merimée's *Chronicle of the Reign of Charles IX* is light, pleasant reading with more depth than the work of Dumas. The character of D'Artagnan is somewhat comparable to that of Cyrano de Bergerac.

Ekwensi, Cyprian. JAGUA NANA. 1961. Novel. Nigerian.

Author: Ekwensi was born in 1921 in Minna, Nigeria, and educated at a number of colleges in Africa and at the Chelsea School of Pharmacy, London University. Lecturer and Pharmaceuticist, he has worked for the Nigerian Broadcasting Corporation and other African corporations. During the Biafran war he came to the United States on several occasions in money-raising efforts. He is presently Chairman of the Bureau for External Publicity in Biafra. His writings include six novels which have been translated into nine languages and a number of plays and scripts for BBC radio and television. In addition to *Jagua Nana,* his best known works include *Burning Grass* (1962), *Beautiful Feathers* (1963), *Iska* (1966), and *Africhaos* (1969).

Work: Jagua Nana has been translated into Italian, German, Serbo-Croatian, and Portuguese. The novel takes us into the heart of Lagos, a city alive and prosperous, with the Tropicana as its center of action. Jagua Nana, beautiful, fashionable, and optimistic, is the heroine. She, along with Freddie Namme and many others, has come to Lagos in search of a better way of life than their own Iboland afforded.

Jagua pursues bright lights and good times at the Tropicana; Freddie, a school teacher, pursues books and lectures. They fall in love and, even though she is a prostitute, she is Freddie's mistress first. He accepts her "business" because of the profits which she shares with him. Despite her intellectual poverty, Jagua provides the spark for the realization of Freddie's dream of studying law in England. By so doing, he hopes to become a leader who will ameliorate conditions in Nigeria. With Jagua's encouragement and financial assistance, Freddie goes to England.

There Freddie meets and falls in love with pretty Nancy Oll, to whom he becomes engaged and whom he later marries. After two years' study in England, Freddie brings Nancy home to Lagos. Determined to improve social conditions, he engages in a political campaign against Uncle Taiwo, who is now "keeping" Jagua. Openly bitter and hostile, the campaign explodes, leaving Freddie murdered by the opposition. Uncle Taiwo, the winner, is also found dead later. Before being killed, however, he has given Jagua a bag of campaign money which she uses to advance her own lot and that of her people.

Earlier, during a visit to Freddie's family, the Royal House of Namme, Jagua learns of a thirty-year feud between the House of Namme and the House of Ofubara. The Chiefs are relatives who had been split on the rightful Yanaba of Bagana. After a romantic liaison with Chief Ofubara, Jagua effects a reconciliation of the two Houses which takes place amid great rejoicing in all Bagana. Jagua realizes that in unity there is strength and that herein may lie the resolution of existing problems.

The novel is heavily detailed and peopled, but the character of Jagua is clearly delineated throughout. Paradoxically, it is she who effects whatever social gains are made. Finally, after many heart-rending experiences, much shame and unscrupulous living, Jagua settles in Onitsha to be near her mother and her brother. The birth and death of an illegitimate son in her later years opens the way for a less reckless life in the future.

Comparative: Jagua Nana is a refreshing departure from the heathen exorcism and social injustices emphasized in many African novels. Its theme embraces social, intellectual, political, and aesthetical values as these relate to a changing culture.

Jagua Nana, in spite of many adversities, desires "to live life while she lives" and may be compared to Moll Flanders, the beautiful prostitute in Defoe's novel. Jagua and Freddie are reminiscent of Mildred and Philip in Maugham's *Of Human Bondage*. The feud between the Royal Houses reminds one of the quarrel between the Montagues and Capulets in Shakespeare's *Romeo and Juliet*.

Ekwensi, Cyprian. PEOPLE OF THE CITY. 1954. Novel. Nigerian.

Author: See *Jagua Nana.*

Work: People of the City concerns Amusa Sango, crime reporter for the *West African Sensation* and representative of the educated young African gone urban. The novel exposes the endless injustices in the social, political, and economic realms which keep ambitious Africans in pathetic circumstances. The setting is a West African city (possibly Lagos) where Sango, like scores of others, has come, aspiring to fame and trying to realize freedom and peace from the bondage he and traditional villagers experience. Accompanying Sango in a panorama of scenes and events are Aina, seductively beautiful and with whom he has a romantic affair; Bayo, his first trumpet player; and Beatrice the First, an ebony beauty who likes "high life and drinks and music." There are Elina (the girl back home) and finally Beatrice the Second, whom Sango later marries. But these are not all. For Sango must contend with Lajide, his wealthy landlord, who kept eight wives but also wanted Beatrice the First. This clash of desires runs through the novel, resulting in Lajide's ousting Sango from his home.

Meanwhile Sango continues writing, boldly reporting the social ills perpetrated by unscrupulous politicians. It is because of his forthright condemnation of the trigger-happy British government in conjunction with Mr. Nekam's strong leadership that the coal crisis in the Eastern Greens is settled. The violence and terror result in a kind of unity between workers and politicians, ending "death, danger, and disaster" for the miners.

Sango's reporting has continued successfully up to this point. Here he falls —he dares to report crime as he sees it and is fired. Sango's spirit is broken; however, a note of joy sounds as the happy Beatrice the Second and Sango leave the city to travel to the Gold Coast.

Comparative: The tone is sad; even the lights and gaiety of the All Language Club cannot penetrate the darkness, the restlessness, and the anxiety of these Africans as they face reality. We find a close parallel in Ekwensi's *Jagua Nana.* A Western work which reveals injustice and corruption, is Upton Sinclair's *The Jungle;* Sinclair Lewis's *Elmer Gantry* also examines a kind of corruption and is an effective novel.

Euripides. IPHIGENIA IN TAURIS (IPHIGENEIA HE EN TAUROIS). ca. 414-412 B.C. Drama. Greek.

Author: Born in Salamis, likely on the day of the Greek victory near that island, Euripides (ca. 485-407 B.C.) received an excellent education, studying philosophy under Anaxagoras and rhetoric under Prodicus. Beginning his public career as a dramatist at the age of twenty-five, he won first prize in 441 and continued to exhibit plays until 408 B.C. when he went to the court of Archelaus, king of Macedonia. He died there at the age of seventy-five. Euripides seems the most modern of the Greek tragedians, presenting men and women in every day situations rather than as ideal and heroic characters. Aristotle called Euripides the most tragic of the tragedians. We have considerable fragments of some fifty of his ninety known plays, and nineteen complete ones.

Work: Iphigenia, daughter of Agamemnon and Clytemnestra, has been priestess at Tauris (north of the Black Sea), where all strangers are sacrificed to Artemis, ever since that goddess had whisked her away from her father's knife at Aulis, where she was to have been sacrificed to obtain winds for the Greek passage to Troy. As the play opens, two young Greeks are captured and brought to the temple. Because her brother Orestes was so young when she was sent to Aulis, Iphigenia does not recognize him or his companion Pylades. The youths are fleeing the Furies who pursue Orestes for his revenge slaying of his mother Clytemnestra (Agamemnon's murderer). Apollo has promised Orestes respite if he brings the Taurian statue of Artemis to Athens.

Gradually, Iphigenia and Orestes recognize their relationship, and together they devise a strategem to escape the savage king Thoas. In an ingenious speech, Iphigenia claims that because the holy image of Artemis has been polluted by the presence of a matricide, she must take both image and prisoners down to the sea for purification; Thoas and his followers must remain behind for fear of pollution. Thus the three Greeks clamber aboard the awaiting ship of Orestes. Thoas, hot in pursuit, is persuaded to let them go only by the sudden appearance of Athene.

This play has been called romantic comedy and tragicomedy because of its exciting plot, appeal to sensation, climax by recognition, exotic setting, and range of effects from amusement to pathos. Melodramatic in its intrigue, resolution, and simplified characterizations, the play nevertheless demonstrates how brilliantly Euripides used pathos, indeed the whole arsenal of argument and rhetoric. As in other of Euripides' plays, the gods, though directly petitioned, do not respond to human need. If there is justice, it is arbitrary. The nostalgia for homeland, the demonstrations of the power of friendship, and the lyrical odes are memorable.

Comparative: The plot resembles that of *Helen,* another play by Euripides. The play may also be used to discuss the demarcation between comedy and tragedy and the relationship of theatricality to credibility. Many other plays deal with the cursed House of Atreus, notably the *Oresteia* of Aeschylus; Euripides also wrote an *Orestes,* an *Electra,* and *Iphigenia in Aulis.*

The last-minute reprieve is a common device in comedy and melodrama, observable, for example, in John Gay's *Beggar's Opera* and consequently in Brecht's *Threepenny Opera.* Goethe composed an *Iphigenia in Tauris* in prose in 1779 and in poetry in 1787; his Iphigenia escapes by telling Thoas the truth and bringing out the best in his nature.

Euripides. MEDEA (MEDEIA). 431 B.C. Drama. Greek.

Author: See *Iphigenia in Tauris.*

Work: Background information is essential to an understanding of this tragedy, though most of the following is referred to in the play. Medea, a "barbarian" princess from Colchis (east of the Black Sea) and a sorceress, falls in love with Jason, who has come seeking the golden fleece held by her father, King Aeëtes, also a sorcerer and son of the sun god Helios. Through her desire to help Jason, Medea murders her own brother. Later, in Iolchus, Jason's uncle, Pelias, refuses Jason his rightful kingdom and Medea persuades the daughters of Pelias that they will rejuvenate their father by cutting him up and boiling him. The scheme fails, and Jason and Medea are exiled. They go to Corinth where after some years Jason decides to accept the daughter of King Creon in marriage and hence the right of succession to the throne. Here the play begins.

Medea's nurse laments the chain of events which began with Jason's trip to Colchis. Now Medea is a broken woman—jealous, angry, despairing of her future, remorseful over her past deeds for Jason, certain that her foreign status now works against her. Like the nurse, the chorus sympathizes with Medea and fears she may harm herself. Jason enters and is reviled by the chorus, by the nurse, and by Medea for his treachery and the transparent expediency of his explanations. Promised asylum in Athens by King Aegeus, who just happens by, Medea plots revenge. Feigning reconciliation with Jason, who wishes to make final settlement, she sends their two sons to carry gifts to the princess (including a poisoned robe which will kill the wearer and all who touch her). She then resolves to kill the children, lest they fall into vengeful hands. Thus she cruelly punishes Jason, her real victim. Medea is miraculously provided with a chariot by Helios and flies away bearing the bodies of the slain children, denying Jason even the comfort of giving them funerals.

The horrific power of the tragedy stems neither from suspense nor character but from the unspeakable deeds committed in full consciousness and with premeditation. The tragedy is that of a whole society, not of an individual. Jason is base, and Medea has committed terrible crimes; what shocks is the primitive power of the fury which drives Medea. She is too extreme to be a tragic heroine, though in the beginning one sympathizes with her and loathes Jason. Forces which are neither reasonable nor controllable drive Medea to actions which destroy an entire society. The chorus fears what will happen but is powerless.

Comparative: Dürrenmatt's *The Visit* is comparable in its story of a long-range revenge consciously taken, and the Electra of Sophocles is driven by a similar rage for revenge. *Medea* can also be compared to such tragedies of revenge as Shakespeare's *Hamlet* and *Titus Andronicus,* and to Thomas Kyd's *Spanish Tragedy,* all of which descend from Seneca's melodramatic tragedies. Like Aristophanes' Lysistrata, Medea is intelligent, complex, and unusually clever. Both women articulate the injustice of the limitations on the roles of women in society, and both determine their own destinies by stepping beyond those prescribed roles. Lysistrata, of course, remains controlled by her reason whereas Medea's fury overwhelms her rationality.

Euripides. THE TROJAN WOMEN (TROADES). ca. 415 B.C. Drama. Greek.

Author: See *Iphigenia in Tauris.*

Work: In the prologue, Poseidon reveals to Athene his regret over the defeat of Troy. Athene assures him that the Greeks will shortly be punished for their desecration of Trojan temples and tombs and their murder of innocent victims. Hecuba, the aged queen of Troy, summons the Trojan women, and they speculate on their futures as slaves to the Greeks. In the ensuing four episodes, the tragedy of Troy as a collective victim of the Greeks is remorselessly demonstrated. Talthybius, the Greek messenger, informs the women what the Greeks have decided: Cassandra, virgin priestess, will be Agamemnon's concubine; Polyxena (another of Hecuba's daughters) will be sacrificed on the tomb of Achilles; Andromache will be given to Neoptolemus, the son of Achilles; Hecuba will go to Odysseus.

In an exciting scene that contrasts with the misery and drabness of the captive women, Cassandra bears in torches, joyful at the thought of her coming marriage, consumed with prophetic visions of the suffering to descend on Agamemnon and Odysseus. Andromache laments her lot and the death of Polyxena, only to have her sorrow augmented by the announcement that her son (and Hector's), Astyanax, must be thrown from the walls to prevent the survival of any future avenger of Troy. Pompous Menelaus arrives, gloating over the recapture of Helen; she enters, exhibiting neither fear nor guilt, and defends herself against Hecuba's venomous hatred. Helen refuses to accept blame for the disaster, claiming that forces larger than herself worked on and through all of them. Menelaus promises that Helen will be punished when they return to Sparta, but no one believes him. Talthybius, bearing Astyanax's body for Hecuba to bury, leads the captives to the ships. Hecuba, having mourned the last Trojan son and restrained by the Greeks from leaping into the flames of the now burning city, summons her last shreds of dignity to lead the Trojan women away into captivity as the towering walls collapse.

Throughout the tragedy, the chorus has but one theme: Troy, its former grandeur and god-favored status, its heroes and civic harmony. The play focuses on a single intense moment in the whole Trojan drama, and sorrow builds from shock to shock until the conclusion seems a vast collective threnody. So powerful is this play's denunciation of the effects of war, so stirring is it to this century's conscience, that it remains the most frequently performed of Euripides' plays.

Comparative: The tragedy has a moral structure like that of *Agamemnon* by Aeschylus, where the hero's sin is first related and then demonstrated in action after action. In this play, the Greeks repeatedly demonstrate their arrogance and *hubris* in their treatment of the Trojans. Only Synge's *Riders to the Sea* concentrates so absolutely on irretrievable communal loss by mothers, sisters, and widows.

Flaubert, Gustave. THE LEGEND OF ST. JULIAN HOSPITATOR (LA LÉ-GENDE DE ST. JULIEN L'HOSPITALIER). 1876. Story. French.

Author: Flaubert (1821-1880) was a Norman and the son of a surgeon. He studied law in Paris but at twenty-five gave up that career to devote himself to writing. Each work he produced was the result of years of searching for perfection. He isolated himself from his fellow writers and friends but maintained a long friendship by correspondence with George Sand. *Madame Bovary* (1857) was completely misunderstood when it appeared, and the author was prosecuted in the courts. It has since emerged as one of the great novels of modern literature. Interesting semi-successes are *Sentimental Education* (1869) and *Salammbô* (1862).

Work: This story, a medieval religious legend, is the second of the trilogy *Trois Contes.* Julian, raised in a high-towered castle, is the object of prophecy from birth—he will become part of an emperor's family; he will become a saint. His boyhood and education are typically medieval. He is taught to hunt and to use weapons, and he discovers the sensual delights of killing. Every creature falls to his arrows or spears. One day he shoots a stag which refuses to die and which delivers the Oedipal prophecy that Julian will murder his mother and father. Later, he mistakenly believes that he has killed his mother, and he flees home to become a soldier of fortune. Thus it is that he meets and marries an emperor's daughter.

Soon after his marriage Julian leaves the palace on a night hunt. While he is away, his mother and father come seeking him. His wife treats them honorably and gives them her own bed in which to sleep. Julian, coming home by dark, feels his father's beard on his pillow; suspecting infidelity, he kills both man and woman, thinking to have killed his wife and her lover. He now becomes a wanderer, haunted by nightmare.

Years later Julian comes to a wild river and settles there to operate a ferry for distressed travelers. One day he is forced to ferry a leper, who begs him for food and then for his bed. The leper then demands that Julian lie nude with him to warm his body. Julian does—and the leper turns into an angel, who grows swiftly and radiantly, pushing the little hut apart as the heavens open and lift Julian upwards.

The descriptions in this tale are brilliant and chiseled, and the characters truly have the mythological quality Flaubert wanted. The story exhibits the quintessence of medievalism as we visualize it: supernatural, superstitious, brutal, and mystical.

The tale reveals the deliberate effect and the keen, detached observation of Flaubert, his fondness for romantic removal in time and place, and the mythic mysticism which makes his stories legendary and universal.

Comparative: The prophecies remind one of those given to Aeneas in Virgil and to Oedipus in Sophocles. The motif of talking animals also appears in the *Ramayana,* in the *Panchatantra,* and in Aesop's fables. The important kiss of love at the story's climax is found in Hesse's *Siddhartha,* in Dostoevski's "The Legend of the Grand Inquisitor," and in Katov's sublime gesture of brotherly love in Malraux's *Man's Fate.* Medieval tales with the same restrained emotional quality are found in stories by Isak Dinesen and Anatole France.

Flaubert, Gustave. MADAME BOVARY. 1857. Novel. French.

Author: See "The Legend of St. Julian Hospitator."

Work: This famous novel concerns a woman's attempts to escape from a stifling world of reality into a world of acted-out dreams. Vigorously controlled writing enabled Flaubert to set as foils against one another the romantic imagination of Emma Bovary and her bourgeois environment, dispassionately creating brilliant portraits of each.

The second wife of Charles Bovary, an unsuccessful medical man, is Emma Rouault, reared on a farm, convent-educated, and expectantly waiting for a life filled with romance and beauty. Charles does not provide such a life; neither does the dreary little town of Tostes where Charles pursues his practice. The couple move to Yonville, near Rouen. Except for one ecstatic evening at a fete at the neighboring chateau of Vaubyessard, life for Emma is just as dull in Yonville as it had been in Tostes.

Emma throws herself into household decorating, clothing design, and the study of music and languages; she even tries religion again but finds every avenue of escape unsatisfying. Her child, Berthe, is only a momentary pastime. Escape finally takes the form of Rodolphe, with whom Emma has her first serious affair. After this lover extricates himself, the unhappy, desperate Emma falls in love with Léon, formerly of Yonville and now studying law in Rouen. Ostensibly visiting the city weekly to study music, she visits Léon and maintains a passionate liaison.

Meanwhile, due to her demand for beautiful things with which to surround herself, Emma Bovary has fallen into the clutches of the merchant Lheureux. Faced with the end of her love affair with Léon and with the financial ruin of herself and faithful, dull Charles, Emma obtains arsenic and kills herself. After her death, Charles finds the evidence of her extravagance in love and money but excuses uncomprehendingly the ruin that Emma has left to him and to little Berthe.

Memorable characters of the petite bourgeoisie: Homais, the clever little pharmacist who gets his coveted medallion of the Legion of Honor; Rodolphe, the hick counterpart of the slick seducer of romantic fiction; poor, timid

Léon, never anything except what Emma imagined him to be; and, of course, Charles Bovary himself. The county fair scene in which the remarks of the crowd in the street, the platitudinous oratory of the officials on their platform, and the amorous conversation of Emma and Rodolphe in their room are presented simultaneously, with the language of each intermingling so that speech and actions comment ironically on each other, is justly celebrated as a remarkable creation of "special form" in the novel, a technique that influenced many other novelists including James Joyce.

Comparative: The dispassionate revelation of character through trivial events and the ironic contrast between the romantic imagination of the principal characters and the real and petty world in which they live—so beautifully achieved in this novel—is also found in Chekhov *(The Cherry Orchard)*, in Ibsen *(The Wild Duck)* and in James Joyce *(A Portrait of the Artist as a Young Man)*. The central female figure can also be compared with Zola's treatment of a woman and her life in *Nana*, Thomas Mann's Tonie in *Buddenbrooks*, and Tolstoi's *Anna Karenina*.

Flaubert, Gustave. A SIMPLE HEART (UN COEUR SIMPLE). 1877. Story. French.

Author: See "The Legend of St. Julian Hospitator."

Work: A novella in scope, this story, the first of the *Trois Contes* describes with details of incident and setting the life of a devoted serving girl, Félicité. The style is simple and dispassionate but not unsympathetic.

Félicité, a simple Norman farm girl without family, is taken in by Mme Aubain, a widow with two children, Paul and Virginia, and devotes her life to this family. Her life is one of monotonous daily chores, although it is interrupted by a few significant events: Félicité's discovery of a nephew who goes on a voyage and dies, Virginia's illness and death, Paul's rascally youth and maturity, Madame Aubain's death.

Félicité forms one consuming attachment after another for her adopted family or for acquaintances who are having ill fortune, and a series of symbols arises around her fixations: her love of the church, the cast-off remembrances with which she decorates her room, and finally a parrot which had been given to her mistress and which Félicité loves and ultimately comes to confuse with Christ. In her room she maintains a sort of altar of everything and everyone she has known and loved. When the parrot dies, it is stuffed and even becomes a part of the altarpiece in the public Corpus Christi day celebration. At the celebration of this feast, Félicité, completely alone and deprived of all she has loved, dies, breathing in the incense of the procession that goes by her window. Her story is an extremely moving tale, saved from bathos by Flaubert's masterful control of distance.

With this work and *Madame Bovary,* Flaubert proved himself master of a new method, which combined an impersonal style and accurate observation, even documentation, of his characters. This method profoundly influenced literature after his time, and "Un Coeur simple" beautifully represents that carefully managed style and amazing selection of necessary details.

Comparative: Félicité changes her entire character each time a new love enters her life, and she is consumed by the devotion she offers. A similar treatment is found in Chekhov's story, "The Darling." A companion motif, in the symbol of Loulou the parrot, is found in the stuffed dog of Lampedusa's *The Leopard,* an excellent historical novel in which style, manner, and the handling of the passing of time are reminiscent of "A Simple Heart." Balzac's *Eugénie Grandet* gives an equally deep look at French provincial life and an equally valid statement of a wasted existence. Grandet's servant, Bib Nanon, is similar to Félicité.

France, Anatole, pseudonym of Jacques-Anatole-François Thibault. THE PROCURATOR OF JUDEA (LE PROCURATEUR DE JUDÉE). 1892. Story. French.

Author: Anatole France (1844-1924) was born in Paris, the son of a bookstall merchant along the Seine. His father interested Anatole in the eighteenth century, and he later discovered a liking for classical scholarship that led him to write such short stories as this and his novel *Thaïs.* The Dreyfus case stirred him to an interest in the victims of society; hence his novella *Crainquebille.* Stylistically, and in his recreation of the classical and historical, Anatole France has few equals. He was awarded the Nobel Prize for Literature in 1921.

Work: Laelius Lamia meets at the baths of Baiae an old man being carried in a litter. He recognizes his friend, Pontius Pilate, now retired from a lifetime of service to the Roman Republic. The two reflect on their experiences and the history and future of Rome and its colonies. Casual talk leads Lamia to a sudden memory and a question: "'Jesus was crucified for some crime. I don't quite know what. Pontius, do you remember anything about the man?' After a silence of some seconds—'Jesus?' he murmured, 'Jesus—of Nazareth? I cannot call him to mind.'"

Pontius Pilate's ignorance of the major event in which he participated, the judging of Christ, is a startlingly effective literary stroke.

Comparative: This story is among the works that begin the literature of disillusionment which flourished after World War I. Nietzsche had proclaimed, "God is dead!" and themes such as these echoed his statement. Dostoevski had already examined the possibility of Christ's return to earth in "The Legend of the Grand Inquisitor." D. H. Lawrence later wrote a similar short story of disillusionment, the intense and powerful "The Man Who Died"— a story about Lazarus and the question of eternal life. Andreyev wrote an expressionistic and compelling account of the same material in his fable "Lazarus."

Frank, Anne. THE DIARY OF A YOUNG GIRL (HET ACHTERHUS, lit., "The Warehouse"). 1947. Autobiography in diary form. Dutch.

Author: Most of what we know of Anne Frank's brief life (1929-1945) is contained in her *Diary,* which begins on her thirteenth birthday. She was born into a prosperous Jewish family and until the advent of the Nazis apparently had a normal childhood. Anne's father has described the circumstances surrounding the survival of her diary, overlooked on August 4, 1944, when five policemen broke into their hiding place, took the silverware and the Hanukkah candlestick, but discarded books, magazines, and newspapers— including the diary. The diary was found and preserved by family friends. Anne herself died in the extermination camp at Bergen-Belsen in March 1945, two months before Holland was liberated. Her father was the only occupant of the secret annex to survive imprisonment. The two Dutchmen, Kraler and Koophuis, Mr. Frank's business associates, who had aided in concealing the little group and were arrested with them, also survived.

Work: More than a generation has passed since this diary was written (1942-44), but the effect of this simple yet powerful first-person account of a Jewish girl's coming of age in Nazi-occupied Amsterdam has not diminished. Knowing, as we do, of Anne's capture and death in the Bergen-Belsen concentration camp, both her fears of imprisonment and her occasional optimistic hopes for the future take on added poignancy.

Anne's diary opens on her thirteenth birthday, when it was given her as a present. Shortly thereafter, as the Nazi purge against the Jews becomes intensified and Anne's older sister, Margot, receives a call-up notice, the family goes into hiding, moving into prepared quarters in the "secret annex" —several small rooms in the rear of the warehouse and office building occupied by Mr. Frank's business. Sharing these cramped quarters are Anne, her mother and father, Margot, Mr. and Mrs. Van Daan, their son Peter, and Albert Dussel, an elderly dentist. For two years these eight people live in close confinement, not even daring to go outdoors for a breath of fresh air.

Their contact with the outside world comes from Mr. Frank's business associates—Elli, Miep, Mr. Koophuis, and Mr. Kraler—who continue to operate the business and who remain loyal to the little group in hiding, bringing them provisions, news of the outside world, and library books. Their most valued possession is a small radio, customarily tuned to English stations for news of the war. Now and then the threat of discovery freezes them with fear, but on the whole they live normally. Their discussions of politics, philosophy, and literature are interspersed with sharp little quarrels that subside into good humor and acceptance of the situation. There are games of Monopoly, school work, reminiscences, and plans for the future. Anne and Peter fall in love, a tender affair that shows surprising depth because of the mature responsibilities under which they live. The diary ends suddenly; it was one of the worthless "papers" left lying on the floor when their hiding place was discovered by the Gestapo and plundered of everything valuable.

Comparative: Although Anne Frank's *Diary* is unique in that it is the spontaneous creation of a sensitive and talented young girl enmeshed in the holocaust, the work lends itself to comparison in several areas. First, it may be compared with other accounts, real or fictional, of young people attaining maturity. Among these are Güiraldes's *Don Segundo Sombra* and Joyce's *A Portrait of the Artist as a Young Man.* Second, it may be included in a study of works on war, possibly those dealing with its effect on innocent victims, including, for example, Hersey's *Hiroshima,* Kuznetsov's *Babi-Yar,* or even *The Trojan Women* of Euripides. It certainly lends itself to specific comparisons with other literature about the Nazi concentration camps, for example, Nelly Sachs's *O the Chimneys,* dedicated "to my dead brothers and sisters" and containing the striking poems "O the Chimneys," "A Dead Child Speaks," "You Onlookers," and "World, Do Not Ask Those Snatched from Death," and Ka-tzetnik 135633's *Star Eternal* (the author, Karol Cetyński, wished to be identified not by his name but by his concentration camp number). Finally, the stories Anne wrote during the period she was in hiding have been collected and published under the title *Tales from the House Behind.*

An adaptation for the stage, *The Diary of Anne Frank* by Frances Goodrich and Albert Hackett, provides the material for an interesting comparison in the handling of narrative and dramatic techniques. The film version of the book can also be used to extend the discussion.

García Lorca, Federico. BLOOD WEDDING (BODAS DE SANGRE). 1933.
    Drama. Spanish.

Author: García Lorca was born near Granada in 1898 and disappeared in 1936 in the Spanish Civil War, presumably killed. During his short life, he had published his first poetry at twenty, produced his first play at twenty-two, taken a law degree, and attracted attention with his drawings. He spent several years lecturing and directing plays in Argentina, Cuba, and the United States.

Work: Two families, each with tragedy in its past, meet through a marriage, and double death comes to them again. Leonardo, unable to resist the bride of another man, abducts her on her wedding day. The bridegroom and his relatives pursue Leonardo in a moonlit, expressionistic scene of horror, and the two young men kill one another. The women—Leonardo's wife, the bride, and the bridegroom's mother—are left to mourn and do so in the high-strung, old world manner behind shuttered windows and heavy doors.

The bare outline of the play is deceptive, for what lies behind it is highly tragic. The play manifests the closed-in, masculine world of Spain, where men pursue death, where honor is maintained at any price, and where women may not betray their feelings except in a conventional and dramatic manner. García Lorca uses many symbols to convey his meaning: he expresses amazement at the strength of a little blade; the horse is a sign of a man's virility and pursuit of death; death is an old woman known to all; violins represent the whispering trees and the two lovers wandering beneath them; woodcutters are symbols of society's destructiveness; and water is less absolution than expiation sought and paid for. Abstraction is carried to the point where only one of the characters—Leonardo—is named; indeed, one character who appears in the play is not even listed in the *dramatis personae.*

Comparative: Shakespeare's *Romeo and Juliet* uses similar material. One of many treatments in ballad literature is Keats's "The Eve of St. Agnes." Woman, victim of man's violence, is the theme of Euripides' *The Trojan Women,* and extended comparisons can be found there. As symbolist, García Lorca follows Maeterlinck in, for example, *The Intruder.*

García Lorca, Federico. THE HOUSE OF BERNARDA ALBA (LA CASA DE BERNARDA ALBA). 1934. Drama. Spanish.

Author: See *Blood Wedding.*

Work: García Lorca is said to be the most translated Spanish poet of this century. He is also among the most traditional of modern Spanish writers, selecting as his themes danger, superstition, blood, and death. This particular drama, first performed in 1945, is perhaps the culmination of his poetic and dramatic method, for it moves through symbols and symbolic situations, and its characters are semi-abstract. This story of five sisters who are cloistered by a protective and jealous mother has as its most important personage a man who never appears in the drama—one man from the menacing outside world of violence that women peep at through shuttered windows.

Five daughters of Bernarda, widow and mother, are kept secluded and are denied husbands. To Bernarda there are two worlds, one of women who must be protected and the other of roistering men. But to the daughters, "to be born a woman is the worst possible punishment." Bernarda's eldest daughter, Angustias, aged thirty-nine, is being courted by Pepe as a financial matter. Jealousies break out among the daughters, and the youngest, beautiful Adela, falls in love with Pepe. Adela takes a turn at the window, "playing bear" at night after Angustias has gone to bed, and Pepe lurks around the house waiting to see her. Oncia, the old maidservant, who bore sons while Bernarda bore only daughters, acts as a chorus and prophesies tragedy. Adela's secret is discovered, and she challenges her mother's authority for the first time. Pepe is heard riding away from the house, and Martirio, a jealous sister (note the name), shoots at him. She misses, but Adela thinks he is killed and rushes into another room and hangs herself.

Stallion, lamb, and window become effective symbols in the drama. The demented but noble grandmother, who looks at life in terms of birth and creation in contrast to this infertile household of women, is herself representational of the conflict.

Comparative: The hatred of men that Bernarda shows is paralleled in Strindberg's *The Father.* Bernarda's tyranny is like that of Grandet in Balzac's *Eugénie Grandet.* The situation of the women finds echoes in Molière's *The Miser,* in the plays of Beaumarchais, in Moratín's *The Maiden's Consent,* and in Pérez Galdós's *Doña Perfecta.* The futility and frustration of the many heroines find some common ground with Chekhov's *The Three Sisters.*

García Márquez, Gabriel. ONE HUNDRED YEARS OF SOLITUDE (CIEN AÑOS DE SOLEDAD). 1967. Novel. Colombian.

Author: García Márquez (1928-   ) was born in the small town of Aracataca, Colombia, and as a child was educated by Jesuits in Bogotá. A mediocre student in high school, he did no better studying law at the University of Bogotá. From there he went into newspaper work, read Joyce and Kafka, wrote stories, and reported and edited for *El Espectador* of Bogotá. In 1954 he was sent to Rome as a correspondent; there he discovered the Experimental Film Center, which led him to take a director's course. Losing his job because of a new dictatorship in Colombia, he settled in Paris and saw hard times before finding work as an editor in Caracas, Venezuela. For a while in 1959 he worked for the Cuban news agency, *Prensa Latina,* in Bogotá. Once again militant party politics caused his resignation, and in 1961 García Márquez went to Mexico to write for the films. Presently his home is listed as Barcelona, Spain. *One Hundred Years of Solitude* was published in the United

States in 1970 after its Spanish language debut in 1967. His work has been published in over twenty languages and in eight Spanish-speaking countries.

Work: García Márquez admits to the heavy influence of William Faulkner and his Yoknapatawpha cycle. *One Hundred Years of Solitude* centers on the mythical town of Macondo, carrying with it the idea of total solitude as well as that of a geographical entity and a population with a mythology. García Márquez attempts to give us the story of a whole continent in his tales of the generational conflicts of the Buendía family. The founder of Macondo, José Arcadio Buendía, has fled over seemingly impossible routes with his wife-cousin Úrsula, to become entrapped forever in this swampy area surrounded by impenetrable mountains. Across the generations we deal with Aureliano, José's great great grandson and the last of the Buendía line, who realizes that the Buendías have been enclosed for a century in glass cages of solitude.

The history of Macondo and the Buendía house comes from the pen of Melquíades, a gypsy magus, who sets down the story in a nearly undecipherable manuscript which will attract future generations with its mysterious legacy.

One Hundred Years of Solitude is a prodigious undertaking containing every kind of character, from gypsies and ghosts to necromancers, cannibals, levitating priests, and incestuous lovers. As if that were not enough, its Chagall-like scenes offer rains of yellow flowers, golden chamber pots, flying carpets, and of course, the obligatory appearance of the wandering Jew.

Comparative: All of García Márquez's other writings connect with the Macondo cycle in some way: *La hojarasca (Leaf Storm)*, 1955; *El coronel no tiene quien le escriba (No One Writes to the Colonel)*, 1957; *Los funerales de la mamá grande (Big Mama's Funeral)*, 1962; *La mala hora (The Evil Hour)*, 1961.

The work of García Márquez has been compared to that of Faulkner, Günter Grass, and Virginia Woolf. In its compression of history *One Hundred Years* has been likened to both Wilder's *The Skin of Our Teeth* and Bunyan's *Pilgrim's Progress.*

Ghālib. GHAZALS OF GHĀLIB. Edited by Aijaz Ahmad, with versions from the Urdu by Aijaz Ahmad, W. S. Merwin, Adrienne Rich, William Stafford, David Ray, Thomas Fitzsimmons, Mark Stand, and William Hunt. Columbia University Press, 1971. Poetry. Urdu.

Author: Ghālib, a *nom de plume* of Mirzā Asadullāh Khān, was born in 1797 in the city of Agra, India, and died in Delhi in 1869. He began writing Urdu and Persian verse as a child. Surrounded by carnage, he wrote a poetry primarily of losses and consequent grief. In sensibility, it is a poetry of endurance in a world growing increasingly unbearable. During the last decade of his life he carried on an extensive correspondence from Delhi in a style which he said "transformed correspondence into conversation." These letters have since been published. His Urdu verse has become popular only since the beginning of the twentieth century, and we now consider it to be strikingly modern. Ghālib himself prophesied that his verses "like wine that has grown old" would win recognition only after his death.

Work: While there are numerous translations of Ghālib, the Ahmad edition is the best and marks a new phase in the history of translation from the Urdu. Literal translations of the poems with notes are provided along with freer translations, interpretations, and recreations by outstanding American poets. Close fidelity to the original is found in the work of Adrienne Rich and William Stafford, but students will also be able to see the vitalization of an Urdu poet in the recreations by American poets who have based their work on the literal translations.

The *ghazal* is a poetic form composed of couplets, each independent of any other in meaning and complete in itself as a unit of thought, emotion and communication. The only link is in terms of prosodic structure and rhyme. All lines must be of equal metrical length. According to convention, a *ghazal* must have at least five couplets, but there is no maximum length.

Comparative: The most meaningful comparison that can be made is to consider the literal translations and the notes along side the versions created by American poets. Students may also be encouraged to write their own *ghazals* or poetic interpretations based on the literal translations.

T. S. Eliot once said that the most important thing that can happen to a nation is a new form of poetry. The *ghazal,* as introduced by Aijaz Ahmad and his American collaborators, has had a profound effect on several contemporary poets in America. Students may, for example, want to look at the work of Adrienne Rich, Robert Bly, and Robert Lowell.

Gide, André. THE IMMORALIST (L'IMMORALISTE). 1902. Novel. French.

Author: André Gide (1869-1951), a sickly child, was raised by strict Protestant women, overcame tuberculosis, and came to accept his homosexual inclinations through the influence of Wilde. Considered one of the most important and controversial contributors in modern European literature, he had his first book published anonymously at the age of eighteen. Gide founded the *Nouvelle Revue Francaise* and served as its director until 1941. He won the Nobel Prize in 1947.

Work: Michel, a young, protected scholar who has failed to realize his potential, marries Marceline to please his father. On their honeymoon in North

Africa Michel's latent tuberculosis emerges, and he nearly dies. Marceline nurses him back to health, and in the process of discovering the value of life, he explores daringly and indulgently his repressed self. He sacrifices everything to self-realization, though he is not fully aware of the implications of what he discovers.

The couple travels compulsively, and Michel grows in his Nietzschean philosophy as his wife declines and dies. His growing interest in the clandestine, secretive, and perverse reflect those heretofore unrecognized qualities in himself. He takes pleasure in watching an Arab boy steal from Marceline; he joins in poaching on his own land; he fails to look after his more serious scholarly and business affairs; he is indifferent to his wife's death. What he has discovered in regaining his life is that he has destroyed his old self and that the new one, which had been latent all the while, is dangerous and pleasurable. At the end of the novel he waits for friends to help him explain what has happened.

Opposites such as Puritanism and perverted hedonism, order and chaos, freedom and responsibility, are exposed in classically clear language through a deliberately imperceptive narrator. The literary technique and the psychology of character are masterfully and economically achieved and are very contemporary—though the novel was written at the turn of the century.

Comparative: In the use of a narrator who is less aware than the reader, *The Immoralist* reminds us of Dostoevski's *Notes from Underground* and Mann's *Death in Venice.* The neurotic compulsions of Dostoevski's narrator and of Mann's artist also bear comparison. The eruption of previously suppressed impulses, the simultaneous drive toward self-realization and self-destruction, the ambiguities of freedom and discipline, and the conflict between the world of art and the world of reason are themes central to these novels and of major importance in many modern novels.

GILGAMESH. ca. 2,000 B.C. Epic poem. Asian.

Author: Unknown. The work has been collected from clay tablets and inscriptions from Nineveh and other archaeological sites.

Work: This near-perfect epic poem about the hero of the city-state of Uruk in Mesopotamia near the time of the tower of Babel demonstrates many of the themes and devices we have come to associate with the classical epic; thus it looks toward Homer. It is also interesting for its correspondence to biblical stories and its depiction of an epic hero who is a believable human being, concerned with the fear of death and love for a friend.

Enkidu is created by a goddess and thrown down to live in the wilds with animals. He is powerful and feared, and hunters set a trap for him in the person of a harlot, who tames him and teaches him the ways of human life.

Hearing of the strength of the prince Gilgamesh, Enkidu sets out for Uruk to defeat him; but through their combat they become friends and brothers. Together they leave to vanquish Humbaba, the monster of the cedar forests. Enkidu with his own hands throws open the gates of the heavenly mountain, and the two heroes kill Humbaba, with winds and storms fighting at their sides. Next against them comes Ishtar's Bull of Heaven, which they also slay.

Now, however, Enkidu falls ill because his strength was drained from him when he touched the holy gates. He languishes and dies. Gilgamesh, distraught by grief for his friend and by fear of his own death, makes a journey to talk with the immortal Utnapishtim (Noah). Gilgamesh must go through the mountain Mashu (Hades), where night is eternal, and cross the ocean with the ferryman Urshanabi (Charon). From Utnapishtim he learns that death is final, but he also learns from the sage the story of the flood in which only Utnapishtim and his wife survived. Gilgamesh is granted safe passage back to Uruk, which he greets gratefully in the manner of Odysseus. After the passage of time, he dies.

Comparative: Combat, laments, invocations, heroic epithets, numerical devices, poetic repetitions, the descent to hell, the battle with a monster, the respect shown the gods, and the nobility of the hero—these are epic devices one finds in *Gilgamesh.* It should be noted that the heroes here are differentiated and humanized and undergo marked character changes during the sequence of events; in this respect *Gilgamesh* is superior to some medieval epics (though not the *Nibelungenlied*) and most resembles *Beowulf.* Compare this work with the *Song of Roland, Poem of the Cid,* the *Odyssey,* and the *Nibelungenlied.*

Giraudoux, Jean. ONDINE. 1939. Drama. French.

Author: Giraudoux (1882-1944) was born at Bellac and educated in Paris; he became head of the Press Service in the French Foreign Office and later worked in the diplomatic service. He was a novelist *(Suzanne and the Pacific),* short story writer, and playwright. His use of irony may remind us of André Gide, but his subject matter is drawn from his own experience—Bellac and bureaucracy. Although he is most famous for his plays, it was not until 1928 that Giraudoux, at the age of forty-six, turned to drama.

Work: This three-act tragic comedy was drawn from Fouqué's novella *Undine* (German). The heroine, a pagan water creature, marries into the unnatural world of men and women, and by her honesty and love destroys both herself and her Babbitt-like husband.

Hans, a knight wandering through a forest, comes to a fisherman's cottage where he meets the old couple's adopted daughter, Ondine, a watersprite.

Ondine falls in love with him, though not really knowing what love is. The Old One (Neptune) and other ondines warn her that she will destroy herself for love, but she goes off with Hans when he returns to court. There she meets Bertha, Hans's fiancée and a woman of the world who knows all about the practices of knighthood and courtly protocol. These niceties Ondine considers unimportant compared with the love which she lavishes on Hans. Faced with the choice between conforming with normalcy and loving this capricious nature creature, Hans is unfaithful to Ondine.

Brokenhearted, Ondine returns to her native waters. Eventually she is captured, given a mock trial and condemned to death. The Old One appears in the capacity of a court magician and tells Ondine that she will be taken away and that Hans will die. And so it happens—at the third call of Ondine's name by supernatural voices from above the stage, Hans falls dead. Ondine, now recalled to her own self, looks with neutral interest and bemusement at the body of Hans and repeats the lines which she had spoken on meeting him: "Oh, I like him so much. . . . How I should have loved him!"

The tragedy of this play is mitigated by the cleverness of its lines. In the translation of *Ondine,* Maurice Valency sums up the personal conflict in a brilliant introduction: "the drama of nature which strives to domesticate itself for the sake of man. . . . This is our dilemma. As men, we love Ondine always, but we cannot do without Bertha. We take Ondine into our arms, hoping to find Bertha. We marry Bertha, looking for Ondine. And so, at every moment, we deceive them, the ideal and the real. . . ."

Ondine, then, is another examination of the modern conflict between man and nature, between what is real and what is fancied, between what men love and what they marry—a charming and witty Gallic examination through magical spectacles, not always rose-colored, of the human condition.

Comparative: The search for the ideal appears in Alain-Fournier's *The Wanderer* and in Goethe's *Faust.* Another encounter with nature personified is found in Hudson's *Green Mansions.* The trial scene, especially the travesty of justice that occurs when human justice meets a truth too large for it, is also a theme in two plays about Joan of Arc—Anouilh's *The Lark* and Shaw's *Saint Joan.* Finally, it is interesting to compare Fouqué's original tale with Giraudoux's twentieth-century dramatic version.

Goethe, Johann Wolfgang von. FAUST, PART ONE (FAUST, ERSTER TEIL). 1808. Drama. German.

Author: Goethe (1749-1832) was born at Frankfurt-on-Main of an elderly, withdrawn father disappointed in public service and a volatile, imaginative young mother. Johann was first educated by parents and tutors and then at the University of Leipzig. His education and interests were wide, covering

law, the occult, and art. From 1775 Goethe lived at the ducal court at Wei-
mar, where he held a cabinet-level post that allowed him time to write, to
travel occasionally, and to carry on scientific experiments in plant biology,
physiology, and optics. His best-known works, aside from his lyric poetry, are
The Sorrows of Young Werther (1774), *Wilhelm Meister's Apprenticeship*
(1795-1796), and *Faust, Part One* (1808) and *Part Two* (1832).

Work: Goethe builds an allegory from early legends, unifying them into a
powerful drama of a man's aspiration toward the complete experience of life
and the attainment of all knowledge.

From the prologue set in Heaven, reminiscent of the book of Job, we learn
that Mephistopheles is one who "always wills evil and always does good,"
one who is "the power that denies." Is he the devil? We will use that name for
convenience. At any rate, Mephistopheles is given authority to attempt the
corruption of Doctor Faust, the middle-aged medieval scholar, who in his
great knowledge has reached a state of disillusionment. Disguised as a poodle,
Mephistopheles accompanies Faust back to his suite after a walk. The devil
reveals himself and later reappears to strike a bargain with his hoped-for
victim: he will give the restless Faust all he seeks in wisdom and experience
in return for his soul. Faust, however, cannily limits the bargain, stating that
the devil will own him completely only when Faust finds an experience so
fair that he asks that it shall never end.

A series of incidents now reveals the supernatural to Faust: he and Mephistopheles fly through the air on steeds; Faust is offered and drinks an elixir
of youth; costly gems are secured from their burial place in the earth to
tempt Gretchen, the teenage girl whom Faust sees and desires. Gretchen's
elderly friend Martha and Mephistopheles serve as pander and pimp to lure
the young girl to a rendezvous with Faust. Gretchen's mother is given a
sleeping potion to favor the lovers and dies as a result. Valentin, Gretchen's
brother, attacks Mephistopheles and Faust for defaming his sister, and Faust
kills him. Gretchen finds herself pregnant, disposes of her baby by drowning
it in a pond, is imprisoned for the murder of her mother and child, and loses
her mind from guilt and grief. Faust, enlisting the aid of Mephistopheles,
appears before the girl in prison and tries in vain to lead her to escape.

The whole is told in an amazing variety of verse forms, including ribald
doggerel that foreshadows the verse of Brecht in *The Threepenny Opera,*
striking ballads such as "The King of Thule," and delicate lyrics, in addition
to the varied and marvelously effective narrative verse. Faust's musings upon
the human condition are pungent and profound.

Faust, Part Two continues the hero's pilgrimage through contemporary
and classical Europe until the moment of his salvation. In constructing an
earthworks to rescue land from the sea in the Low Countries, he finds himself
at last of use to humanity and free from the power of Mephistopheles: "I
find this wisdom's form:/ He only earns his freedom and his life/ Who takes
them every day by storm."

Comparative: Deals with the devil occur frequently in American literature—Washington Irving's "The Devil and Tom Walker," Nathaniel Hawthorne's "Young Goodman Brown," Stephen Vincent Benét's "The Devil and Daniel Webster." They also occur in works such as Ivo Andrič's *The Bridge on the Drina,* Adalbert von Chamisso's *Peter Schlemihl,* and Thomas Mann's penetrating twentieth-century novel *Dr. Faustus,* a less exuberant work uncomplicated by the Gretchen episode and ending with Faustus the loser. The relentlessness of Faust's pursuit also reminds one of Michel in Gide's *The Immoralist.*

The Faust theme of aspiration toward total experience and complete knowledge can be added to Cervantes's duality of Sancho Panza and Don Quixote, and to Don Juanism to provide the recognized canon on the nature of humanity.

The Faust story has become the property of folklore, opera, and ballet. In particular, Charles Gounod's opera *Faust* (1859) is loosely based on Goethe's play.

Goethe, Johann Wolfgang von. THE SORROWS OF YOUNG WERTHER (DIE LEIDEN DES JUNGEN WERTHERS). 1774. Novella. German.

Author: See *Faust.*

Work: As much as any single fictional work, this novella may be said to have introduced romanticism. As a youth overpowered by a hopeless love and poignantly aware of nature's beauty as well as its latent destructiveness—love and nature both leading him toward suicide—Werther began a vogue of romantic melancholy that remained fashionable for almost a century. An interesting aside—Werther's story was one of Napoleon's favorite literary works.

Young Werther retires to a rustic village and there meets and falls in love with Charlotte. Even though he learns that she is engaged, he courts her; when she marries Albert, Werther is unable to end his idolatry. A strange love triangle emerges, with each of the three "intelligent and well-meaning people" protecting and respecting one another. Werther is a delightful young man, rare and sensitive, and the novella, written in the form of letters sent to a friend, gives the reader the privilege of knowing this hero confidentially. Albert, pragmatic as well as idealistic, is devoted both to Werther and to Charlotte; his reasonableness provides a foil to Werther's "ungovernable passion for all that is dear." Charlotte is completely beautiful in character. So we have three splendid young people sensitive to one another and trying courageously to discipline themselves. Werther eventually finds that nature is cruel, as society and all humanity are cruel. Unable to bear further disillusionment, he kills himself.

Comparative: Another sensitive psychological love triangle, but one that is obscured by the complexities of French court life, is Mme de Lafayette's *Princess of Cleves* (1678). Another novel with something of the mood of *The Sorrows of Young Werther* and with a hero in desperate search of the ideal is Alain-Fournier's *The Wanderer.* A young passion, lesser but comparable, is the subject of Turgenev's *Spring Torrents.* Almost equally responsible for creating the wave of romanticism are Chateaubriand's *Atala* and *René*— indeed, "Wertherism" and *mal de René* are terms to describe the same morbidly sensitive psyche. For fun, read Thackeray's "The Sorrows of Young Werther," a four-verse parody of Goethe's novella.

Gogol, Nikolai Vasilievich. THE INSPECTOR GENERAL (REVIZOR). 1836. Drama. Russian.

Author: Gogol (1809-1852) was born and educated in the Ukraine, the setting for most of his early works. At the age of nineteen he felt called to perform great services for Russia and moved to St. Petersburg, but his first literary work was scorned. After an aborted trip to America he became a minor government clerk. He achieved popularity, however, with his two volumes of stories about Ukrainian peasants, *Evenings on a Farm near Dikanka* (1831 and 1832). From 1834 to 1835 he taught history at Petersburg University, and in 1835 he published *Mirgorod,* containing the romantic Cossack tale "Taras Bulba." In the same year he turned his attention to city life with *Arabesques,* his Petersburg tales. Gogol's great comedy, *The Inspector General,* staged in 1836, satirized the corrupt provincial bureaucracy. His attack on pettiness and corruption continued in the novel *Dead Souls* (1842) and the short story "The Overcoat" (1842). Despite these satires, Gogol felt that the existing political and social order was sacred and that moral regeneration must take place within that order. He was deeply disturbed when his works were used by liberals to advocate reform. From 1836 until 1849 Gogol spent much time outside of Russia, including a pilgrimage to Palestine in 1847. He returned to Moscow, where he died in 1852 after several years of deep despair and religious fanaticism.

Work: Gogol's simple plot was suggested to him by Pushkin and involves the corrupt officials of a provincial town who mistake a penniless minor official, Khlestakov, for a government inspector sent to check up on them. The officials compete with one another in attempts to bribe and influence Khlestakov, the mayor going so far as to thrust his daughter upon the all-too-willing imposter, who makes his getaway just before the arrival of the real inspector-general is announced to the stunned bureaucrats.

Like Gogol's story "The Overcoat," this play immediately sparked an argument: the liberals hailed it as a satire on government corruption and proof of the need for reform; the conservatives proclaimed it an unfair attack on themselves. But here as with "The Overcoat," the reader should remember that Gogol was primarily a moral and not a social critic, and he saw the reformers and the corrupt officials as equally culpable. The world for Gogol is a corrupt place, where few can feel morally superior. It is not that people are evil, as indeed Khlestakov is not, but that they are weak and easily carried away by their own vanity and lies. As Gogol wrote: "All men are Khlestakovs—for at least a few minutes, or a moment only. It is so hard not to become a Khlestakov, even if only once." Khlestakov is not a con man; he is merely a weak, passive, and amoral human being. Similarly, the attempt of the officials to influence him is a very human response. The moral equivocation shown by Gogol's characters and their desire to hide their guilt from the inspector general are only slightly different from humanity's attempts to appear innocent before the ultimate Inspector General. Indeed, when the truth is finally learned at the end of the play, the mayor's response is addressed as much to the audience as to the snickering officials: "What are you laughing for? You're laughing at yourselves!"

Comparative: Gogol's comedy belongs to a long line of works which poke fun at hypocrites and at vain, petty bureaucrats and functionaries, most notably the comedies of Molière *(The Physician in Spite of Himself, The School for Wives, Tartuffe,* and *The Bourgeois Gentleman)* and those of Beaumarchais *(The Barber of Seville* and *The Marriage of Figaro).* In England, Gilbert and Sullivan made fun of corrupt officials in their operettas, and, in Russia, Bulgakov did the same in *Master and Margarita.*

Ossip, Khlestakov's wily servant, may be compared to many of Molière's servants and to Beaumarchais's Figaro, and both Ossip and Khlestakov may be found in the hero of Gogol's *Dead Souls,* Chichikov.

Comedy resulting from a case of mistaken identity is found in Plautus' *The Twin Menaechmi,* Shakespeare's *The Comedy of Errors,* Molière's *The Physician in Spite of Himself,* Beaumarchais's *The Barber of Seville,* and Carl Zuckmayer's *The Captain of Köpenick,* which at times almost seems a German version of Gogol's play.

Gogol, Nikolai Vasilievich. THE OVERCOAT (SHINEL'). 1842. Story. Russian.

Author: See *The Inspector General.*

Work: The story originated from an anecdote Gogol heard at a party. A civil servant who had saved to buy a new shotgun lost it on his first hunting trip and almost died of despair until his colleagues took up a collection for a new gun. Gogol transformed this material into the story of a poor government clerk's love for his new overcoat and his death after its theft.

The story of the lowly clerk Akaki Akakievich, his loneliness and poverty, is easy to misread, as Gogol's liberal readers did and as some modern socialist realist critics have done. Such readers regard Akaki's sacrifices to buy his new overcoat and his vain attempts to get a police bureaucrat to pay attention to its theft as the story of a good, simple man in an impersonal and corrupt bureaucratic society. And indeed, there are moments, such as when Akaki pleads with his taunting fellow workers to be left alone, when the heroic view of Akaki seems possible. But Gogol was more interested in moral than in social evil, and from a moral viewpoint Akaki, with his vanity, pettiness, and lack of human affection (the coat becomes a love object for him), seems no better than the other characters. It is as easy to scorn Akaki as it is to sympathize with him. Gogol's intentions are, to some extent, lost in translation because so much of his attitude toward his hero is revealed in the language itself (e.g., Akaki's name is a mildly obscene pun). But a careful reader will still perceive that Akaki's misery is largely his own fault, not that of the system, and that his single-minded devotion to an overcoat does not generate sympathy. Finally, the epilogue which Gogol added to the story, in which the bureaucrat, after hearing rumors that Akaki's ghost is haunting the streets, has his coat ripped from his back, represents poetic, not spiritual, justice.

Comparative: Gogol's work falls midway between the romanticism of the preceding literary age and the realism of the following period. In the works about Ukrainian peasants and their folklore one sees similarities with romantic writers in general and with his countryman Pushkin in particular. The supernatural elements of both the Ukrainian and Petersburg tales show the influence of E. T. A. Hoffmann, whose works are widely read in Russia, and, again, of Pushkin (e.g., "The Queen of Spades").

But "The Overcoat" is not purely a romantic work. In its concern with the poor and downtrodden little man it looks back to the romantic hero, yet the story has more in common with the social concerns of the next generation of writers. As Dostoevski was to exclaim years later, "We have all come out from under Gogol's overcoat." In its method of characterization and depiction of atmosphere, Gogol's story is linked to the short stories of Balzac, Maupassant, Dickens, Turgenev, Dostoevski, Tolstoi, and Chekhov. It is easy to see the modern descendant of Akaki in the little tramp of Charlie Chaplin's films and, with a more existentialist orientation, in K., the hero of Kafka's *The Castle.*

THE GREEK ANTHOLOGY (also, PALATINE ANTHOLOGY). 10th Century A.D. Poetry. Greek.

Work: The Greek Anthology, a collection of over 4,000 short poems in fifteen books, was made in the tenth century by Constantinus Cephalas, a learned Byzantine. The manuscript was discovered in the Palatine Library in

Heidelberg in the seventeenth century. There are poems on gods, mosquitoes, growing up, love, death, and nature; there are inscriptions, lampoons, satiric verse, epitaphs, rhetorical exercises, and much occasional verse. As one might expect, the quality varies, but poems by great poets appear: Aeschylus, Plato, Bacchylides, Simonides, Theocritus, Meleager—some 320 authors in all. Written with works dating from as early as 700 B.C. to as late as 900 A.D., the collection contains a remarkable variety of Christian, pagan, Athenian, and Byzantine authors.

No complete paperback translation is available, but Dudley Fitts has translated over a hundred of these poems in *Poems from the Greek Anthology in English Paraphrase;* Kenneth Rexroth's *Greek Anthology Poems* contains literal and free translations along with some illustrations. Willis Barnstone's *Greek Lyric Poetry* is a "best buy," including many poems from *The Greek Anthology* and some from other sources.

Comparative: A collection as vast as this is by its very nature comparative, in theme, form, and period. And, of course, comparisons can be made with other collections of poetry, for example, with the magnificent collection of 3,000 years of Chinese poetry, *Sunflower Splendor,* edited by Wu-chi Liu and Irving Yucheng Lo.

Grimm, Jacob and Wilhelm. THE FROG KING AND OTHER TALES OF THE BROTHERS GRIMM (KINDER- UND HAUSMÄRCHEN). 1812-1814. Tales. German.

Authors: Jacob Grimm (1785-1863) and Wilhelm Grimm (1786-1859), probably because they were almost the same age and had similar interests, remained unusually close throughout their lives. Their father, who died while they were still children, had intended that they study law, and, following his wishes, they studied at the University of Marburg. There, however, they became involved in two related currents in German thinking of the day: nationalism and romanticism. Eventually the brothers became librarians and university professors in Berlin, occupations that gave them the opportunity to pursue their interests in the German language and in German folklore. Wilhelm married, but Jacob remained a bachelor. Although the brothers collaborated in gathering the tales, Wilhelm put most of them into final literary form. Jacob's research in linguistics led him to formulate a theory known as Grimm's Law, which accounts for variations in certain consonant sounds in Germanic languages.

Work: These tales collected from *Kinder- und Hausmärchen (Children's and Household Tales)* contain most of the well-known favorites: "Hansel and Gretel," "Cinderella," "Little Red Riding Hood," "Tom Thumb," "Snow White." The collection also includes many fascinating lesser-known tales, such as the violent and somewhat frightening "Juniper Tree" and the whimsical "Span of Life." The collection derives its title from the tale, "The Frog King, or Iron Henry," more widely known as "The Frog Prince." The tales in this collection come straight from the oral tradition; that is, the Grimms listened to and took down verbatim the words of peasants known for their ability as storytellers. When different versions of the same story were discovered, the Grimms combined elements or attempted to determine which version was more authentic.

The tales are of many different types—metamorphoses, beast fables, religious tales, ghost tales, "trickster" tales, and rags-to-riches tales. Students will be interested to learn that in the earliest versions of many of the stories, the evil force is a wicked mother, motivated by jealousy, and not a wicked stepmother. The change in later versions was probably made so that the tales would be more palatable to the mothers who told them to their children. Readers can learn a great deal from examining motifs, character types, themes, settings, and the Freudian implications of the tales in this collection. Children's taste in stories is another excellent topic to discuss in relation to this collection.

Comparative: The folktales collected by the brothers Grimm and the fairy tales of Hans Christian Andersen make an obvious comparison. In some instances two versions of the same story may be compared, but an over-all impression of both collections is also rewarding. The Grimm collection may also be compared with *Les Contes de ma mère l'Oye (Mother Goose Tales)* of Charles Perrault (1628-1703). Further comparisons may be made with Aesop's *Fables.* Advanced students with access to library facilities may want to look at the research of Stith Thompson, who in his *Motif Index of Folk Literature* and other works has identified motifs common to the folklores of many nations. Finally, students may be interested in more up-to-date uses of folktales— Disney films, Maurice Maeterlinck's *The Blue Bird,* and Sir James M. Barrie's *Peter Pan,* to name a few.

Hauptmann, Gerhart. FLAGMAN THIEL (BAHNWÄRTER THIEL). 1888.
  Novella. German.

Author: Gerhart Hauptmann (1862-1946) was awarded the Nobel Prize in 1912 "in recognition of his fruitful, varied, and outstanding production in the realm of dramatic arts." In his plays and in his early fiction Hauptmann was a pioneer in the naturalist movement. His works, which generally deal with the working classes, show the sordid as well as the admirable aspects of the lives of common people, emphasizing the forces, economic and psychological that work against them. Hauptmann was born in Silesia, the setting of *The Weavers* and many of his other works. He did not find his vocation easily, ranging from farming to sculpture to history before he began free-lance writing. He achieved his first real success with two stories, "Carnival" and "Flagman Thiel." Fame came with the play *Before Dawn* in 1889. Other notable works are *The Sunken Bell* and *Till Eulenspiegel.*

Work: The beauty of nature, impartial or indifferent to human affairs, is contrasted in this story with the potential destructiveness of human passions and technology, personified by the railroad. Flagman Theil, Herculean in build but gentle and religious, marries Minna, a frail woman who dies in childbirth two years later. Within a year Thiel remarries to provide a mother's care for Toby, his infant son. Lena, his second wife, is a strapping, healthy woman who soon subdues her husband through the passion he feels for her. When she bears him a son, she begins to mistreat Toby. Thiel, aware of what she is doing, fails to act because of the sexual power she holds.

Meanwhile, in his flagman's hut in the Brandenburg Forest, Thiel maintains a virtual shrine in memory of his first wife. He is resolved that Lena will never set foot in the hut or the surrounding area. However, when he loses the land on which Lena has customarily planted the family's potatoes and is offered a strip of land near his hut to replace it, he changes his mind and Lena comes with the two children to garden. She sets Toby to watch over the infant, and the day passes uneventfully until suddenly Thiel hears the shriek of the express applying its brakes. When Thiel learns that Toby is dead, he falls unconscious. He is carried home, and Lena attempts to care for him. Later, the townspeople find her and her infant murdered, and Thiel is apprehended on the railroad track where Toby had been killed, holding the child's little hat. He is forcibly removed and taken to an insane asylum.

Throughout the story, scenes of nature alternate with scenes that show the frightening power of the railroad. Thiel seems almost a pawn, caught between the two, but ultimately destroyed by—and the destroyer of—the woman for whom he had felt such passion.

Comparative: The theme of a man destroyed by passion for a woman is common in literature—the biblical account of Adam and Eve, the later account of Samson and Delilah, and the classical story of Jason and Medea—to name only three. Hauptmann's achievement with "Flagman Thiel," however, transcends extensive comparison with these because of its admixture of natural description with the portrayal of human passions. In the evocative descriptions of nature Hauptmann resembles Joseph Conrad or Thomas Mann *(Death in Venice);* however, he is also a pioneer in the literary movements of realism and naturalism and as such may be generally compared with Maupassant and Zola.

Hauptmann, Gerhart. THE WEAVERS (DIE WEBER). 1892. Drama. German.

Author: See *Flagman Thiel.*

Work: Set in Silesia in the 1840s, this play records the uprising of a group of downtrodden weavers against their oppressors. Kept near starvation by the low wages paid by their rich employers, the weavers are led in their revolt by two young men: Jaeger, the ex-soldier, and Baecker, the red-headed weaver. The rallying call for the weavers is a song, "Bloody Justice," directed against Dreissiger, their employer.

Initially there are sharp words between Dreissiger and Pfeifer (an ex-weaver who is Dreissiger's manager) and the angry weavers. Old and young, male and female, join the revolt, and Pfeifer, Dreissiger, and his wife are forced to flee. Pastor Kittelhaus, who has sympathized with Dreissiger, is beaten by the mob when he tries to tell them it is God's will that they submit. Eventually a group of about fifteen hundred marches into nearby towns, growing larger as it moves, destroying the homes of the wealthy who have preyed upon the weavers. In Bielau an aged weaver, Old Hilse, refuses to join the revolt, though his daughter-in-law and son do. The rioters now are pursued by a company of soldiers. Old Hilse, adhering to traditional ways, takes his place at his loom and weaves, despite the danger of stray bullets. He is mortally wounded and falls across his loom as his granddaughter runs in with the news that the weavers have driven off the soldiers with a barrage of paving stones.

Comparative: In its sympathetic portrayal of the downtrodden proletariat, this play may be compared with Steinbeck's novel, *The Grapes of Wrath,* which deals with dust-bowl Americans dispossessed of their farms; with Giovanni Verga's novel, *The House by the Medlar Tree,* which deals with Sicilian fishermen; or with Mariano Azuela's novel, *The Underdogs,* which deals with Mexican peasants turned revolutionaries. An especially good comparison may be made with Heinrich Heine's short lyric "The Silesian Weavers," which deals with the same revolt.

The Weavers has approximately forty speaking parts, most of them small, and is, therefore, excellent for classroom presentation. It may be compared with another short play, Synge's *Riders to the Sea,* which also deals with working-class life and is highly effective in classroom presentations.

Heine, Heinrich. POETRY AND PROSE OF HEINRICH HEINE. Translated by Uwan and Untermeyer. Citadel Press, 1948. Lyric Poems. German.

Author: Heinrich Heine (1797–1856) was born in Düsseldorf, the son of a Jewish shopkeeper who equated poets with bums. By the time he was twenty-seven, Heine had written *A Journey through the Harz Mountains (Die Harz-reise),* a narrative in brilliant prose interspersed with lilting, clever poetry. The work brought him quick success. His genius seemed to be best suited to lyric poetry and prose with a light, ironic touch, and his barbs might be directed at the state, at society in general, or at himself. While still a student Heine had migraine headaches. In his thirties he began to suffer from creeping paralysis. At forty-eight he was no longer able to walk; one arm was paralyzed; one eye was blind and the other could only stare straight ahead. He lived on for eight years, and in those years wrote some of his best poetry.

Work: Because Heine was a Jew, Hitler ordered his name stricken from the many popular songs to which his poetry had been set and the word "folksong" substituted. His name has, of course, since been restored. Heine's love of Germany is revealed many times, but perhaps best in this short lyric, written after his last visit home:

> I used to have a lovely fatherland
> There oak trees seem
> gigantic; violets nod gently, too.
> It was a dream.
> It spoke in German and in German said
> (you could not know
> how sweet it sounded to me): "I love you"
> I dreamed it, though.

> (translated by Kenneth Oliver)

Heine's longer poems offer a rich variety of poetic narrative and comment. During his last, long eight years of intense suffering Heine wrote this:

> Good fortune is a giddy maid,
> Fickle and restless as a fawn;
> She smooths your hair and then the jade
> Kisses you quickly, and is gone.

> But Madam Sorrow scorns all this;
> She shows no eagerness for flitting,
> But with a long and fervent kiss
> Sits by your bed—and brings her knitting.

> (translated by Louis Untermeyer)

Comparative: Heine's work corresponds in some ways to that of Robert Frost. His language and themes are simple, though their implications are not. Like Frost, his poetry appears to have come easily and naturally, almost spontaneously. Again as in Frost's poetry there are occasional barbs and a gentle but effective irony. Unlike Frost, Heine turned his sharpest irony against himself.

As a romantic, Heine's work may be compared with any of the English or American romantic poets. He is, perhaps, most like Byron, but like other romantics he wrote ballads, nature poetry, poems centering on the inner self, and poetry that commented on society.

Heine's life is as interesting as his poetry and has been the subject of many fine biographies. Biographically, Byron again offers interesting comparisons.

Hesse, Hermann. SIDDHARTHA. 1922. Novel. German.

Author: Hermann Hesse (1877–1962) was born in Calw, in the Black Forest area of Germany. A precocious child and difficult to manage, he was sent away to school and in 1891 won one of the coveted places at Maulbronn School, from which students usually went on to seminary study. Before a year had passed, however, Hesse had undergone an identity crisis and run away. He returned home, but the next few years were tumultuous.

In 1895 Hesse obtained employment in a bookshop in the university town of Tübingen and began to write. In 1899 he moved to Basel in Switzerland, and in 1904 he married. By this time he had published several books and was able to support himself through his writings. As his success increased, he was able to travel, not only in Europe but, in 1911, as far as India, a part of the world in which his parents and maternal grandfather had served as missionaries. His experiences there influenced his writings, most notably *Siddhartha.*

Returning to Switzerland, Hesse settled his family in Bern. The outbreak of World War I caused Hesse, a pacifist, great anguish. In 1916 he suffered a nervous breakdown and underwent psychoanalysis. In 1923 Hesse became a Swiss citizen. He received the Nobel Prize for Literature in 1946, "for his inspired writings which, while growing in boldness and penetration, exemplify the classical humanitarian ideals and high qualities of style."

Hesse's best known works are *Beneath the Wheel* (1906), *Demian* (1917), *Siddhartha* (1922), *Steppenwolf* (1927), *Narcissus and Goldmund* (1930), *Journey to the East* (1932), and *The Glass-Bead Game* (also translated as *Magister Ludi*) (1943).

Work: Like many novels with a quest theme, *Siddhartha* may be read at several levels. On the surface it is the story of the search by Siddhartha, son of a wealthy Brahmin, for meaning in life.

While still a young man, Siddhartha, accompanied by his close friend Govinda, leaves his home to become a Samana, a member of an ascetic order of wandering beggars. After several years of this life Siddhartha, not having found what he is searching for and still accompanied by Govinda, hears Gotama Buddha preach. Govinda becomes a disciple of the Buddha, but Siddhartha, realizing that he must find his own way, leaves. He comes to a large river which he must cross and is impressed by the tranquility of the ferryman, Vasudeva. After spending a night in the ferryman's hut, he continues on his way. Nearing a town, he sees a sedan chair in which sits a beautiful courtesan, Kamala. To win her love, Siddhartha takes service with Kama, a wealthy merchant. Siddhartha too becomes wealthy through business and gambling and enjoys the favors of Kamala.

Years later, Siddhartha once more hears the call and sets out penniless. He comes again to the bank of the river and the hut of the ferryman, but this time he stays, aiding Vasudeva in his work.

Years pass, and Gotama Buddha dies. Kamala, who has become religious, approaches the ferry with the son she had borne Siddhartha, but she is bitten by a snake and dies. Siddhartha attempts to raise his eleven-year-old son, but the boy is unhappy and eventually runs away and returns to the city. Siddhartha follows him but stops at the sight of the familiar grove where he and Kamala had spent much time. Vasudeva finds him and takes him back to the river.

Finally Siddhartha hears the whole song of the river—time is an illusion; past, present, and future are one; all nature is one. Realizing that Siddhartha has attained the object of his search, the aged Vasudeva leaves him and goes off into the forest.

Eventually Govinda wishes to cross the river, and he and Siddhartha meet again. The book ends as Govinda touches Siddhartha's forehead and suddenly realizes that he is in contact with all humanity and that Siddhartha is a great holy man.

At deeper levels, the book may be interpreted as embodying Hesse's philosophical view of the unity of all creation, as presenting various manifestations of Buddha, or as showing that the road to peace and wisdom is found through first-hand knowledge of life and the living.

Comparative: Like most of Hesse's works, *Siddhartha* falls into the category of quest literature and, more specifically, into that type of fiction that borders on the philosophical. A similar search for the meaning of life occurs in Maugham's *The Razor's Edge*, where again the wisdom of the East is important. An important sub-theme, the continuity of generations, is also treated in Turgenev's *Fathers and Sons*. A greater affinity than is generally realized exists between *Siddhartha* and *Huckleberry Finn*. In both a river is instrumental in fostering the protagonist's maturity and self-awareness.

Because of its Indian setting, *Siddhartha* also lends itself to comparison with the work of native Indian authors, such as Tagore, especially his *Gitanjali*, a collection of religious poems embodying Indian philosophy.

Hesse, Hermann. STEPPENWOLF (DER STEPPENWOLF). 1927. Novel. German.

Author: See *Siddhartha.*

Work: Employing an unusual format, far in advance of its day, Hesse tells most—but not all—of the story of Harry Haller, the Steppenwolf of his title. One part of Haller's personality resembles that of a wolf of the steppes, ill-at-ease in society and desirous of self-gratification. Another part resembles that of a bourgeois conformist. As might be expected, the two are often in conflict. But these are only two facets of Haller's personality, as he comes to realize before the end of the book. The means by which he gains a better understanding of himself are usually bizarre, sometimes absurd, and always interesting.

Hesse's novel may be divided into three somewhat irregular parts. The first, an introduction, presents a view of Haller from the standpoint of his landlady's nephew. This objective view shows Haller's life from the outside— he is a middle-aged loner, an unobtrusive lodger who reveals virtually nothing of himself. One day he vanishes, leaving behind nothing but a manuscript, which comprises the rest of the book. This first-person account of Haller's life is entirely subjective. Through it we learn how he gradually became aware of the warring elements in his personality and how he learned to overcome his suicidal tendencies. His reformation began as he wandered the streets one night and encountered the Magic Theater, over the entrance of which an illuminated sign read, "Entrance not for everybody" and "For Madmen Only." A man gives Haller a booklet titled "Treatise on the Steppenwolf. Not for Everybody." This treatise constitutes the third part of the book, though it is contained within the second, and casts further light on the character of Harry Haller.

Later, Harry is helped toward self-understanding by Hermine, a prostitute, who also represents one part of his personality; by Maria, another prostitute who becomes his lover; and by Pablo, a jazz saxophone player. Harry learns to dance, to enjoy sensual pleasures, and almost—but not quite—to develop a sense of humor. Near the end of the book Harry attends a masked ball, at the end of which he enters the visionary world of the Magic Theater. His bizarre experiences there are climaxed by the stabbing of Hermine, and followed by his prosecution, condemnation, and "execution"—he is condemned to eternal life and laughed out of the court by the Immortals. With Harry's realization that some day he will learn how to laugh, the book ends.

Comparative: This complex book lends itself to comparisons with many works. There is much about it that is Faustian, though Harry Haller's search is for self-knowledge. In its use of the absurd it resembles Kafka's *The Trial.* With regard to style and theme it may also be compared with its predecessor, *Siddhartha.* Similarly, it may be discussed in relation to Hesse's *Narcissus and Goldmund,* which represents a further step in the author's artistic maturity.

Like most of Hesse's works, *Steppenwolf* falls into the broad category of quest literature; in this case the quest is for a meaning in life derived through self-knowledge, and thus the work is existential and may be compared with such works as Camus's *The Stranger.* Indeed, in some ways Haller seems to be a middle-aged Meursault.

Certainly a major theme of *Steppenwolf* is alienation, and the exploration of this theme leads us to other works by Camus, to Kafka, and to Dostoevski's *Notes from Underground.*

Homer. ILIAD. ca. 850 B.C. Epic Poem. Greek.

Author: Even Homer's personal existence has been a subject of scholarly dispute, for little is known about him, though seven cities (among them Smyrna and Chios with the best arguments) claimed him as a native son. Evidence suggests that he lived in Ionia (western Turkey) in the eighth century B.C. Homer was universally revered even in classical times as the author of the *Iliad* and the *Odyssey.*

Work: Both the *Iliad* and the *Odyssey* are oral epics meant to be recited and based on a long tradition of recitation. The form itself is characterized by elaborate similes, epithets, and recurrent passages; digressions from the plot relate the individual histories of gods and men. There are long speeches and catalogues. The style is leisurely, the author objective. These two epics are the finest of a cycle of works now lost that dealt with portions of the Trojan War. Greeks and Romans alike studied and memorized the epics of Homer, not only for stories of heroism, but for knowledge of the gods, of military strategy, and of rhetoric. Above all, Homer is valued for the majesty of his language and for the depth of his psychological insight.

The 15,693 lines of the *Iliad* cover forty-seven days during the tenth year of the Trojan War. Agamemnon, King of Mycenae, commands 100,000 men bent on retrieving Helen, wife of his brother Menelaus, who has run off with Paris to Troy. The true subject of the *Iliad,* however, is the wrath of Achilles, the greatest Greek warrior, and its consequences. Years before, Achilles had been offered one of two fates: to live a long and peaceful life without glory, or to die young and much renowned. During the *Iliad,* he recognizes the true meaning of choosing the latter.

As the poem begins, a plague has ravaged the Greek troops. Calchas, a soothsayer, reveals that Agamemnon has offended Apollo by capturing and refusing to return Chrȳsēis, a priest's daughter. Agamemnon refuses to return her unless he is awarded another war captive of equal worth. This response leads Achilles to accuse him of putting personal pride above the army's welfare. Agamemnon then seizes Briseis, the captive of Achilles, and the great warrior, publicly humiliated, renounces fighting on the grounds that Briseis matters to him as much as Helen to Agamemnon and Menelaus. Further, Achilles prays to his mother, Thetis (a sea divinity), that Zeus and the other Olympians will show the Greeks how indispensable Achilles is to their campaign. His prayer is granted. Though the other warriors fight valiantly, they are continually beaten back by the Trojans. Patroclus, Achilles' closest friend (and the embodiment of the humane side of Achilles) pities the suffering warriors and finally dons Achilles' armor and joins the fighting. Routing the Trojans, Patroclus is killed by Hector, and Achilles turns his wrath upon that Trojan leader. In violent fighting Achilles kills Hector, who prophesies his imminent doom. Patroclus and then Hector are given elaborate funerals,

Achilles having agreed to return Hector's body to his father, Priam, the Trojan king who comes in the night to Achilles' tent. In that encounter the two enemies recognize their common mortality as fathers and sons and admire each other's beauty and bravery. The humanity of Achilles is fully restored as his absolute will is balanced once again with a sense of common humanity.

While the gods loom large in the epic, it is important to note that they differ from ordinary mortals only in their immortality and power; clearly they are less noble and moral than the mortal heroes. Further, mortals are not their pawns.

The tale of the wrath of Achilles is told against the background of the Trojan War, but earlier episodes of the war are recounted as well as foreshadowings of the future. Homer humanizes the colossal scale of the long war by limiting the tale to graspable length and by using individual scenes which epitomize the effects of war on both sides: e.g., Hector's farewell to his wife and son (Bk. 6), Helen's overview of the troops (Bk. 3), and Thersites' insolence (Bk. 11). His use of similes reduces the heroic and gigantic to homely and conceivable scale.

Comparative: The influence of Homer is incalculable. To sixth-century Athenians, his epics were already ancient classics, annually recited at public festivals. Greek lyric poets and tragedians openly acknowledged their indebtedness to him for plots and characters. Rome's first literature was a translation of the *Odyssey,* and Roman writers borrowed story lines from his epic, as have many writers since. Virgil's *Aeneid,* a literary epic, derived both its inspiration and certain technical devices directly from Homer, though of course Virgil created something grand and original as well.

Beowulf and the *Song of Roland* are heroic epics like those of Homer, whereas Milton's *Paradise Lost* and Tasso's *Jerusalem Delivered* descend from Virgil's literary epic. Byron, Pope, and Tennyson are but three British poets to work directly with Homeric material. In our time, Tolstoi, Mann, Proust, and Durrell have written epic works, though Tolkien's *Lord of the Rings* is currently the most popular.

Homer. ODYSSEY. ca. 850 B.C. Epic poem. Greek.

Author: See the *Iliad.*

Work: The action of the poem occupies forty-one days in the tenth year after the fall of Troy. Odysseus is marooned on the isle of the nymph Calypso while his faithful wife Penelope is besieged with a horde of insolent and carousing suitors. As the poem opens, Athene reminds Zeus of the predicament of Odysseus, and the gods (except Poseidon) agree to set in motion his return. Calypso is told to release Odysseus; Athene suggests to Telemachus,

Odysseus' son, that he seek out news of his father and take steps to get rid of the suitors who are wasting his father's property. Telemachus learns from Menelaus and Helen in Sparta that Odysseus is alive but stranded on Calypso's island. Meanwhile the suitors set an ambush for Telemachus, who escapes. Odysseus, rejecting Calypso's offer of immortality, sets out in a raft and arrives at Phaeacia, where the princess Nausicaa takes him home. He is feasted by the generous sea-faring islanders. Eventually he reveals his identity and recounts his famous adventures—among these are his adventures with the Lotus-eaters, the Cyclops, and Circe; his visit to Hades where he encounters his mother and Agamemnon, Achilles, and Aia; and his meetings with the Sirens and with Scylla and Charybdis, the Oxen of the Sun (Bks. 9-12).

Transported back to Ithaca by the Phaeacians, Odysseus proceeds cautiously, disguised as a beggar, to test the loyalty of his subjects and his family. (Odysseus recalls how Agamemnon was slaughtered at his homecoming.) Eumaeus, his swineherd, is especially helpful, though only his dog and his old nurse actually recognize him. Odysseus and Telemachus slaughter the reckless suitors, who have disregarded warnings and continued their disregard for the gods, for property, and for the sacred rights of hospitality. Penelope and Odysseus are reunited after an elaborate testing and recognition scene. The next day Odysseus meets his father, and three generations make peace with the islanders.

Like Achilles, Odysseus was confronted by two choices; in his case, between immortality and his return to human life. Choosing the latter, Odysseus demonstrates a personality more various than any other Homeric character and vastly different from that of the warriors of the *Iliad*. His skill in oratory, his persuasiveness, his guile, craft and cunning are much admired by the gods, especially Athene. Mortals admire his physical prowess and beauty. While mortal folly is a central theme of the *Odyssey*, Odysseus always stops short of defying the gods. The magical and exotic settings contrast vividly with the domestic focus of the scenes in Ithaca.

Comparative: See the *Iliad*.

Horace (Quintus Horatius Flaccus). ODES. 30-23 B.C. Poetry. Roman.

Author: Though his father belonged to the freedman class, Horace (65-8 B.C.) was given the best education then available in the world—first in Rome, then in Athens. After the defeat of the republican army at Philippi (ca. 42 B.C.), he found himself landless and poverty stricken, obliged to get a clerkship in the Roman equivalent of the civil service. He began writing, and his lyrics soon attracted the attention of Virgil, who brought the young poet to the attention of the influential Maecenas, Augustus' political advisor and Virgil's patron. Maecenas later became Horace's friend and patron, giving him in 33 B.C. a small estate in the Sabine hills, where he lived the rest of his life.

In 35 B.C. Horace published his first collection of *Satires,* dedicated to Maecenas. His second appeared in 30 or 29 B.C. and his *Epodes* (iambic verses) at almost the same time. Between 30 and 23 B.C. he published three books of odes, also dedicated to Maecenas. After some further satires and epistles, he published a fourth book of odes (ca. 13 B.C.) celebrating the secular games of 17 B.C. and the victories of Augustus' stepsons. The famous "Art of Poetry" is probably the third epistle of a second book of letters in verse, written not earlier than 12 B.C. Horace died in November of 8 B.C. and was buried near his recently deceased friend Maecenas.

Work: Horace's four books of *Odes* (or *Carmina,* their ancient title) were the first large-scale, serious effort at Latin lyrics. He chose for his model the Aiolian poets, Sappho and Alkaios and adopted their Greek meters to his own Latin usage. These are monodies—poems meant to be sung or recited by a single voice—rather than choral odes like Pindar's. The subject of these 103 odes range from drinking songs to commentaries on wise and virtuous conduct (frugality, bravery, patriotism, piety). Book I,4 is a little spring song reflecting on the brevity of life; I,8 is an erotic poem; I,9 concerns a wintry scene. II,15 laments the corrupting effects of luxury. Though his subjects, moods, and meters vary, it is for the perfection of his verse and the depth of his feeling that Horace continues to be admired.

Comparative: In English poetry, compare Horace's *Odes* with Andrew Marvell's "Upon Cromwell's Return from Ireland" (1681). Pope's "Ode on Solitude" (ca. 1700) is based on Horace's *Epode II.* Compare the work with Pindars' *Odes,* or William Collins's "Ode to Evening" (1746). These use the Horatian four-line stanza as well as the tone and certain themes found in Horace. Keats's odes are in a direct line of descent from Horace in their use of a solitary speaker, vivid detail, and high ideals.

   Contemporary taste does not run either to the calm, elegant style of Horace or to the moderation of his philosophy. His influence was strong from the fifteenth century onward in Italy, Spain, and France, Ronsard being the best known of the French imitators. Horace remains the source of more eloquent phrases in European literature than any other classical author.

Hugo, Victor. LES MISÉRABLES. 1862. Novel. French.

Author: Hugo (1802–1885) wrote almost as voluminously as Dumas, but better. His best-known works include the dramas *Cromwell, Hernani,* and *Ruy Blas,* poetry collected in *Rays and Shadows,* and this novel and *Notre Dame de Paris (The Hunchback of Notre Dame).* As a humanitarian, Hugo ranks with Tolstoi; as a lyric poet he is perhaps France's best. He passed many years in exile because of his political views and completed *Les Misérables* abroad.

Work: Jean Valjean is released after nineteen years in the galleys for stealing a loaf of bread. After his escape, he rehabilitates himself and begins a life of service to humanity; however, he is pursued by a relentless detective, Javert, who has a compulsion to capture Jean, just as Jean has a melodramatic urge to confess his true identity even when he is a successful businessman. The chase leads all over Paris (which complicates the hero's attempt to rear Cosette, an orphan he has taken under his protection), through a battle at a revolutionary street blockade, and finally through a harrowing episode as Jean carries the wounded Marius, suitor to Cosette, through the sewers of Paris. Pathetically, the story ends neatly wrapped up with the change of heart and suicide of Javert, the marriage of Cosette and Marius, and the revelation to all of Jean's true nobility of soul despite his criminal past.

A melodramatic novel of pursuit and escape in nineteenth-century Paris, *Les Misérables* makes a sentimental plea for the poor and oppressed. Interestingly enough, it was the favorite novel of many American Civil War soldiers. Critics such as Pater and Meredith have considered it one of the world's great literary achievements. Hugo's prose often reads like an outline as he attempts to keep in motion nearly a dozen life stories. The characters, though they wear their emotions like labels, are vividly drawn.

Comparative: For other studies of the poor and oppressed, see Dicken's *Oliver Twist* and Dostoevski's *Crime and Punishment*. For a novel with a similar background and a similar character (Doctor Manette), see *A Tale of Two Cities*. For another figure of heroic fatherhood, see Balzac's *Le Père Goriot*.

Ibsen, Henrik. THE WILD DUCK (VILDANDEN). 1884. Drama. Norwegian.

Author: Ibsen (1828-1906), a father of modern drama, was born at Skien, Norway, into an impoverished family which was to sink into bankruptcy. At sixteen he became a druggist's apprentice in Grimstad and helped to edit a weekly journal there. From 1851 to 1857 he was stage director of Ole Bull's theater in Bergen, for which he wrote a play each year. Later, he became director of the Norwegian Theater at Christiana (now Oslo). He left Norway in 1864 to become a voluntary exile in Italy, Germany, and Austria for twenty-seven years, during which time he wrote his greatest plays. He returned to Christiana when he was sixty-three. His major plays reveal the psychological aspects of personality and emphasize the necessity for individual fulfillment. Additional major plays include *A Doll's House* (1879), *Ghosts* (1881), *An Enemy of the People* (1882), *Hedda Gabler* (1890), and *The Master Builder* (1892).

Work: Behind Hjalmar Ekdal's photography studio is an improvised garret forest made up of discarded Christmas trees and inhabited by pigeons and rabbits, and most remarkably, by a wild duck. Here Hjalmar's elderly father, obviously beaten by the disgracc heaped upon him through the unscrupulous manipulations of his former business partner, Werle, dresses in his officer's uniform and now and then goes hunting, as he had for bigger game in days gone by. Hjalmar's daughter, Hedwig, who does not realize that she is rapidly losing her sight, and his wife and mainstay, Gina, are the other members of the immediate household.

Werle, who is also going blind, has recently prevailed on his estranged son, Gregers, to come home for a visit. But Gregers, retaliating against his father's manipulations, breaks off his visit and finds lodging in a vacant apartment in Hjalmar's house—much against the wishes of Gina. Gregers disastrously introduces the truth into the Ekdal family illusions: Gina had been his father's mistress. Hjalmar, unquestionably a weakling and dreamer, threatens to leave Gina (and Hedwig), but he returns like a runaway little boy on next to no pretext at all.

Hedwig, at the urging of Gregers, seems to agree to kill the wild duck, thus symbolically freeing the family from the specious happiness under which they had been living. Instead, once in the garret, she kills herself. But what ought to have had tragic proportions becomes material for yet another illusion to Hjalmar.

The sobering argument of Relling, a doctor who occupies lodgings in Hjalmar's house, that people must not be robbed of their illusions, stands in sharp contrast to Gregers's theory that truth frees the individual.

Comparative: Tennessee Williams's *The Glass Menagerie* and Arthur Miller's *Death of a Salesman* also show a world of illusion shattered. Eugene O'Neill's *The Iceman Cometh* illustrates the inability of persons to cast off illusion. Ibsen's own *An Enemy of the People* develops a similar theme, focusing again on the damage that a truthsayer such as Gregers can do. Mrs. Candour in Sheridan's *The School for Scandal* and Alceste in Molière's *The Misanthrope* are other examples of people who tell the truth at all costs. Pangloss in Voltaire's *Candide,* like Gregers, cherishes the fiction of an ideal, even when its terrible effects are demonstrated. Old Ekdal's happy life of illusion can be compared to that of Don Quixote. And James Thurber's *The Secret Life of Walter Mitty* clearly contrasts fantasy and reality.

But another comparative study might also be considered. Ibsen, in *Ghosts,* presents a directly opposing view—that the concealment of truth, the refusal to face up to facts, is destructive of happiness, even of life. An analysis of *Ghosts* and *The Wild Duck* makes an exceptionally interesting study.

Ibsen, Henrik. AN ENEMY OF THE PEOPLE (EN FOLKEFIENDE). 1882.
   Drama. Norwegian.

Author: See *The Wild Duck.*

Work: Dr. Stockmann is the hero of his small town, for he originated the idea of the spa that is bringing financial prosperity to the community. As a devoted scientist, however, he finds that the local tanneries have made the medicinal waters unhealthful, and he intends to publish his findings. He is surprised to learn that Hovstad and Aslaksen, newspapermen, are against the publication of these facts because the publicity will compromise the public interest. Even Peter Stockmann, his brother and the mayor of the town, turns against him. The doctor loses his appointment as medical director of the baths; his daughter is dismissed from her teaching assignment; his sons are sent home from school; neighbors mob his house and stone the windows. Still ignorant of the wisdom of tempering righteous wrath with caution, Dr. Stockmann makes a John Paul Jones speech about having just begun to fight and states the only lesson he has learned: "The strongest man in the world is he who stands most alone."

Comparative: Comparisons might be made between Stockmann and the young doctor in Sinclair Lewis's *Arrowsmith,* who also meets popular hatred. The corrupt citizens of Ibsen's small town find peers in Pérez Galdós's *Doña Perfecta* and Sartre's *The Flies.* The broad theme of social hypocrisy is so common in literature that we mention only a few examples: Dostoevski's "The Legend of the Grand Inquisitor," Swift's "A Modest Proposal," and Anatole France's *Crainquebille.*

Ionesco, Eugène. THE BALD SOPRANO (LA CANTATRICE CHAUVE). 1948. Drama. French.

Author: Ionesco was born in 1912 of a Rumanian father and a French mother. He was educated in France, returned to Rumania for a period, and then settled in France. He worked for a time as a proofreader in a Paris publishing house before devoting his full time to writing. His sometimes irritating but compelling dramas have had continuing theatrical success. Ionesco relies less than most playwrights on words, choosing instead to communicate through powerful visual images. In his own words: "I have, for example, tried to exteriorize the anxiety . . . of my characters through objects; to make the stage settings speak; to translate the action into visual terms. . . . I have thus tried to extend the language of the theater."

Work: Mr. and Mrs. Smith sit in an English middle class interior, discuss their English middle class dinner, and read from their English middle class newspaper. They tell pointless anecdotes and never quite complete the meaning of anything they say to one another. As their conversation dwindles to zero, in come Mr. and Mrs. Martin, who add new, absurd, and incomplete topics to those of Mr. and Mrs. Smith. (Ionesco is precisely indicating average thought processes and everyday conversation.) The Fire Chief comes to call and amuses the company with a series of preposterous fables. The maid recites a nonsense poem. As this dismal bourgeois evening progresses, it is punctuated by the striking of an erratic clock. (What difference does time make in an Ionesco play, what difference to lives like these?) The Fire Chief concludes his visit. The four friends begin talking nonsense syllables. The lights go off. The gabble of voices ceases. The lights come on again. Mr. and Mrs. Martin now sit in the postures the Smiths had assumed at the beginning of the play. They begin speaking the Smiths' opening lines.

Ionesco calls this play an "anti-play." It is entirely undramatic; there is no situation, no conflict. Two conventional couples, bored and boring, sit in a nondescript living room and discuss nothing.

Comparative: Ionesco's themes are everywhere in contemporary writing but may also be traced back: (1) the isolation of the individual is found, for example, in Conrad; (2) the breakdown in the meaning of words, so that in an increasingly complex society we no longer know what another person is trying to say, is a comic device used from Molière (*Le Bourgeois gentilhomme*, for example) to the present; (3) absurd bourgeois pretentiousness—and mediocrity—is a theme of modern literature after Balzac; see also Flaubert's *Madame Bovary* (especially Homais the pharmacist); (4) the nightmare within the externally reasonable situation was exploited by E. T. A. Hoffmann, Kleist, and Kafka and is used increasingly by writers today. Also compare Ionesco's work to those of Brecht; and note that indirect, inconclusive conversation in theater—a new realism—stems from Chekhov's plays.

Ionesco, Eugène. THE LESSON (LA LEÇON). 1951. Drama. French.

Author: See *The Bald Soprano.*

Work: With tongue in cheek Ionesco subtitles this one-act "A Comic Drama." The play emphasizes the lack of communication in modern life and its inherently destructive tendencies.

An eighteen-year-old girl comes to a famous professor, aged fifty or sixty, for tutoring for her degree. The session begins amiably as the girl demonstrates her ability to add two and two, and two and three. The maid comes in to warn the professor of the dangers of beginning with mathematics as "tiring, exhausting." The professor continues the lesson.

Throughout the session, the interchange of question and answer becomes increasingly intense, more inaccurate, more frustrating. Unable through mathematics (the ultimate ideal) to establish communication, the professor launches into linguistics. The desperation and inadequacy of the dialogue increases. As fears and tension mount, the young student develops a protective, psychosomatic toothache, and the old professor releases a flood of language, which fails to convince himself or his student. To demonstrate finally some of the complexities of language, he grabs an imaginary knife (a remarkably primitive symbol) and stabs the girl. She dies. The unimaginative maid helps him to dispose of the body, again warning of the excitements of mathematics as another young pupil rings the doorbell. The maid goes to answer the door, and Ionesco's cyclical plan (a symbol of futility) is recognizable as the play ends where it begins.

To imagine the play as stage-effective, readers must increase the tempo of their reading in the last few pages of the play, so that the words speed past as they do in the oral production.

The Lesson may be taken as an attack against new symbols (a belief in the potency of exact sciences) and a plea for a return to the old, easy, conventional symbols of human speech, of clichés, which, no matter how hackneyed, at least allowed one person to speak with some agreement to another. The play portrays the terror of a total lack of human communication and the only possible results—murder and death.

Comparative: See the entry for Ionesco's *The Bald Soprano* and the suggestions for comparison there. The striking force of this play with its few characters is reminiscent of Strindberg's *The Stronger* and Cocteau's *The Human Voice*, while the antagonisms seem as great as those in Strindberg's *The Father*. For the theme of the lesson itself, see Pablo's unreal and dreamlike instruction of Haller in Hesse's *Steppenwolf.*

Ionesco, Eugène. RHINOCÉROS. 1958. Drama. French.

Author: See *The Bald Soprano.*

Work: A dry little inland French town, with no marsh in miles, is suddenly invaded by an epidemic in which the gossipy, quarrelsome inhabitants are, one by one, turned into rhinoceroses. As they metamorphose, they become "natural" and likable, qualities they never had as human beings. One man holds out against this destruction of the human race, however. Bérenger, the town drunk, was always a nonconformist and in this instance he shows his determination to remain one. He sees all his friends—Jean the ultraconformist, Dudard the conservative, Boeuf (naturally, with his name, one of the first to change) the big businessman, and even his dear Daisy—disappear into the amiable herd of the behemoths. The play ends with a triumphant shout: "You won't get me! I'm not joining you; I don't understand you! I'm staying as I am. I'm a human being,"—and with a whimper: "I've only myself to blame; I should have gone with them while there was still time. Now it's too late!"

Comparative: This play is a humorous counterpart of Kafka's *Metamorphosis.* Another modern look at the perils of nonconformity is found in Camus's *The Stranger.* The theme of the involuted and contemptible little town may be found in Pérez Galdós's *Doña Perfecta* and in Sartre's *The Flies,* and the specific theme of the supernatural infecting such a small town appears in Giraudoux's *The Enchanted.*

The question of whether brute nature is to be preferred to human civilization is frequently asked in modern literature but goes back at least to Voltaire's comment to Rousseau: "Your book makes me want to walk on all fours."

Expressionist theater generally seeks its effects through the use of stage facilities, here in the gradual change of Jean into a rhinoceros (Act II), made possible by modern lighting and sound effects. *The Emperor Jones* of Eugene O'Neill, with its use of lighting and increasing drum tempos, is another good play to use in the study of these techniques; and this study may well be carried on into Miller's *Death of a Salesman* with its lap-dissolves that show movements into past time.

Juvenal (Decimus Junius Juvenalis). SATIRES. ca. 125 A.D. Poetry. Roman.

Author: Scant information exists about Juvenal's life (ca. 60–140 A.D.), and this is derived from a brief and untrustworthy biography of late antiquity. Born southeast of Rome during the reign of Nero, Juvenal seems to have had an excellent education. His poverty is clear, as is his frustration about it. Apparently he did not leave Rome for the better life available in the country, as he recommends in Satire iii. He may have turned to declamation in his adult years, and he may have been exiled to Egypt for a time by one of the emperors under whose reign he lived (Domitian and Otho being among the worst.) He seems to have taken up writing in his maturity rather than in his youth.

Works: Juvenal published over a hundred separate satires in five volumes over a period of about twenty years preceding 128 A.D. Of these, only sixteen survive, all in dactylic hexameter. Juvenal was a master of rhetorical composition, and his eloquence is as striking as his merciless tone. The structure of the satires is loose, though patterned by the enumeration and description inherent in the genre. On the one hand, Juvenal is well acquainted with Rome and its corruption; on the other, he lacks neither humor nor tenderness. Violent prejudices (against women, against foreigners) exist in his satires alongside outrage at human vice (greed, snobbery, fanaticism) and deepest pessimism about Rome's capacity for reform. Indeed, his lack of proportion is one of his vivid qualities: mere folly and affectation are treated with as much vituperation as outright crime and vice. His range of topics, even among the surviving satires, is remarkable: Satire i gives his reasons for writing satire; ii and v attack aristocratic vices; iv burlesques the emperor's Privy Council. Book II is a long satire against women; Book V,xiv deals with parental duty.

Comparative: Juvenal's influence is so pervasive that much of our understanding of the genre "satire" is derived from his poems. No discussion of satire can avoid him; no writer of satire can ignore him. Juvenalian satire is opposed in its extremity, moral indignation, and pessimism to Horace's more urbane and tolerant satire. In tone and sweep of vision he is comparable to Swift. Samuel Johnson's *The Vanity of Human Wishes* (1749) is a famous imitation of Juvenal's Satire x. Even standard terms like "bread and circuses" come from Juvenal.

Kafka, Franz. METAMORPHOSIS (DIE VERWANDLUNG). 1915. Novella. German.

Author: Franz Kafka (1883-1924) was born into a German-speaking Jewish family in Prague. Educated in law, Kafka accepted a minor government post because of his ill health and held it until he entered a sanitarium. Always delicate and sensitive, he was prevented by indecision from marrying and never became confident about his work (much of which he destroyed). He died of tuberculosis near Vienna. Kafka's works customarily show a human being confronted by a vast, usually bureaucratic force against which his struggles are powerless. The grotesque backgrounds which he created have left their mark. His other major works include *The Trial* (1925), *The Castle* (1926), and *Amerika* (1927), all published posthumously through the efforts of his literary executor, Max Brod.

Work: Gregor Samsa is a commercial salesman and the sole support of his bankrupt father, a self-pitying semi-invalid, of his weak mother, and of his artistic and refined sister. One morning Gregor awakens to find himself flat on his hard-shelled back, waving insect legs in the air—metamorphosed. Still able to speak in a near-human voice and to move and think in a semi-human fashion, he tries to approach his parents and sister in despair and grief but meets misunderstanding, disgust, and hatred. It is as if his metamorphosis had disclosed what his family actually thought of him behind the veil of convention. Gradually Gregor deteriorates, losing his human faculties and acquiring increasingly those of the insect, yet still pitiably conscious of his plight, still attempting to communicate, still trying to show tact and consideration. Locked in his room and fed the garbage he craves, he crawls on the ceiling, cherishes a few human mementos, and resigns himself. When he inadvertently enters the family living room, his enraged father throws apples at him; one of them penetrates the hard shell of his back, hangs and rots there, and brings on his slow death. One day the chambermaid pokes him with her broom, finds

Gregor dead, and disposes of him in the dustbin. The family, greatly relieved of the embarrassing situation, goes out for a celebrative excursion in the country. While one automatically thinks of the metamorphosis as taking place in Gregor, the changes in the members of his family are equally important.

Comparative: Ionesco in his play *Rhinoceros* shows an entire community undergoing a transformation in which, as in Kafka's story, a lower order emerges to be compared with the supposedly preferable human level. Other works of modern literature that point out the weaknesses of humans through animal characters are George Orwell's *Animal Farm,* Karel Čapek's *War with the Newts,* and Mikhail Bulgakov's *The Heart of a Dog.* Some older works also use the device of transformation. Ovid's *Metamorphoses* plays on such changes but without the grimness and realism of Kafka's treatment. Apuleius' picaresque novel *The Golden Ass* (ca. 160 A.D.) jovially recounts the misadventures of a man who is turned into a donkey with all of his mental faculties intact, but he does not suffer insectival deterioration that gives Kafka's tale its shuddering poignancy. For further treatment by Kafka of the theme of extreme human alienation, see his short story "The Hunger Artist" and his novel *The Trial.*

Kafka, Franz. THE TRIAL (DER PROZESS). 1925. Novel. German.

Author: See *Metamorphosis.*

Work: "Someone must have traduced Joseph K., for without having done anything wrong he was arrested one fine morning." These opening words introduce the nightmare world of Joseph K. Accused of an unnamed crime, confronted by what is literally a bureaucracy of bureaucracies in the law courts, he seeks vainly for justice or some logical explanation of what is happening to him.

This novel is told from the third-person limited viewpoint of Joseph K., as indeed it must be, since only he gives continuity to its free-floating episodes.

Joseph K., a respectable banker nearing middle age, awakens one morning to find strangers in his apartment; he is told that he is under arrest. What his crime is he never learns (for Joseph thinks through Kafka's baffling style— a style that symbolizes in its intelligent wandering in its exploration of all avenues leading from each idea, the lack of human communication). Once he is charged with the crime, he tries to begin a defense, but the courtroom is run as a parody of the law and operates by rules that seem to bear no relationship to Joseph's case. The scene is nightmarish, but beneath the extravagance there peeps out now and then something like a salient truth.

From this point, Joseph's entire attention is monopolized by his "case." His duties at the bank become unbearable. Two minor love affairs, as strange and inconclusive as his relationships with the court, provide momentary distractions. His life becomes a series of inexplicable night calls on court officials and attorneys and shabby back-street rendezvous with the official court painter and the official court bailiffs. The crime with which he is charged appears monstrously clear, but only now and then. Is he charged with being a human being? Does he bear all humanity's guilt? Though Kafka did not complete the novel, he wrote a conclusion in which Joseph is escorted from his quarters by two top-hatted officials, taken to the edge of a quarry, and there formally executed—still amazed at his predicament, still gentle, still full of bewildered acceptance of the ways things have turned out.

Comparative: The Trial can best be compared with other works by Kafka. It seems to fall midway among his three novels—all incomplete at his death. Students should be directed first to *Amerika* and then to *The Castle* for further examination of Kafka's themes and techniques.

Because Kafka was a pioneer in the literature of the absurd, echoes of his style are found in the modern theater of the absurd, in the works of such playwrights as Beckett, Pinter, and Stoppard. Comparisons may also be made with many modern novelists who use the techniques of the absurd to comment upon man's condition. Joseph K.'s search for justice in an indifferent, bureaucratic world can be compared with that of the hero in Ken Kesey's *One Flew Over the Cuckoo's Nest,* in Joseph Heller's *Catch-22,* and in Kurt Vonnegut's *Slaughterhouse Five.* Finally, the sense of alienation in *The Trial* is in the vanguard of modern existentialist literature—certainly, Joseph K.'s alienation lends itself to comparison with that of Meursault in Camus's *The Stranger.*

Kang, Younghill. THE GRASS ROOF. Published in English in 1931. Autobiography. Korean.

Author: Younghill Kang (1903-1972) was born in Korea where he spent his early childhood and adolescence. He came to New York when he was eighteen and lived much of his life in America. He worked for the *Encyclopaedia Britannica* and the Metropolitan Museum of Art and taught literature at New York University. A writer and a poet, his last achievement was the translation of the Korean Buddhist poet Han Yon-gun. Kang's outlook was that of a citizen of the world.

Work: In Korean and Japanese fiction, the demarcation between autobiography and fiction is not clear. The "I" novel, as it is called in Japan, may be only thinly disguised autobiography. Thus this work, though Korean, may be as much novel as autobiography. The story is of the childhood and youth of a boy growing up at the beginning of this century when Korea was going through a turbulent period. In the words of Younghill Kang, "the people had been happy in the same customs, dwellings, foods, and manners for over a thousand years. Life in such country districts as mine was a long unbroken dream, lasting thousands of years, in which the same experiences, the same thoughts, the same life came unceasingly like the constantly reappearing flowers of spring, whose forms and attributes were the same, although the individuals were changing." But during these years the unbroken dream was shattered and, according to Isabella Bishop, an American traveler in Korea, there was in that country "an array of powerful, ambitious, aggressive, and not always over-scrupulous powers bent it may be on overreaching her and each other, forcing her into new paths, ringing with rude hands the knell of time-honored custom, clamoring for concession, and humiliating her with reforms, suggestions, and panaceas of which she [saw] neither the meaning nor the necessity."

Against this background Kang writes of his personal conflict with and gradual gravitation towards science and technology. He returns for a time to the security of Buddhism, exchanging his Western shoes for the comfortable elastic grass shoes of Korea. But in the end, he finds no comfort in the past and is compelled to recognize that the childhood utopia is over. As his friend tells him, the disease of civilization is upon Korea; there is no turning to the wisdom of Confucius or the non-attachment of Buddhism. Kang was not destroyed; he remained a humanist, but the traditional culture of Korea was at an end, as was childhood.

Thomas Wolfe, author of *You Can't Go Home Again,* reviewed the work when it first appeared in America. He wrote of Kang: "He has made a record of man's wandering and exile upon the earth, and into it he has wrought his vision of joy and pain, and hunger, and in this is the first and most lasting importance of his book."

Comparative: See the note under Richard E. Kim's *Lost Names* for other works set under conditions of colonialism or occupation. For another author who writes vividly about nature and the family, consider Colette, especially *Break of Day.* Although by different authors, Kang's *The Grass Roof,* Li's *The Yalu Flows,* and Kim's *Lost Names* form a trilogy on the theme of tradition and change.

Kartini, Raden Adjeng. LETTERS OF A JAVANESE PRINCESS. Originally published in Dutch in 1911; Indonesian translation published in 1922. Letters. Indonesian.

Author: Kartini (1879-1904) was the daughter of a high Javanese civil servant in the Dutch colonial government. She was granted the unusual privilege of attending a colonial elementary school until she was twelve. For the following four years her education continued in seclusion, at home, following Javanese tradition. Fluent in Dutch, she carried on a correspondence—a very literary one—with Dutch friends. Through her work she became a spokesman for Indonesian nationalist aspirations and for feminism. She is a national heroine, and Kartini Day is celebrated in May by Indonesians all over the world. A reading of her letters was given by the American actress Julie Harris in a program arranged and produced by the Asian Literature Program at Asia House in 1967.

Work: Through these letters echoes the *cri de coeur* of a young girl who suffered intensely under a traditional culture which placed heavy restrictions on her because of her status and sex. Hildred Geertz has written of this work: "In Kartini's case, the adolescent fumbling for a style of life which could simultaneously satisfy all of her competing desires and ideals was paralleled by a series of social changes in Java which just as urgently needed new formulations of societal purpose and style. Kartini's individual crisis of identity responded to a crisis in Javanese cultural identity, and, as her writings became known, contributed to it.

> Where Kartini stood as she wrote these letters—where she was located socially, what emotional state she was in, and what kinds of ideas and ideals she held—must all be seen in terms of the confrontation of the Javanese with the Dutch. When the letters begin Kartini is twenty, still caught in the alternating optimism and despair of a thoughtful, rebellious adolescent. When the letters abruptly end with her death four years later, she has become a woman. She has discovered for herself who she is, whom she loves, and for whom she must fight.

Both her life and the letters end on a tragic note, for Kartini, at twenty-five, died in childbirth.

Comparative: Kartini was a product of Javanese and Dutch culture and shares a kindred spirit with Anne Frank, a Dutch girl, who suffered (and died) under the occupation of Holland by the Nazis. Kartini's letters and Anne Frank's diary each present the search for identity of a young adolescent dominated by forces over which there is little control. Works which show this search against the background of colonialism include three Korean works —*The Grass Roof* by Younghill Kang, *The Yalu Flows* by Mirok Li, and *Lost Names* by Richard Kim—and the Philippine novel *The Lost Eden* by José Rizal. In each of these we find a search for identity—private and national— in a culture dominated by a foreign power or by war. For comparisons with other Indonesian writers see *Anthology of Modern Indonesian Poetry,* edited by Burton Raffel, and *The Complete Poetry and Prose of Chairil Anwar,* edited and translated by Burton Raffel.

Kawabata, Yasunari. THE MOON ON THE WATER (SUIGETSU). 1953.
Story. Japanese.

Author: Yasunari Kawabata was born in 1899 and committed suicide in 1972,
not long after the suicide of Yukio Mishima. He studied English literature at
Tokyo University, was President of the Japanese P.E.N., and is credited with
the discovery of a number of young writers, including Mishima. In 1968 he
was awarded the Nobel Prize for Literature.

Work: Most readers are familiar with Kawabata's novels *Snow Country* and
Thousand Cranes; however, "The Moon on the Water" is a very distinctive
story which reflects Kawabata's sensibility and the continuity of themes in
Japanese fiction. It is a philosophical story, one concerned with the nature
of illusion and reality and the non-duality of inner and outer reality. Like
many Japanese works, the story is dreamy, elegiac, loosely knit. Kawabata
himself once commented on another work, "My novel has an ending any-
where in it and yet it does not seem to end." His statement can be applied
to this story as well.

Briefly, Kyoko gives her husband, who is very ill, two mirrors. He finds
that the mirrors contain a world: "It was not only Kyoko's vegetable garden
that her husband had observed through the two mirrors. He had seen the sky,
clouds, snow, distant mountains, and nearby woods. He had seen the moon.
He had seen wild flowers, and birds of passage had made their way through
the mirror. Men walked down the road in the mirror and children played in
the garden."

The mirrors create a new life for the invalid, and Kyoko joins her husband
in this world. "Kyoko used to sit beside his bed and talk about the world in
the mirror. They looked into it together. In the course of time it became
impossible for Kyoko to distinguish between the world that she saw directly
and the world in the mirror. Two separate worlds came to exist. A new world
was created in the mirror and it came to seem like the real world." Kyoko
remains attached to this reflection of the world even after the death of her
husband with whom she shared the mirrored land.

Comparative: This story is best read along with other Japanese works that
explore the nature of reality. An exploration of this theme is found, for
example, in Murasaki's *The Tale of Genji* and in Kobo Abé's *The Woman in
the Dunes.* The work may also be compared with *A Cloude Dream Nine,* the
Korean classic novel.

Since it is a story of sensitive people, it may be effectively compared with
a sensitive character in any literature. The boy in Steinbeck's "Red Pony,"
or Rolvaag's *Giants in the Earth,* for example, offers both contrasts and
similarities to enrich the reading.

For further reading in Kawabata, the story "The Izu Dancer" and his
novel *The Sound of the Mountain* are highly recommended. "The Izu Dancer"
may be read with Kafū Nagai's *The River Sumida,* Mirok Li's *The Yalu Flows,*
and Younghill Kang's *The Grass Roof,* particularly for an understanding of
adolescence in an East Asian society.

Kawabata, Yasunari. THE SOUND OF THE MOUNTAIN (YAMA NO OTO).
1954. Novel. Japanese.

Author: See "The Moon on the Water."

Work: The central character of this novel is Shingo—father, husband, and grandfather as well as aging businessman in post-war Japan, where old values are shattering. As with much of Kawabata's work, this novel is concerned with impermanence—the passing of time, the brevity of beauty. It is Kawabata's intention to evoke *mono no aware,* to allow the reader to be moved aesthetically and morally as he shares the beauty and sadness that are in the world. *The Sound of the Mountain* is his greatest achievement, rich, complicated, poetic, and compelling.

Comparative: This novel invites comparison with Kawabata's earlier short story "The Izu Dancer." He once said of that story, after his second or third novel, that all else was emotional overflow. In a sense this is true. The theme of "The Izu Dancer" is the same as that of *The Sound of the Mountain:* the impermanence of beauty and the poignancy of that knowledge. This theme is also found in Murasaki's *The Tale of Genji.* A most interesting comparison concerning the concept of time may also be made with F. Scott Fitzgerald's *The Great Gatsby:* Gatsby who thought one could recapture the past and Kawabata's Shingo who knows one loses a little more happiness each year.
Also see Kawabata's Nobel Prize speech, *Japan the Beautiful and Myself.*

Käzantzakis, Nikos. ZORBA THE GREEK (ALEXIS ZORBA). 1946. Novel.
Greek.

Author: Käzantzakis (1883-1957) was born on the island of Crete, the son of an uncultured peasant. He grew up during the Greek struggle for independence from the Turks, and following the 1897 Rebellion his family fled to Naxos, where he was educated at a French Catholic school and learned both French and Italian. He studied law in Athens (1902-1906) and philosophy in Paris (1907-1909), where he was a student of Henri Bergson and was strongly influenced by the philosophy of Nietzsche. Between the World Wars he traveled widely and published numerous philosophical tracts, literary essays, travel books, translations of French, German, and Italian literature, and his monumental epic, *The Odyssey: A Modern Sequel* (1938). Following World War II he served briefly as the Greek Minister of National Education and Director of Translations from the Classics for UNESCO. Repeatedly sponsored for the Nobel Prize, he never received it, although his work was highly praised by several Nobel laureates.

Work: The novel describes the growing relationship between two men, an unnamed sensitive young writer, committed to thought rather than action, and the aging Zorba, a man who has knocked about the world and who believes that philosophy is only a poor substitute for living. The story of their meeting, their attempts to operate a lignite mine, the poet's efforts to deny his human desires and Zorba's passionate affair with the elderly Madame Hortense, the failure of the mine, and the subsequent separation of the two men are the means through which Käzantzakis portrays the gradual change produced in the poet by Zorba, a truly existential hero, a man totally committed to life and to the world of the senses. As Zorba puts it: "It makes no difference whether I have a woman or whether I don't, whether I'm honest or not, whether I'm a pasha or a streetporter. The only thing that makes any difference is whether I'm alive or dead." Zorba, unlike the ascetic poet, lives with his whole body, not just his head. While the poet struggles to deny his human nature and live only through the spirit and words, Zorba maintains that this life is to be lived to the fullest and to be experienced with one's entire being. It is this commitment to the totality of human experience that Zorba embodies, and at the end of the novel the poet asks Zorba to teach him to dance, a celebration and expression of the whole person. Zorba's last words are only a continuation of the ethic by which he has lived: "I've done heaps and heaps of things in my life, but I still did not do enough. Men like me ought to live a thousand years. Good night!"

Comparative: Zorba's commitment to life and experience places him among the ranks of the existential heroes who teach that each moment is to be lived and enjoyed to the maximum and that we cannot worry about things beyond human understanding or knowledge. He seems to put into practice many of the ideas expressed by Camus in his essay *The Myth of Sisyphus* and in his novels *The Stranger* and *The Plague.* It should be remembered that Camus and Käzantzakis greatly admired each other.

The conflict between the abstract or the world of the intellect and the world of human joys and sorrows is a frequent theme in literature. Goethe's Faust sells his soul to the devil to experience life; Hesse's Magister Ludi in *The Glass Bead Game* and his Harry Haller in *Steppenwolf* reject the intellectual world of scholarship and art for the everyday world, and Michel in Gide's *The Immoralist* learns, if only momentarily, to scorn intellectual sterility and to appreciate the simple pleasures and pains of life.

Khayyām, Omar. THE RUBĀIYĀT. Translated by Edward FitzGerald. 1859.
     Poem. Persian.

Author: Omar Khayyām, born in the eleventh century at Nīshāpūr, Persia, died in 1122. His name means "tent maker." The FitzGerald translation awoke interest in Khayyām's poetry even in his own country, where he had been respected as a mathematician, astronomer, and philosopher. FitzGerald (1809-1883), an Englishman, translated other works, but *The Rubāiyāt* remains his most important achievement.

Work: Little poetry of the nineteenth century had such a large influence as FitzGerald's translation and rearrangement (often called a "poetic transfusion") of Khayyām's eleventh century verse. Many of these vivid quatrains *(rubāiyāt)* have an almost proverbial quality, and taken together they represent a series of views on the wonderful, puzzling nature of life with its brevity and beauty, of death with its mystery, of a God whose creatures (perhaps whose toys) we are. Omar Khayyām calls us to awaken to life and to participate:

> Before the phantom of false morning died
> Methought a Voice within the Tavern cried,
>   "When all the Temple is prepared within,
> Why nods the drowsy Worshipper outside?"

Although we are called to experience life to the full, life may not fulfill the promise it seems to offer:

> The Wordly Hope men set their hearts upon
> Turns ashes—or it prospers; and anon,
>   Like Snow upon the Desert's dusty Face,
> Lighting a little hour or two—is gone.

The poet has no answers, and doubts the answers of the sages:

> Myself when young did eagerly frequent
> Doctor and Saint, and heard great argument
>   About it and about; but evermore
> Came out by that same door where in I went.
> . . . .
> Strange, is it not? that of the myriads who
> Before us passed the door of Darkness through,
>   Not one returns to tell us of the Road,
> Which to discover we must travel too.

Yet a germ of faith is expressed in the fine sequence of stanzas built on the image of God as the Potter and man as the Pot:

> "Why," said another, "Some there are who tell
> Of one who threatens he will toss to Hell
>   The luckless Pots he marred in making—Pish!
> He's a Good Fellow, and 'twill all be well."

In spite of doubts, the poet offers a vision of a better life, speculating that man might have made—or might still make—a better world:

>   Ah, Love! could you and I with Him conspire
>   To grasp this sorry Scheme of things entire
>   Would we not shatter it to bits—and then
>   Remold it nearer to the Heart's Desire!

And he concludes with the assertion that he, for one, would live this life, be it what it may, to the full.

Comparative: The story of Job offers a view of man's life and his relation to God which suggests a fruitful and provoking comparison. Ecclesiastes, with its words on the vanity of life, is also comparable to part of *The Rubáiyát.* Tagore's mystical love of life is similar in some ways yet sharply different in others. The poetry of Herrick and Donne and portions of *The Greek Anthology* offer views that stimulate comparative comment. And it should not be overlooked that themes and views within *The Rubáiyát* itself may well be set side by side for analysis and comparison. Finally, any work which offers a philosophical-religious concept of life (e.g., Tolstoi's *The Death of Ivan Ilyich)* invites comparison.

Kim, Richard E. LOST NAMES. 1970. Novel. Korean.

Author: Richard Kim was born in Korea in 1932 and served as an officer in the Korean army from 1951 to 1955. He received a master's degree from Harvard and was a Guggenheim fellow. His novels also include *The Martyred* and *The Innocent.* He has taught in California and at the University of Massachusetts. He has returned to his native Korea several times over the last years.

Work: Like other works by Richard Kim, this novel concerns the moral dilemma of a people faced with an oppression which destroys their culture, taking away their language and even their names. The meaning of survival and the definition of courage are the main questions in this novel. Specifically, this is the story of one Korean family and how it survived the colonial period of Japanese annexation. The work, however, is universal in its implications and suggests that great human tragedy is experienced by the oppressor as well as the oppressed, by the victimizer as well as the victim.

Comparative: This novel may be read within the context of other works that came out of occupation and oppression. See *The Diary of a Young Girl* by Anne Frank, a work written under the Nazi occupation of Holland; Kartini's *Letters of a Javanese Princess;* and José Rizal's *The Lost Eden.* The work may also be read as part of a "Korean trilogy" along with *The Grass Roof* by Younghill Kang and *The Yalu Flows* by Mirok Li.

La Fayette, Marie-Madeleine, Comtesse de. THE PRINCESS OF CLÈVES (LA PRINCESSE DE CLÈVES) 1678. Novel. French.

Author: Married to Count de La Fayette, Madame de La Fayette (1634–1693) bore two children, but left her husband in the country to live in Paris. There she became prominent in society and a good friend of La Rochefoucauld, author of *The Maxims*—a friendship which strengthened her literary career. Though she wrote several other novels, she is best known for *The Princess of Clèves*.

Work: Perhaps the finest novel of the seventeenth century in France, this novel of sensibility deals with the struggle between passion and reason against an authentic background of court life. It is considered a model of clear, formal style.

Madame de Chartres, a widow, presents her daughter at court and arranges for a marriage with the Prince de Clèves, a man her innocent daughter respects but does not love. Shortly after her marriage, she meets the Duke de Nemours and experiences the beginnings of a new emotion she has not felt for her husband. Her husband recognizes that his wife has fallen in love with the Duke, mistakenly believes she is unfaithful, and dies of a broken heart. After a period of mourning, the Duke pursues his suit for the Princess, but she, filled with remorse and fearful of the destructiveness of passion, retires to a convent and dies soon after. This simple story is played against a background of court affairs and political intrigue.

Comparative: The theme of the destructiveness of passion, of the struggle between passion and reason, is similar to that of Racine's *Andromaque*. The conflict between love and duty was a salient concern of seventeenth-century French writers, both in the novel and in drama. The language is formal and epigrammatic, the feelings intense, the psychology simple and sharp, and the tone objective and moral. Contrast this neoclassical style with that of Romantic writers on the subject of love (Goethe's *The Sorrows of Young Werther*, for example). Compare it, too, with other stories of women in love—Undset's *Kristin Lavransdatter*, Lawrence's *Women in Love*, Euripides' *Medea*.

La Rochefoucauld, François, Duc de. THE MAXIMS (RÉFLEXIONS OU SENTENCES ET MAXIMES MORALES). 1665. Essays. French.

Author: La Rochefoucauld (1613–1680) had the misfortune to plot against Richelieu, join the *Fronde*, and assist at the siege of Paris. Thus disgraced and ruined financially at forty, he retired in exile to the country and began writing his memoirs. When at last he returned to Paris, he joined the glittering salons of Mme. de Sablé, the Countess de La Fayette, and others, and refined there his wit and learning.

Work: In this collection of pithy comment on life, morals, and society, La Rochefoucauld speaks in the two voices he favors, the cynical and the moral.

The cynical:

19. We all have strength enough to endure the troubles of others.

73. You can find women who have never had a love affair, but seldom women who have had only one.

133. The only good copies are those which show up the absurdity of bad originals.

269. Few men are sufficiently discerning to appreciate all the evil they do.

273. Some people are thought well of in society whose only good points are the vices useful in social life.

The moral:

114. We cannot get over being deceived by our enemies and betrayed by our friends, yet we are often content to be so treated by ourselves.

122. When we resist our passions it is more on account of their weaknesses than of our strength.

168. Hope may be a lying jade, but she does at any rate lead us to the end of our lives along a pleasant path.

La Rochefoucauld is credited with refining the French language and directing French tastes toward consciousness and logic. His publication belongs to the corpus of wisdom literature and takes its place among varied collections, from the biblical Proverbs and Ecclesiastes through Voltaire's *Philosophical Dictionary*, Ambrose Bierce's *The Devil's Dictionary*, Pascal's *Pensées*, and Franklin's *Poor Richard's Almanack*.

Comparative: The cynical La Rochefoucauld belongs to the world of Voltaire, Shaw, Oscar Wilde, Bierce, and Sheridan (see especially the social comedies such as *The School for Scandal*). The writing of the moral La Rochefoucauld may be compared to the biblical Proverbs, to Pascal's *Pensées,* and to Franklin's *Poor Richard's Almanack,* among many others.

Finally, comparisons may be drawn with *Poems from the Greek Anthology* and Montaigne's *Essays* for wisdom in a similar vein.

LAZARILLO DE TORMES. 1554. Novel. Spanish.

Author: Unknown, but probably Juan de Ortega or Diego de Mendoza. The author concealed his identity because his was a dangerous book, exposing as it does the foibles of nobility and churchmen when the Inquisition was so close at hand.

Work: This work is one of many candidates for the honor of being the "first novel." This delightful novel about the *pícaro* at least partially sires Cervantes's *Don Quixote* and Fielding's *Tom Jones. Lazarillo de Tormes* is engaging in its light approach but filled with sharp portraits of life during this time and of the slow decay taking place in Spain.

As a young boy, Lázaro is given to a blind beggar by his widowed mother who can no longer care for him. The beggar, an unscrupulous trickster, beats and starves poor Lázaro but opens his eyes to the difficulties of life and teaches him that only the shrewd person can survive. In fact, Lázaro becomes so smart in the ways of the world that he throws over the old beggar. Life is not easy, however, under his new master, a churchman who is so stingy that even crusts of bread are kept under lock and key. Lázaro cheats, steals, and lies to keep himself alive until his duplicity is discovered. The next master Lázaro picks is a proud and richly dressed nobleman. Only when he wolfishly bolts the food that Lázaro has begged does the *pícaro* learn that this master is hiding starvation behind a facade of pride and blood, a condition wholly symptomatic of the situation in Spain. Lázaro, growing ever more skilled in deceit, next works for a peddler of bulls (indulgences for forgiveness of sins sold to the poor and ignorant). Eventually, Lázaro becomes a constable ("For nowadays nobody prospers except those who work for the government"), marries a wife whom he shares with the Archpriest, and settles down in the lap of luxury, winking his eyes at the peccadilloes necessary to success.

Comparative: It is impossible to name all the analogues, but *The Golden Ass* of Apuleius is a worthy predecessor. Almost as successful, though longer, more deliberate, and more self-consciously artistic, is Lesage's *Gil Blas.* We have already mentioned *Don Quixote,* in which Sancho Panza is a *pícaro,* and *Tom Jones.* The *pícaro* becomes more glorified in romantic literature, such as Dumas's *The Three Musketeers* and Rostand's *Cyrano de Bergerac,* where soldiers of fortune replace the lower class knave. A comparison to Figaro in *The Barber of Seville* by Beaumarchais is worthwhile.

The picaresque novel still thrives: Schulberg's racy *What Makes Sammy Run?,* John Braine's *Room at the Top,* Hervey Allen's *Anthony Adverse,* and Thomas Mann's *Felix Krull* are modern versions.

Lermontov, Mikhail Yurievich. A HERO OF OUR TIME (GEROI NASHEGO VREMENI). 1840. Novel. Russian.

Author: Lermontov (1814-1841) was born in Moscow and received a good education. A sickly child, he was sent to the Caucasus and fell in love with the mountains. He began writing at the age of eight and by seventeen had produced fifteen long poems, three dramas, a novelette and over three hundred lyrics. Essentially an idealistic youth, the harsh facts of nineteenth-century Russia led him to a position of skepticism and cynicism, much like his early hero, Lord Byron.

In 1837, following Pushkin's death, Lermontov published a poem accusing the czar's court of complicity. He was arrested and sent with the army to the Caucasus. He was allowed to return after a few months, and his lyrics soon made him famous. In 1840, *A Hero of Our Time* and Lermontov's first book of verse were published. Following a duel, he was again sent to the Caucasus where he distinguished himself in dangerous cavalry operations. Returning from a leave, he was killed in a duel with a friend, a duel set up as an exact recreation of the one described in the novel.

Work: The novel is a collection of five episodes arranged to reveal gradually the character of Pechorin, the book's hero. The first tale, "Bela," is told by an old soldier, Maxim Maximich, who had served with Pechorin. The story of how Pechorin abducted the native girl Bela, caused her to fall in love with him, and then abandoned her, introduces the hero as a Don Juan figure, but one who is searching for an ideal love. Bela's failure to satisfy his ideal vision, a situation no doubt inspired by Rousseau, only causes Pechorin to become more cynical about his ideals, and he laughs at the girl's death. In the second tale, "Maxim Maximich," the old soldier is coldly treated by his friend, who is compared to "one of Balzac's thirty-year-old coquettes . . . after a tiring ball." Pechorin is clearly suffering from romantic ennui. The remaining tales are from Pechorin's diary and give us the hero's own thoughts. "Taman" is a Byronesque adventure tale. In "Princess Mary," the most important of the tales, we learn that Pechorin, like Lermontov, is or was essentially idealistic, but harsh reality has turned him into a skeptic. Cooly rational, he has lost all enjoyment of life and suffers a deep boredom. He therefore cultivates artificial adventures like that of "Taman," searching for danger, seducing women, making enemies. On one occasion, at the loss of a woman, he shows emotion, but he quickly explains it in rational terms. In the final episode, "The Fatalist," Pechorin attempts to determine if life is predestined by assisting in an experiment with fate that ends in the death of a young officer.

Comparative: Pechorin is a member of the long line of Romantic heroes that stretches from Goethe's Werther, who remains idealistic and is destroyed, through Chateaubriand's René and Constant's Adolphe, who remain fairly idealistic, to the cynicism of Lord Byron's Childe Harold. But as Lermontov said of himself: "No, I'm not Byron; I'm different, I'm still unknown, a man apart. Like Byron by the world rejected. Only I have a Russian heart." Pechorin follows in the footsteps of Pushkin's Onegin, for he would be a useful member of society if only society were better and allowed him to express himself. Such is the situation in many works on the Don Juan theme, most notably Shaw's *Man and Superman.*

Li, Mirok. THE YALU FLOWS. An Asian Literature Program Book with an introduction by Bonnie R. Crown. W.W. Norton, 1975. Autobiography. Korean. (Originally written and published in German.)

Author: Mirok Li (1898-1950) was born in Korea and died in Germany, where he had lived in self-exile because of Japanese colonialism and the annexation of Korea by Japan in 1910. In addition to this book, he wrote tales of Korea, published in Germany under the title *Iyagi.* Li wrote in German, and has achieved wide recognition in Germany. On his deathbed, in 1950, his longing for Korea was so intense that he recited the opening lines of the Korean national anthem.

Work: This is the story of a young boy growing up in a closely knit Korean family, his relationships with his father, mother, and sister and with his friends. It is also the story of the conflicts experienced by this young man during a time when Korea was intimidated by powerful nations and be-wildered by the new scientific thought that was alien to the humanism of its time-honored national culture. While the work is firmly rooted in the Korean tradition, it is at the same time a universal statement of conflict and growth. If there is a moral, it is that human values must endure despite the suffering inflicted by political institutions and indifference. It is also a work touched by the Buddhist belief in the impermanence of beauty.

Comparative: It is highly recommended that *The Yalu Flows* be read as part of a Korean trilogy which would include Younghill Kang's *The Grass Roof* and Richard Kim's *Lost Names.* Each celebrates the survival of the human spirit in spite of the power of technology and politics. The novel may also be read, along with these two works, in a consideration of the literature of childhood memories. See also *To Kill a Mockingbird* by Harper Lee and *A Member of the Wedding* by Carson McCullers as other statements of the universal experiences of childhood and adolescence. In conjunction with the themes of war, occupation, and colonialism expressed in this Korean trilogy, see *Friederich* by Hans Richter, Anne Frank's *Diary of a Young Girl,* and Kartini's *Letters of a Javanese Princess.* Finally, this work, along with those mentioned above and many, many others, may be read in an exploration of the theme of rites of passage.

Lui, Wu-Chi and Irving Yucheng Lo, co-editors. SUNFLOWER SPLENDOR: THREE THOUSAND YEARS OF CHINESE POETRY. Indiana University Press, 1975. Poetry. Chinese.

Authors: The poems in this anthology represent 3,000 years of literary histo-ry, including poems by Mao Tse-tung, who died in 1976. The familiar names of Li Po and Tu Fu will be encountered as well as those of Chinese poets with a growing reputation in this country—Yang Wan-li, Su Tung-p'o, Han-shan, ard Lu Yu.

Work: This work has particular importance in the history of translation, for it set a new standard of excellence and accuracy in the translation of Chinese poetry, which in effect began in English with Arthur Waley and Ezra Pound. *Sunflower Splendor* not only takes the reader of poetry beyond the chinoiserie stage of translation and the admirable translations of Waley and Pound, but it is also noteworthy for the collaboration of Chinese and Western scholars.

While an anthology of this sort obviously does not give readers the opportunity to know any one poet well, it does introduce the range of forms used by Chinese poets and the subject matters they have chosen over a 3,000 year period. In addition, Chinese poetry, like Japanese, Vietnamese, and Korean poetry, provides an excellent introduction to poetry in general because it is direct and accessible. Chinese poetry, in spite of great cultural differences, is easier for students to grasp than Western poetry, which often tends to be intellectual and abstract. Chinese poetry reflects the "practicality" of the Chinese mind; it is poetry that is always close to the people, to their daily activities, to their values—especially loyalty and duty—and to nature. Finally, Chinese poetry draws on the intellectual, ethical, and religious framework of Chinese life—upon Confucian, Buddhist, and Taoist traditions, sometimes separately, sometimes in combination. It is through this poetry, then, that students come to understand these traditions and to know the Chinese people.

Comparative: One reviewer has called this anthology "a library of poems" that deserves a lifetime of reflection. Rather than comparing these poems with those of other nations, a more complete reading of the individual poets included in *Sunflower Splendor* is recommended. Consider, for example, *Heaven My Blanket, Earth My Pillow: Poems from Sung-Dynasty China* by Yang Wan-li, translated by Burton Watson or his translation of *Sun Tung-p'o: Selections from a Sung Dynasty Poet.* For excellent translations of love and protest poems (not included in *Sunflower Splendor*) turn to *Love and Protest: Chinese Poems from the Sixth Century B.C. to the Seventeenth Century A.D.* edited by John Scott, whose translations rival those of Ezra Pound. To consider contemporary Chinese literature, particularly its relevance to a new society in China, see *Twentieth Century Chinese Poetry: An Anthology* edited and translated by Kai-yu Shu.

Machiavelli, Niccolò. THE PRINCE (IL PRINCIPE). 1513. Essay. Italian.

Author: Niccolò Machiavelli (1469–1527) was a Florentine who from his early twenties served the city-state of his birth. He was upright, honest, a good father, and a responsible though errant husband. He was a notable writer of prose and poetry, a political thinker, an ambassador, a civil servant, a playwright. He is widely considered to be the man who bridged the gap between the Middle Ages and the Renaissance, a man who had his intellectual roots in the Middle Ages but nevertheless espoused the humanism of the Renaissance. In his day, Italy was divided into city-states which were often at war with each other. Machiavelli dreamed of and worked toward Italian unity. It is ironic that such a man should in the popular mind be considered cynical, corrupt, and evil. His very name has become a pejorative adjective— Machiavellian.

Work: Though Machiavelli wrote a number of other pieces, he is best known for his political treatise, *The Prince.* Dedicated to Lorenzo the Magnificent, it is a pragmatic and practical book that advises a head of state on how to rule. It is filled with maxims and advice, such as "It is safer to be feared than loved." Such advice may not be moral but it is probably sound, for it takes into account human nature and the needs of the time. Machiavelli dreamed of a strong leader and a unified Italy. He didn't pretend to be writing a moral treatise; he wrote, instead, of the laws of politics and the psychology of the commoner. Interestingly, *The Prince* also has literary merit, for Machiavelli employed strong imagery, relied on directness and terseness to achieve a vigorous prose, and made ample use of explanatory examples.

Comparative: *The Courtier* by Castiglione, a book of advice to those who wish to be successful courtiers, shares the directness and some of the cynicism of *The Prince.* Hitler's *Mein Kampf* is an inside look at the plans of a man who boldly mapped the course of his own ambitions. Nixon's *Six Crises,* a book written after the fact, conveys the same cold, political astuteness as *The Prince.*

Maeterlinck, Maurice. THE BLUE BIRD (L'OISEAU BLEU). 1909. Drama. Belgian.

Author: Maurice Maeterlinck (1862-1949) received the Nobel Prize in 1911, chiefly for his dramatic works, which are "distinguished by a wealth of imagination and a poetic fancy which reveal, sometimes in the guise of a fairy tale, a deep inspiration, while in a mysterious way they appeal to the readers' own feelings and stimulate their imaginations." Born into a middle-class family in Flanders, educated for the law—a profession which never appealed to him—Maeterlinck went to Paris, where he was influenced by the Symbolist movement. Returning to Belgium, he wrote and printed his first play, *Princess Maleine* (1889), which was an immediate success. From then on he was playwright, philosophical thinker, and author of monographs that combine science and imagination—the best known of these are *The Life of the Bee* (1901) and *The Life of the Termite* (1927), the latter posing some frightening questions for mankind.

Work: This play may at first be dismissed as a fairy tale; however, it possesses allegorical and philosophical elements that more than once touch upon existential questions.

The basic story follows the quest of a boy and a girl, who live at the edge of the forest, for an elusive blue bird that symbolizes happiness. In their search the children are sometimes aided, sometimes impeded, by a variety of allegorical characters. They are, in fact, accompanied on most of their adventures by Light, who serves as their guide, Fire, Water, Bread, Sugar, Milk, Dog, and Cat. Dog's adoration of his young master is especially interesting since he has the power of speech and can therefore express his love and faithfulness in words.

The story is set on Christmas Eve, and the children are sent on their journey by the fairy Berylune, who needs the blue bird to heal her sick daughter. Among the places they visit is the Land of Memory, where they meet their dead grandparents and their seven dead brothers and sisters. In this touching part of the play, Maeterlinck implies much about death—and life. Other highlights occur in the Forest, where Dog saves the children from being killed by personifications of all the beasts and trees who have been injured or exploited by man; in the Graveyard, where the children wait in fright for the dead to rise at midnight, only to find all the graves empty; and in the Kingdom of the Future, where they meet children waiting to be born. Nowhere, however, can they find the blue bird.

The fantasy ends when they awake on Christmas morning, and the boy gives his pet dove to a neighbor whose sick daughter has wished for it. The bird assumes a blue color and the little girl is cured, but the bird escapes. The boy asks the theater audience to return it if they find it, for it will be needed for happiness later on.

Comparative: The most obvious comparison is with Grimm's fairy tales, a comparison which shows how Maeterlinck updated the fairy tale. The play may also be used as an introduction to the masque; it has, for example, a number of elements in common with Milton's *Comus:* innocent protagonists, forest setting, extra-human characters, to mention a few. Also masquelike are the ornate settings, the dances, and the appeal to the audience at the end.

In theme the play, with its elusive blue bird, may be compared with Hawthorne's short story, "The Artist of the Beautiful," where it is beauty that is elusive. The play is also in the direct line of quest literature, beginning with the quest for the Holy Grail and represented in modern times by a man's search for meaning in life, as depicted, for example, in Hesse's *Siddhartha.* Finally, the play's implicit questions about death and the human condition are forerunners of modern existentialist thought. Maeterlinck himself is quoted as saying that in his drama he wanted to convey "what is astonishing in the mere fact of living."

**Malraux, André. MAN'S FATE (LA CONDITION HUMAINE). 1933. Novel.
French.**

Author: Malraux, born in Paris in 1901, was a student of Oriental art and
languages. He did archaeological work in Indochina and China and was involved in the Kuomintang Revolution. This experience contributed to the
background for this novel and for *The Royal Way* and *The Conquerors,*
among others. Malraux joined the Loyalists at the outbreak of the Spanish
Civil War in 1936, helping to organize their air force and serving as a machine
gunner. During World War II he served in the Tank Corps, was captured by
the Germans, escaped, and joined the resistance movement. He later held
cabinet posts in the government of Charles de Gaulle.

Committed to the idea of *l'homme engagé,* Malraux is also devoted to art
and is the author of important works in that area, among them the three-
volume *Psychology of Art,* which later appeared as a single volume, *The
Voices of Silence* (1951).

Work: This is the story of Ch'en, a revolutionary who makes terrorism his
religion and who dies as a human bomb underneath Chiang Kai-shek's car.
It is also the story of Kyo Gisors, half-French, half-Japanese, his wife May,
and his father, Old Gisors, who believes "that the essence of man is anguish
. . . but that opium frees you from it." It is also the story of Hemmelrich, a
German phonograph merchant, and his Oriental wife and sick son. Other
people drift in and out of the novel—Ferral of the French Chamber of Commerce, Baron de Clappique the smuggler, among others—but the character
who emerges finally as the hero is Katov, the Russian organizer of the Shang-
hai insurrection, who knows blood brotherhood and, as he is about to be
thrown alive into the furnace of a locomotive, gives his cyanide capsule to
two frightened comrades.

The novel is constructed around divisions of time instead of in chapters,
and it covers, sometimes swiftly, sometimes hour by hour, the period from
March 21 through April 12, 1927. It is generally proletarian in sympathy,
but Malraux's world is peopled with complex characters, each of whom
comes through with rare individuality.

The title refers to Pascal's famous image of each man linked with his dying
brother, and *La Condition humaine* may be the most definitive statement
made about war or the individual's duty to his fellow man—at least since the
story of Cain and Abel. This novel won the Goncourt Prize in 1933.

Comparative: Another treatment of human responsibility, under different
circumstances, is found in Maugham's *Of Human Bondage.* Other comparisons
may be found in John Dos Passos' *Three Soldiers* and in Remarque's *All
Quiet on the Western Front* and the related works noted there. The revelatory
kiss of love in Flaubert's "The Legend of St. Julian Hospitator" from *Trois
Contes,* in Hesse's *Siddhartha,* and in Dostoevski's "The Legend of the Grand
Inquisitor" finds its equal in Katov's act of renunciation. Like Rubashov in

Koestler's *Darkness at Noon,* Katov dies having accomplished nothing except self-realization.

Mann, Thomas. DEATH IN VENICE (DER TOD IN VENEDIG). 1912. Novella. German.

Author: Thomas Mann (1875-1955) was awarded the Nobel Prize for literature in 1929 for his contributions to the development of the realistic novel. He was born into a respected Lübeck family; his father was a corn broker and a senator and his mother, of South American descent, came from a family of prosperous international merchants. Despite their background of business and political activity, both parents were unusually interested in the arts, and the theme of the struggle between the artist and the burgher is a common one in Mann's works. His creative output was helped by his marriage to Katja Pringsheim, herself a translator and essayist, by whom he had six children. Forced by his political beliefs to leave Germany under the Hitler regime, Mann eventually emigrated to the United States. He taught at Princeton and became an American citizen. Though he later returned to Europe and settled in Switzerland, he retained his American citizenship. His best-known works are *Buddenbrooks* (1901); *The Magic Mountain* (1924); *Joseph and His Brethren,* a tetralogy (1933-42); *Doctor Faustus* (1947); and *Confessions of Felix Krull, Confidence Man* (1954).

Work: This novella relies for its strength on a combination of setting and psychological analysis. Gustav von Aschenbach, a successful and aging writer, is near the breaking point from years of overtaxing his creative powers. His general debilitation is aggravated by the unusual spring weather throughout Europe—humid, stifling, a premature summer that carries with it a general air of foreboding. One evening, a chance encounter outside a cemetery with an unnamed but strikingly ugly traveler stimulates Aschenbach to undertake a journey of his own.

   Eventually he finds himself at a beachfront Lido hotel convenient to the decadent beauty of Venice, which is described in intricate and artistic detail. The decadence of the ancient city is reflected in the increasing decadence of Aschenbach's mental state. On his first day at the hotel his attention is caught by a strikingly handsome Polish boy, Tadzio. This attraction soon grows into a strong attachment for the boy, who apparently encourages it. Mann's skill at handling what could be a sordid story is evident in the delicate treatment of this attachment—neither the aging man nor the lovely boy ever speaks directly to the other, nor is there any physical contact between them. Rather, the reader is made to feel the effect that the sultry weather and the decadent beauty of Venice have on Aschenbach's emotions. Allusions to mythology underscore his emotional state.

Cholera breaks out in Venice, but its presence is concealed lest the resort business be hurt. All of the interrelated strains of the novella rise to a crescendo which results in Aschenbach's death and gives the work its title.

Comparative: The descriptive passages in this novella are reminiscent of those of Joseph Conrad, especially in "The Lagoon" and *Lord Jim.* The almost surrealistic foreshadowings of the plague in the shape of the mysterious traveler mentioned above, in the Charon-like gondolier who ferries Aschenbach to his Lido hotel, and in the group of performers with their faces painted white are similar to details used by Edgar Allan Poe in "The Masque of the Red Death," another short work dealing with the advent of plague. The foreboding sense of fate and nature allied against the protagonist is similar to that created by D. H. Lawrence in such novellas as *The Fox* (which also contains elements of latent homosexuality) and *The Horse Dealer's Daughter.* An excellent comparison can be made with Henry James's novella, *Daisy Miller,* in which another tourist, a young and vital American girl, succumbs to disease in Rome. *Death in Venice* may also be compared with other works by Mann, especially *Buddenbrooks, Mario and the Magician,* and *Tonio Kröger,* in which he again treats the sensitivity and psychology of the artist.

Mann, Thomas. CONFESSIONS OF FELIX KRULL, CONFIDENCE MAN (BEKENNTNISSE DES HOCHSTAPLERS FELIX KRULL). 1954. Novel. German.

Author: See *Death in Venice.*

Work: This unfinished picaresque novel recounts the always amusing, sometimes outrageous adventures of Felix Krull, equipped by temperament, good looks, and native wit to become a con artist *par excellence.* Since it describes approximately the first twenty years of Felix's life, the novel may be classified as a *Bildungsroman,* but it also contains elements of satire that make it more difficult to categorize.

Born near Mainz, Felix appears from early childhood to be predestined to become a confidence man. At a very early age he poses successfully as a violin virtuoso, though he doesn't play a note. Lacking interest in school, he manages to counterfeit illness so successfully that he almost fools himself. His godfather, Herr Schimmelpreester, an artist, paints Felix in many different costumes—as Greek god, toreador, page, courtier, officer—and for each Felix puts on the personality as well as the costume of the character.

The Krull family has always entertained beyond its means; and when the champagne firm which has formed the basis for the family's fortune goes bankrupt, Felix's father, unable to face ruin, shoots himself. Herr Schimmel-preester arranges for Felix to enter a hotel career in Paris. First, however, Felix must escape compulsory military service. In a scene of pure slapstick, he again draws on his ability to counterfeit illness and is summarily rejected.

En route to Paris, Felix steals a jewel case from a prosperous-looking lady and not much later begins an affair with its owner, who encourages him to steal still more from her. Somewhat later, Felix changes roles with the Marquis Louis de Venosta of Luxemburg, known familiarly as "Loulou." To separate Loulou from his pretty chorus girl mistress, his family has arranged for him to take a trip around the world, but Loulou arranges to have Felix assume his identity and replace him on the tour.

As the novel breaks off, Felix has met the memorable Professor Kuckuck and is ensconced in Lisbon. Felix, who has been paying court to the Professor's charming daughter, suddenly finds that he has won the amorous attentions of her redoubtable mother.

Comparative: As a *Bildungsroman,* this novel may be compared with Joyce's *A Portrait of the Artist as a Young Man;* with Hesse's *Demian,* with which it shares many elements, including the presence of a very attractive older woman; with Dickens's *David Copperfield;* with Rolland's *Jean Christopher;* and with Byron's *Childe Harold* and *Don Juan.* In its presentation of the seamier aspects of life not always understood by its protagonist, it resembles Twain's *Huckleberry Finn*—though Huck's character is far different from Felix's.

Elements of social satire and the exposure of hypocrisy place this novel in a long history of social satire. In particular, students might enjoy comparing it with Thackeray's *Vanity Fair* or with Colette's *Gigi.*

Mann, Thomas. **TONIO KRÖGER.** 1903. Novella. German.

Author: See *Death in Venice.*

Work: Despite its brevity, this novella is one of the finest examples of Mann's technique and provides a wealth of material for discussion. Tonio Kröger is one of the protagonists perennially popular with modern youth—an outsider. In his case, however, his alienation stems from his mixed background; from his father's family he has inherited the Northern European bourgeois temperament, from his mother's, the Southern artistic temperament. Ultimately, Tonio himself realizes this dichotomy and expresses it in a letter to an artist friend: "I stand between two worlds, I am at home in neither, and this makes things a little difficult for me. You artists call me a bourgeois, and the bourgeois feel they ought to arrest me."

Largely through a series of vignettes, each dealing with a key episode in Tonio's progress to literary success and self-awareness, the novella follows him from early youth into maturity. Eventually, Tonio, now an accomplished literary artist, makes a pilgrimage to the northern countries of his youth. In his home town he pays a sentimental visit to the former mercantile house of his family, once a prominent trading house whose softening and decay is discussed in Mann's earlier novel *Buddenbrooks*. Symbolically enough, the house is now a public library just as Tonio is a public literary figure. Going to Denmark, Tonio sees a couple who remind him of his past—of Ingeborg with whom he was in love and of Hans Hansen whom he admired. Seeing the couple, he relives speciously the one occurrence in his lifetime which was not sacrificed to the demands of art and artistic success.

Mann has a great deal to say in this story about the place of the artist in the world and about the compulsions he faces. Tonio, the creative artist, is self-conscious, irritating, and patronizing in his attitude toward commonplace people, but he allows some shoulder-shrugging pain to steal in as he acknowledges what he has been forced to deny himself. The novella is thus a quiet battleground for these two conflicting passions in Tonio's life, and the work becomes poignant and autumnally sad, a sharp blend of romantic nostalgia and realism.

Comparative: Its theme of the alienated man allies *Tonio Kröger* with many works of modern literature, among them Camus's *The Stranger,* Hesse's *Siddhartha* and *Steppenwolf,* Kafka's *The Trial,* Dostoevski's *Crime and Punishment,* and Chekhov's *The Sea Gull.* In addition, the theme of the development of the artist *(Künstlerroman)* may be compared with that expressed by Joyce in *A Portrait of the Artist as a Young Man* and by Gerhart Hauptmann in two plays, *Lonely Lives (Einsame Menschen)* and *The Sunken Bell (Die versunkene Glocke).*

The novella may also be compared to other works by Mann, among them *Death in Venice,* which not only deals with alienation but also employs the same sort of descriptive passages used so effectively in *Tonio Kröger; Tristan,* which, though more nihilistic in outlook, deals with the conflict between the artist and the bourgeois and also employs the technique of the *leitmotif—* brief descriptive phrases used repeatedly in connection with a character until they come to be associated with that character; and *Buddenbrooks,* which deals with the downfall of a merchant dynasty and examines the role of the artist in society.

Marie de France (and others). LAYS OF COURTLY LOVE. 12th Century. Poems. French.

Author: Probably Breton or Norman, Marie de France settled in England after the Norman Conquest and there wrote in verse the narratives she remembered from France. Her characterizations are deft and quick, and real pathos develops from some of the tragedies.

Work: This collection of short narrative poems, designed to be sung, celebrates courtly love. Typical is "The Lay of the Chatelaine of Vergi." A knight is the lover of the Chatelaine, whose little dog runs out to show him when it is safe to visit her chamber. The Duchess of the court, however, falls in love with the knight. He spurns her affection, and she then accuses him of assaulting her honor. Since the knight apparently had no love affair (a rare thing at court and an incident that reminds us of the *Hippolytus* of Euripedes), the Duke is inclined to believe his wife's lie. The knight, who has pledged to keep silent about the affair, fails to respond to the charges, though he knows that confession would remove him from suspicion. Finally, he tells the Duke, who witnesses a meeting between the lovers to satisfy himself. The Duke then repudiates his wife's charges, but she worms out the secret of what he has seen. Filled with hate for her competitor, the Duchess loses no time in revealing to the proud young Chatelaine that her secret is known. In despair at the betrayal of their compact, she imagines that the knight has broken his word, swoons, and dies. Only a chambermaid who has heard her lament can tell the knight why his "friend" has died. The knight, in shame and heartbreak, kills himself. The Duke, enraged that his wife has broken her pledge of silence, rushes into the ballroom and kills her.

These lays stem from the epic tradition—only here the hero is engaged in love rather than war—and they show the gradual rise of the exaggerated manners of the Renaissance. These highly stylized romances, now quaint and with a nostalgic rustle of old silks and brocades, give us an interesting picture of life within the draughty castles.

Comparative: Aucassin and Nicolette, Sir Gawain and the Green Knight, and *The Romance of Tristan and Iseult* are close relatives to the lay, although the lays are less pretentious than the courtly romances. Similar material is found in Boccaccio's *The Decameron.* Patterned after the lay was the *fabliau,* which ridiculed the court and courtly love.

Markandaya, Jamal, pseudonym of Kamala Taylor. NECTAR IN A SIEVE.
1954. Novel. Indian.

Author: Born in 1924, Markandaya is a Brahmin, a member of India's privileged class; however, she tells with insight and sympathy the life stories of lower class people. Educated at Madras University, she worked for a short-lived weekly newspaper. In 1948 she went to London, supporting herself as a proofreader and secretary until the third novel she wrote, *Nectar in a Sieve,* became her first published book. She lives in London with her English husband and her daughter.

Work: This novel of modern India is the story of a pitiless battle against hunger lightened by man's faith and fellow-courage, but it becomes archetypal and symbolic of men in all lands. The novel is sensitively written from a first-person point of view, which instead of limiting perception, often surprises the reader with the depth of the raconteur's sociological and historical understanding.

Rukmani, a young and beautiful woman, is given to Nathan in marriage and taken to a mud hut to live. Life is hard but exciting in the first years of marriage and adjustment. A daughter is born, but for five years no sons come to the couple. Some seasons are good and the rice and melons flourish; in other years, floods or burnouts reduce the people to starvation. Finally, with the advice of Dr. Kenney, an "Ugly American" who lives in the village, Rukmani has sons. The remainder of the novel is the story of how one son after another disappears or dies because of the old enemy, famine, or the new menaces sweeping through India: industrialization, political unrest, and war.

When Nathan's rented land is taken from him, the couple seek housing and sustenance from their son in the city, but the son has disappeared. Nathan dies. Rukmani adopts a young street urchin, Puli (much like Kipling's Kim), and returns to the village where she and Nathan had lived. The novel ends as she forces her memory back through the cycle of everything that has been. Thus we see each tragedy through the eyes of the young person who experienced it and later through the mature vision of the old woman who remembers it. Curiously enough, the result is ennobling and triumphant; one wants to shout with Thornton Wilder's George Antrobus *(The Skin of Our Teeth)*, "Thank God, I'm a human being!"

Comparative: The novel gives an intimate picture of Indian life, the reverse of the Brahminic lives in Chatterjee's *Krishnakanta's Will*. The behavior of characters is sometimes *non sequitur,* and difficult for a Westerner to understand. This curious quality, however, is part of what makes the novel peculiarly Indian.

The novel reminds one of Pearl Buck's *The Good Earth,* except that Markandaya avoids the happy ending. Nathan's personality and role are almost like that of Job, and Hunthi, the jealous woman, is by name and character from the *Mahabharata.* Rukmani's loss of her loved ones parallels the loss in Synge's *Riders to the Sea.* The struggle with famine may be compared with that in Manzoni's *The Betrothed.*

Maupassant, Guy de. BEL-AMI. 1885. Novel. French.

Author: Maupassant (1850-1893) finished military service and worked as a government clerk before deciding on the literary life. He became the friend of

Flaubert, Turgenev, Daudet, and Zola. Before his ruin by overwork and debauchery, he had written over three hundred masterful short stories and six novels. He died insane.

Work: Georges Duroy (Bel-Ami is his nickname), a young and ambitious Paris journalist, successfully and successively exploits Mme de Marelle, Mme Forestier, Mme Walter, and Mlle Suzanne to advance himself socially and economically. Through marriage as well as liaison, he hopes to win a post in the government. Glimpses of every level of society—George's early days of poverty in the *banlieues* of Paris, his provincial background, music hall life, and upperclass circles—make the novel a fascinating exposé of humanity at one time in its history—or any time.

Comparative: As one of the best examples of naturalism, that literary attitude which denied spiritual guidelines and insisted that man was governed only by heredity, environment, and desires, this work has many parallels in current writing; in its material it is as modern as Beckett and Lawrence.

Schulberg's *What Makes Sammy Run?* and John Braine's *Room at the Top* show us how contemporary Maupassant's novel is, for in each the counterpart of young Duroy pulls himself up the social ladder, using the weakness and vanity and idleness of society for his footholds. Aspects of this character may also be found in Hermann in Pushkin's "The Queen of Spades" and in Rastignac in Balzac's *Le Père Goriot.* For another look at the European *demi-monde,* see Colette's *Gigi.*

Maupassant, Guy de. BOULE-DE-SUIF. 1880. Story. French.

Author: See *Bel-Ami.*

Work: In this sardonic story a pretentious society is unable to find virtue in the patriotic action of a prostitute.

When the Prussians occupy Rouen during the Franco-Prussian War, a few of the inhabitants with business interests elsewhere secure passes to travel to Dieppe. Setting out in a coach on a bitter snowy day are M. and Mme Loiseau, wine merchants; M. Carre-Lamadon, cotton dealer; the Count and Countess de Breville; two nuns; Cornudet, a radical politician; and Boule-de-suif ("Butterball"). The last, a well known prostitute, is ignored by the respectable citizens, all of whom, as Maupassant notes, have skeletons in their closets, until she invites them to share her lunch basket. Some sort of democracy is thus established and continues until the party reaches Tôtes.

In Tôtes the coach is inspected by a Prussian hussar who is taken with Boule-de-suif and refuses to allow the passengers to continue their journey unless he enjoys "Madame's" favors. At first the loyal French bourgeois and aristocrats are outraged at the affront; after a day or two of waiting, they are outraged that Boule-de-suif will not comply and organize an attack to undermine her determination. Eventually, for the good of the group, she gives in. As the trip resumes, she is again exposed to the contempt of the carriage-full of hypocrites.

"Boule-de-suif" was included in *Les Soirées de Médan* (1880), a collection of stories by Zola and five authors who were his disciples at the time. The volume became, if not the manifesto of naturalism, at least a superb example. Beyond this, Maupassant shares with Poe the honor of inventing and perfecting the modern short story and defining its theory. His output was so enormous and so consistently good that it is difficult to single out any one story as his best, but many have granted that honor to "Boule-de-suif."

Comparative: The overwhelming hypocrisy portrayed in Maupassant's work may be compared to that of Goneril and Regan in *King Lear*. The boxed-in situation of the travelers suggests comparison with Sartre's *No Exit* and *The Flies* and with Camus's *The Stranger*. The character of the honorable prostitute has been drawn by Sartre and Chikamatsu, and by many others.

Mauriac, François. THÉRÈSE (THÉRÈSE DESQUEYNOUX). 1927. Novel. French.

Author: François Mauriac (1885-1970) was born in Bordeaux and had a strongly conservative Catholic background. His father died when François was an infant, and he was raised by his devout mother. He began writing early and decided to become a professional author. To understand his work, one must keep in mind the ardor of his religious feelings; indeed, Mauriac wished to be remembered as a Catholic who wrote novels rather than as a Catholic novelist. He was a member of the French Academy, and he was awarded the Nobel Prize in 1952.

Work: Thérèse, a provincial girl, is the victim of an arranged marriage to Bernard, a wealthy landowner, who is coarse in his relations with her and who thinks only of land and reputation. Thérèse feels oppressed, and even after she has a daughter, she spends her time reading, smoking, thinking, feeling imprisoned. She begins to hate her husband and her life, and she poisons him. Bernard survives, however, and Thérèse is sequestered at home. Finally she breaks away to live in Paris. Her husband remains, appearances preserved, to live his middle-class, landowner life. Thérèse is a typical Mauriac heroine— sensitive, misunderstood, trapped, pitiful, revulsed by coarse masculine sex— who insists on trying to be herself.

Comparative: Zola's *Nana,* Flaubert's *Madame Bovary,* and Anatole France's *Thaïs* are novels, among many other stories, long and short, which treat heterosexual relationships from the woman's point of view.

Mérimée, Prosper. COLOMBA. 1841. Novella. French.

Author: Mérimée (1803-1870) studied for the law and entered literature by writing a series of literary hoaxes. He produced only one full-length novel *(Chronicle of the Reign of Charles IX)* and devoted himself to novellas and short stories, of which *Carmen* is best known because of its use in Bizet's opera.

Work: Orso della Rebbia, a young officer discharged from the French army, returns to his hometown in Corsica after an absence of many years in the company of Colonel and Miss Neville of England. He and Miss Neville fall in love. Orso is seized upon by his sister, Colomba, who paints vivid and prejudiced pictures of the slaying of their father years before by the treacherous Barricini family. Colomba wants revenge, and Orso is filled with mixed feelings as his new continental ideas conflict with the hatreds engendered by an old vendetta. Pietranera, a sleepy little town, is dominated by two rival "castles" that confront one another across the square like the houses of the Montagues and the Capulets. Violence is sure to erupt.

Since Orso is unwilling to seek revenge, Colomba tricks him into situations where he must declare himself, even at the risk of losing the love of Miss Neville. Finally, the two Barricini brothers ambush Orso, and he kills them both in a gun fight as good as any in the American West. Colomba is beside herself with joy. Orso is forced to take to the *maquis* under the protection of two benevolent bandits until he is able to prove he acted in self-defense. Once cleared, he and Miss Neville go on a honeymoon to Pisa. Colomba accompanies them and one day meets the elder Barricini, who has become mad with grief over the deaths of his sons. Vengeful Colomba delivers one last taunt to the pathetic old man.

Next to Stendahl, Mérimée possessed the cleanest, sharpest style in the new movement called realism, but he chose the romantic for his subject matter. In this tale of vendetta, Mérimée's style becomes a foil for his subtle irony and wit.

Comparative: Like Colomba, Electra goads her brother Orestes into avenging their father's death (note the similarity of names—Orso and Orestes). Both Electra and Colomba are possessed by hatred and are unscrupulous in forcing their brothers to kill. See Sophocles' *Electra* and Sartre's *The Flies.* The single mindedness of Medea might also be used in this comparison of vengeful women. We have already mentioned a similarity to the feud in Shakespeare's *Romeo and Juliet.* An interesting note is the British colonel, a "Colonel

Blimp" type found as a stereotype in Evelyn Waugh, P. G. Wodehouse, Somerset Maugham, and others. Another interesting Mérimée story of the Corsican *maquis* and of primitive vengeance is "Mateo Falcone."

Mishima, Yukio. THE PRIEST OF SHIGA TEMPLE AND HIS LOVE. 1954.
    Story. Japanese.

Author: Yukio Mishima was born in 1925 and committed ritual suicide in 1970. He was a writer and a man of action, though his politics which glorified the Emperor were never taken seriously. He traveled widely and is probably the best known of Japanese writers. Because of his flamboyance, he has sometimes overshadowed more gifted Japanese writers; however, he must be included in any serious study of modern fiction or Japanese literature.

Work: The story is about love and sacrifice; however, it must be understood within its Buddhist context. The Priest, the main character in this story, is approaching death. He has led a pure life and should be permitted to enter the realm of the Pure Land upon his death: "In his dreams he lived nightly in the Pure Land, and when he awoke he knew that to subsist in the present world was to be tied to a sad and evanescent dream." At the end of his life— so close to the Pure Land—he experiences a magnetic attraction for a lady of the court, a woman who has always longed for a love that called for great sacrifice. Before his death, the Priest goes to the woman. He is received by her, and she recognizes that he has made the supreme sacrifice. No greater love could be given than to have sacrificed the Pure Land.

Comparative: This compelling story might be compared with other works on the theme of love and sacrifice. See, for example, "Prelude to Glory" by U Win Pe (a Burmese story) in *Literatures of the Eastern World*. For a comparison with a Western work, consider Colette's short story "Rendezvous." For a further exploration of the Japanese short story, see *Modern Japanese Stories, An Anthology* edited by Ivan Morris, and *Contemporary Japanese Literature, An Anthology of Fiction, Film and Other Writing Since 1945,* edited by Howard Hibbett.

Mistral, Gabriela, pseudonym of Lucila Godoy Alcayaga. SELECTED POEMS OF GABRIELA MISTRAL. Translated by Langston Hughes. Indiana University Press, 1957. Poems. Chilean.

Author: Gabriela Mistral (1889–1957), was awarded the Nobel Prize in 1945 for her poetry. The pseudonym she chose, for fear of losing her teaching job, is derived from the name of the Archangel Gabriel and from the word for sea wind, a combination that seems to suit her emotionally charged verses. Daughter of an elementary school master, she herself became an outstanding, creative teacher and was eventually given a post in the Chilean Department of Education.

Mistral first attracted attention for a series of poems published in 1914 under the title of *Soñetos de la Muerte* and written in despondency over the suicide of her young lover, Romelio Ureta.

She served with a program of educational reform in Mexico and established many lasting friendships there. In the 1930s she became Chile's delegate to the League of Nations. She subsequently taught at Middlebury and Barnard Colleges and represented her government in several diplomatic posts in South America and Europe and on the United Nations Subcommittee on the Status of Women, from which she resigned because she felt the committee was seeking special protection for women rather than equality.

Mistral never married. In 1953 she settled in the United States, where she lived at Roslyn Harbor, Long Island, until her death. Her individual works include *Desolation (Desolación)* 1922; *Tenderness (Ternura)* 1924; *Feeling (Tala)* 1938; and *Wine Press (Lagar)* 1954.

Work: Selected Poems of Gabriela Mistral contains seventy-four of the author's best known works. Though her range is limited to nature poems, holy hymns, lullabys, love songs, naive lyrics and games for children, and poems about the basic needs of human life, there is great warmth and intensity. Often she writes of maternal yearnings, as in "Poem of the Son" or "Children's Hair."

No poet has surpassed Mistral in writing of the trials and loves of motherhood, indeed womanhood, and her celebration of femaleness is especially fresh and timely today. Ironically, she was to be a mother to all children, yet never to one of her own.

Because of the loss of her beloved, death is frequently a theme of Mistral, and it is usually interwoven with religion and hope. For example, in "Prayer" she pleads that her lover, a sinner because he was a suicide, receive the grace of God and be admitted to His presence.

Mistral's poems are generally compact, highly polished, forceful. They work well in English, especially in the gifted translations of Langston Hughes.

Comparative: Mistral's works show the influence of the Bible, Tagore, the Mexican writer Amado Nervo, and Rubén Darío. Certain poems, those concerned with motherhood, the woman's role, and children, compare and contrast well with poems by Sylvia Plath.

Molière, pseudonym of Jean-Baptiste Poquelin. TARTUFFE. 1664. Drama. French.

Author: Molière (1622-1673), born the son of an upholsterer to the King of France, received a fine classical education but entered the stage as soon as he turned twenty-one. For twelve years he led his troupe through southern France, playing in inns and courtyards and developing the techniques he was later to use to great advantage. Returning to Paris in 1658, he presented one of his comedies so successfully that he was granted his own theater by Louis XI. Molière died of tuberculosis, courageously braving his illness to play the lead in his last comedy, ironically, *The Imaginary Invalid.*

Work: Tartuffe, a religious hypocrite, uses the pretext of zealous Christianity to work his way into the good graces of Orgon and his mother, Madame Pernelle, both of whom are gullible and anxious to appear religious. The members of Orgon's household recognize the hypocrisy, but Orgon's blindness is such that he will not listen to reason. Indeed, he makes over his property to Tartuffe, who then threatens the family with expulsion. Elmire, Orgon's wife, contrives to reveal Tartuffe's real nature to her husband, but it is too late. Tartuffe has the deed and can now show his true colors. In a *deus ex machina* conclusion, the all-knowing King, through his Gentlemen of the Guard, imprisons Tartuffe and restores the property to the family.

The five-act drama makes clear both the tendency to place appearances above genuine qualities and the nature of true Christianity. The play was apparently written as an answer to (or attack on) Molière's enemies, of whom he had many, for he had rigorously attacked the hypocrisies of the upper classes. The play was banned, rewritten, and banned again. His enemies, however, could hardly denounce the final version without denouncing the king himself. This drama, then, played a central part in Molière's struggle for personal acceptance as well as for the acceptance of a socially honest and significant comedy.

Comparative: Other plays of Molière *(The Misanthrope, The Ridiculous Précieuses, The Bourgeois Gentleman,* and *Don Juan)* satirize the hypocrisies and pretensions of his time and are a perennial part of the human scene. Voltaire's *Candide,* a century later, offers a different but equally effective satire on our tendency to believe what we want to believe. Robert Frost's *The Mask of Reason* and Archibald MacLeish's *J.B.* offer fine comparisons with the religious theme. Sinclair Lewis's *Babbit* and *Elmer Gantry* are novels with excellent studies of shallowness, hypocrisy, and religiosity.

Molière, pseudonym of Jean-Baptiste Poquelin. DON JUAN. 1665. Drama. French.

Author: See *Tartuffe.*

Work: This prose tragedy in five acts is based on the old legends of Don Juan Tenorio, the compulsive lover who thinks his heart belongs to all womankind.

Don Juan, fleeing from Doña Elvira, whom he has lured from a convent with the promise of marriage but of whom he has now tired, returns with his servant Sganarelle to the town where six months before he had killed the

Commander. He is after new prey, intending to seduce a young bride as she leaves with her husband on their wedding trip. The affair, however, turns out disastrously, and Sganarelle and Don Juan are thrown into the river. They are rescued by a peasant, Peter, and Don Juan immediately begins making love to Peter's intended, Charlotte. Elvira appears and begs anew for Juan's affection. Gusman, her servant, also pleads, and Elvira's brother appears to beg Juan to reform. Don Juan laughs at all of them, even refusing to listen to the warnings of the devoted Sganarelle. The family of the murdered Commander enters, intent on exacting vengeance. In a brazen mood Don Juan visits the tomb of the Commander and invites the memorial statue to come to dinner with him. The statue does and in return invites Don Juan to sup with him. In the last scene, Don Juan fulfills his agreement and meets the Commander's statue, which seizes the rake's hand and drags him down to hell as the earth opens in flames. Sganarelle is left lamenting his back wages.

The drama is episodic with swift action and classically direct conversational explanations and justifications. Character changes, such as that of Doña Elvira (IV,ii), are not convincing because of the rapid and episodic quality of the stage narration.

Comparative: Don Juan's long literary history provides many comparisons: a play by Tirso de Molina, 1632; Mozart's opera *Don Giovanni;* Pushkin's *The Stone Guest;* Byron's *Don Juan;* George Bernard Shaw's *Man and Superman;* and others.

In one excellent passage from Molière, Charlotte speaks rustically to Peter but refines her speech when talking to Don Juan, thus illustrating the eternal adaptability of womankind which Shaw noted in *Man and Superman* and Chekhov noted in "The Darling," and which, interestingly enough, some critics see as the cause of Don Juan's compulsive chase. Sganarelle, like Figaro, merits study: fearful, speaking for the conscience of humanity and yet strangely captive to adventure, money, and perverted loyalty to the Don. A modern descendant of Molière is Courteline (1858–1929) with his world of farce and satire peopled by civil servants, officers, and concierges. Molière's two young lovers find a counterpart in Moratín's *The Maiden's Consent.*

Molière, pseudonym of Jean-Baptiste Poquelin. THE PHYSICIAN IN SPITE OF HIMSELF (LE MÉDICIN MALGRÉ LUI). 1666. Drama. French.

Author: See *Tartuffe.*

Work: In this three-act farce, a drunken woodcutter accidentally turns doctor and effects a ridiculous cure that aids a pair of distressed lovers.

To revenge herself on her husband, the woodcutter Sganarelle, Martine tells two strangers that he is a physician but will admit it only after being beaten. The strangers take Sganarelle, having convinced him that he is a physician, to cure Lucinde, who wants to marry Léandre and has feigned losing her voice to prevent a distasteful arranged marriage. Sganarelle introduces Léandre into the house disguised as an apothecary, and the lovers plan to flee. Sganarelle is exposed and threatened with hanging—but all ends happily in the nick of time. The slight story line is just strong enough to carry the humor and to support the rapid dialogue and the perennially valid jibes at the medical profession.

Molière utilizes here every trick of his trade—imposture, double take, pratfall, mistaken identity, deflation of the pompous—but manages nonetheless to create believable characters. Molière ranks among the four or five greatest comic writers for his light comedies such as this one and for the tragicomedies *Tartuffe* and *The Misanthrope*.

Comparative: The lusty humor of this play may be matched in English theater by Gay's *The Beggar's Opera* or by Goldsmith. Beaumarchais's *The Barber of Seville* and *The Marriage of Figaro* make excellent companion studies. For a current revival of farce, see Courteline's plays.

Molière, pseudonym of Jean-Baptiste Poquelin. THE SCHOOL FOR WIVES (L'ÉCOLE DES FEMMES). 1662. Drama. French.

Author: See *Tartuffe*.

Work: This Italianate comedy in five acts concerns an old man who attempts to rear and educate the perfect wife and loses her to the inevitable young man. The play has a neoclassical quality with little stage action; the absence of action, however, shows off to great advantage the wit of the speeches.

Arnolphe, a pretentious bourgeois, has changed his name to Monsieur Delafield and has had himself appointed guardian to Agnès. He has placed her in a convent school where she has been reared for thirteen years in touching innocence. When she is of age, he intends to marry her, and because she is ignorant of the world's ways he hopes not to suffer the fear of cuckoldry, which, nevertheless, he delights in observing in others. However, Horace, a young man recently arrived in Paris, has fallen in love with Agnès. Horace fails to recognize Arnolphe by his ostentatious new name (the one used by Agnès in referring to him) and innocently betrays the budding love affair to Arnolphe. With the aid of his two servants, Arnolphe sets out to circumvent this love affair and lays plan to marry Agnès immediately.

Horace and Agnès employ every trick to get together. A midnight scene reveals a ladder-and-balcony incident and the beating of Horace. Agnès runs downstairs to commiserate with Horace and is delivered by him to the care of his friend, Arnolphe—since Horace is still unaware of the double identity of

Arnolphe-Delafield. Just when things look their worst for the lovers, a *deus ex machina* arrives: Horace's father, Oronte, has arranged for Horace to marry the daughter of the wealthy Seigneur Enrique, and luckily that daughter turns out to be Agnès, who had been placed in the care of the woman from whom Arnolphe took her in guardianship. Arnolphe must acquiesce. And his friend, the cynical and worldly-wise Chrysalde, offers him this advice: "Since you're so terrified of cuckoldry, the wisest policy is not to marry."

This delightful comedy of young love comments on what marriage ought and ought not to be, and it contains every stock situation at drama's command: the midnight elopement attempt, the double identity, the concealment of Horace in Agnès's wardrobe right under Arnolphe's eyes, and so on. It is a brilliant exposé of the artificialities of seventeenth-century society (and ours) and a statement of how love conquers all.

Comparative: Many of the classical elements of comedy and character found here are also to be found in Beaumarchais's *The Barber of Seville* and Alarcon's *The Three-Cornered Hat.* In Beaumarchais, note the similarity of Figaro to Arnolphe's clever and mercenary servants. Situational comparisons may be found in Sheridan's *The School for Scandal,* in Goldsmith's *She Stoops to Conquer,* and in the plays of Wilde and Coward. Moratín's *The Maiden's Consent* also relied on similar stock situations.

Montaigne, Michel Eyquem de. ESSAYS (ESSAIS). 1580. Essays. French.

Author: Montaigne (1533–1592) was the son of a merchant-mayor of Bordeaux. As a child he was taught Latin before French, but he benefited little from his college education. He became a magistrate of the parliament of Bordeaux, but after the death of his father in 1568 Montaigne retired to the round, booklined tower of his château to write and to assume the responsibilities of a dutiful country squire. The essays, begun in 1572 are the result of years of quiet thinking and much revision.

Work: The essays, of which more than a hundred editions have been published, offer a thorough and impartial look at society, the world, and religion by a man whose motto was "What do I know?" and who proved that he knew a great deal and had intolerance only for the narrow view.

"Of Cannibals" is typical. Here Montaigne chats about the aborigines of the New World (South America), setting their customs, which strike us as odd and horrible, against European manners, which in this sudden confrontation horrify us more than those of the savages. In "Of Custom," he demonstrates how slyly the habits and manners of our peers prevent us from observing the truth—a wonderful lesson for our time, afflicted as it is by the mass media and by insidious advertising.

Montaigne was a Renaissance man, curious to know all things and desirous not for power or riches—a common enough Renaissance attitude—but to realize within himself some of the capabilities of man. It is fascinating to discover how this modest liberal, "thinking out loud" as it were, managed to arrive at the heart of problems. Montaigne insisted on the relativity of reason, and he was a major influence on Pascal, Voltaire, and Emerson.

Comparative: Bacon's essays cover many of the same topics, but his prose is pruned, disciplined, and cold compared to that of Montaigne, which is personal, easy, and often whimsical. Bacon's statements tend to be rigid, but Montaigne's allow or even suggest a contrary opinion. Bacon examines everything as a scientific principle; Montaigne looks at each subject in a context of constant change.

Moravia, Alberto, pseudonym of Alberto Pincherle. TWO ADOLESCENTS (translations of LA DISUBBIDIENZA and AGOSTINO). 1950. Novella. Italian.

Author: Alberto Moravia (1907–   ), a sophisticated novelist much read in Italy, has attained international fame as well. His satirical pen, more often than not, is directed against the complacent middle class. He is a prolific author, having written novels, short stories, film criticism, film scripts, articles, and prefaces. His work as a special correspondent for a number of newspapers has necessitated travel, and he has become familiar with the mores and values of many countries. Every successful novelist invests his novels with psychological insights, and Moravia, perhaps, more so than most. He is especially noted for his mastery of form and the creation of memorable characters. Among his books are *Woman of Rome, The Conformist,* and *Conjugal Love.*

Work: Two adolescents, Agostino and Luca, are the subjects of the two novelettes which together make up this work. The stories are unrelated to each other except that each deals with the rites of maturation. Agostino knows nothing about sex and is overly-devoted to his young, widowed, and beautiful mother, who begins a flirtation (or is it more?) with a young man she meets. The highly sensitive Agostino is driven to associate with a gang of young toughs, who initiate him into their sordid world.

Luca, who is even more shy and sensitive than Agostino, is also beset by the problems of growing up. His first love affair, a pathetic experience, causes him to retreat into a wasting illness. He is finally saved by a compassionate nurse, who gives him more than medical care.

Comparative: Any book about boys bridging the gap between boyhood and manhood will have parallels with *Two Adolescents.* Salinger's *Catcher in the Rye* is such a book, and Goethe's *The Sorrows of Young Werther* and Romain's *Jean-Christophe* are others. Thomas Mann's *Tonio Kröger* is quite a different story, though it too deals with the transition from childhood to manhood.

Murasaki, Shikibu. THE TALE OF GENJI (GENJI MONOGATARI). ca. 1000 A.D. Novel. Japanese.

Author: Murasaki, her real name is unknown, was born around 978 and died around 1026. The sobriquet "Murasaki Shikibu"—which can be translated "Lady Purple"—comes from the name of a character in her novel as well as from an office held by her father. Her father is said to have been a classical Chinese scholar, and she came from a branch of the great Fujiwara family, which ruled Japan in the name of successive emperors through most of the Heian Period. Murasaki herself served at court, where fiction and tales were important in the lives of the court ladies—"to overcome boredom" as Murasaki put it.

In addition to *The Tale of Genji,* she wrote a diary, which has been criticized severely by Japanese specialists for the inaccuracy of its translation but is nevertheless interesting reading. (*Diaries of Court Ladies of Old Japan,* translated by Annie Shepley Omori and Kochi Doi.) At the time of his death in 1976, Ivan Morris, one of the finest translators of Japanese literature, was in the process of retranslating Murasaki's diary.

Murasaki was married, but her husband died after two years; there was one child, a daughter, who became a poetess.

Work: The Tale of Genji is a long novel—perhaps the world's first novel—and it has often been compared to the unrolling of a Japanese scroll. While Prince Genji is the main character, the novel provides an avenue for a meeting with the extraordinary mind and feelings of Murasaki. She has recorded Genji's amorous affairs and gives a view of life at the court where women were very important. There was a tension in court life—a tension between the men and the many ladies in waiting. There were mild flirtations and permanent (or near permanent) alliances, all conducted with regard for the intricate etiquette of the court in an atmosphere of poetry, music, excursions, dance, and above all religion. The belief in the impermanence of all beautiful things pervades. Thus the novel is an accurate portrayal of the aesthetic and emotional life of the court of Heian Japan. It is a novel in which the characters are sensitive to the innate sadness of things, their brevity, the impossibility of love meaning everything in life. The characters are treated sympathetically, indeed empathetically. (For an elaboration of the Japanese concept of empathy, *mono no aware,* an important concept in understanding this novel, see *Literary and Art Theories in Japan* by Makota Ueda, The Press of Western Reserve University, Cleveland 1967.)

In Murasaki's view a novel does not simply consist of the author's telling a story about the adventures of some other person. On the contrary, the storyteller's experience of life, whether for good or ill, and not only events experienced but even those only witnessed or been told of, moves the storyteller to an emotion so passionate that it can no longer be kept shut up in the heart.

When reading this novel, the reader will want to keep in mind the Buddhist belief that attachment brings pain, that there is a special poignancy in happy times because of the knowledge that all is evanescent. And indeed it is with a sense of poignancy that one reads this novel, for one would like to remain forever in the company of Genji, the Shining Prince.

Comparative: While many critics have compared *The Tale of Genji* with *Remembrance of Things Past* by Proust, the aesthetic sensibility might better be compared with *The Lost Lady* by Willa Cather and *The Earthly Paradise* and *Break of Day* by Colette. As writers, these three women have much in common: the delight in beauty, the pursuit of the aesthetic in writing style and in life, and the knowledge of the poignancy of partings.

An interesting comparison can be made with *The Sound of the Mountain* by Yasunari Kawabata. For a contrast in Japanese sensibilities compare *The Tale of Genji* with fiction of the Genroku Period (1688-1703). See, for example, *The Floating World in Japanese Fiction* by Howard Hibbett. For a study of Heian aesthetics, see *The World of the Shining Prince: Court Life in Ancient Japan* by Ivan Morris.

The influence of Murasaki on Japanese contemporary literature can be seen in *The Bridge of Dreams*, a novella by Junichiro Tanizaki in *The World of Japanese Fiction* edited by Yoshinobu Hakutani and Arthur O. Lewis. While there is no competent translation of the Chinese classic *The Dream of the Red Chamber* by Ts'ao Chan to include in this guide as a separate entry, the work nevertheless, makes an interesting comparison with *The Tale of Genji,* especially the distinctions between the writing styles of China and Japan, and between Chinese and Japanese aesthetic sensibilities.

Nagai, Kafū, pseudonym of Nāgai Sokichi. THE RIVER SUMIDA (SUMIDA-GAWA). 1909. Novella. Japanese.

Author: Kafū Nagai was born in Tokyo on December 3, 1879, the unluckiest day in the whole Chinese cycle of sixty days according to the Chinese almanac. His district was on the outskirts of the city and he witnessed during his lifetime the growth of urban sprawl, making his district neither country nor city. Like many writers of the Meiji era, he read French novels and other Western works; yet, his work is deeply rooted in traditional Japanese art, Kabuki theater, classical dancing and music, and the popular art of the traditional storyteller. After trips to America and France he wrote *Tales of America* and *Tales of France* and translated some of the French poets. He died in 1959.

Kafū the Scribbler: The Life and Writings of Nagai Kafū by Edward Seidensticker, contains a critical study of Kafu and translations of several works including *The River Sumida.*

Work: *The River Sumida* reflects the Japanese sensibility in its restrained use of language to suggest rather than to detail—not to fill the cup but to let the reader "empty" the cup or fill in the details. The tale is about Chokichi's childhood and growth in a world where beauty and life are fleeting—the Buddhist concept that is the theme of so much Japanese literature. The story documents Chokichi's discovery of the evanescent nature of life:

> It was clear to Chokichi, as he thought of winter this year and last year, last year and the year before, as he went back through the years—it was clear to him how much happiness a person loses as he grows up. In the days before he started to go to school, he had been able to sleep as long as he wanted on cold mornings—and the cold had not bothered him as it did now. On days when there was rain and a cold wind, he had in fact particularly enjoyed going out to play. How different it was now—how hard to tramp through the frost on Imado Bridge early in the morning, and in the afternoon to hear the cold wind in the old trees of the Matchi grove, and to see the evening light so early! And what new trials would each coming year bring to him? Never quite so vividly as this December had Chokichi known the sorrow of the passing days.

The novella is as much to be appreciated for its style as for its story. In technique, a few sharp details often create a character, much as a few strokes of the Japanese painter's brush create a misty, elegiac scene. Impressionistically, it is as if there were a fog, and one sees the characters and scenes through this mistiness.

Comparative: For fine detail in writing and sensuousness of style, this novella may be compared with *The Break of Day* by Colette. The theme of the transitory nature of reality is found in much of Japanese literature, and this work might be read with Murasaki's *The Tale of Genji* and selections from *The Penguin Book of Japanese Verse* edited and translated by Geoffrey Bownas. The character of Chokichi may be compared with that of other adolescents, for example, in Younghill Kang's *The Grass Roof* and Mirok Li's *The Yalu Flows*.

Natsume, Sōseki, pseudonym of Kinnosuke Natsume. BOTCHAN. Translated by Umeji Sasaki. C. E. Tuttle, 1977. 1906. Novel. Japanese.

Author: Sōseki Natsume was born in Tokyo in 1867. He graduated from Tokyo University, became an English teacher in Japan, and went on to study for three years in London. He returned to succeed Lafcadio Hearn as Lecturer in English Literature at Tokyo University and began his writing career with

Botchan. Among his better known works are *I Am a Cat, The Three-Cornered World, Mon* ("The Gate"), *The Wayfarer, Sanchivō*, and *Kokoro.* He was a student of Zen Buddhism and Chinese classics as well as English literature. His work is noted for its fine psychological analysis of human actions, and his wry humor depends largely on Japanese rituals and manners. He died in 1916, having established for himself a permanent place in Japanese literature.

Work: Botchan is Sōseki's most popular novel among young people, and students in America will prove no exception. As the translator, Umeji Sasaki, observes in his forward: "The hero . . . unites in himself contradictory traits of character: he is rash, driving, hasty, he is like a locomotive puffing and pulling; yet he is honest, simple and frank. He never says or does what he does not mean. He never flatters, he is 'yes' or 'no'. There is no halfway in him. Young folks cannot read the book without loving him."

This novel offers a marvelous contrast to the poetic qualities of fragility and fleeting beauty we often associate with Japanese literature. Instead, Botchan is of human flesh, a person we love, a man we laugh at and with. In addition, he embodies in many ways the new ideals of a new Japan, which, again according to Umeji Sasaki, must "with her honest, simple, frank democratic ways . . . come to speak and act in world terms." In this respect, Sōseki was prophetic, for Botchan was originally published in 1906.

Comparative: This is a novel of manners and might be read with other novels of manners. *Botchan* shares some characteristics with *Monkey*, the Chinese novel attributed to Wu Ch'eng-en, and it may also be compared with films directed by Kon Ichikawa: *Mr. Pu (Pu-san)*, a film based on Taizo Yokoyama's popular comic strip that follows the foibles of a good-hearted school teacher while portraying the poverty, exhaustion, and apprehension of the immediate post-World War II era; and *A Billionaire (Okuman Choja)*, a dark comedy about the postwar struggles of the "little man," here a helpless employee in an income tax office who is forever getting into trouble because of his honesty. Sōseki Natsume's famous novel *I Am a Cat* is also available on film. For information about the availability and sources of films write to the Japan Society, 333 East 47th Street, New York City.

Neruda, Pablo, pseudonym of Ricardo Eliezer Neftalí Reyes y Basoalto. SELECTED POEMS. Edited by Nathaniel Tarn. 1970. Poetry. Chilean.

Author: Pablo Neruda (1904-1973) was awarded the Nobel Prize for literature in 1971. Born in Parral, Chile, son of a railroad worker, Neruda attended schools at Temuco and the Instituto Pedagógico in Santiago during the twenties. He was a student of the poet Gabriela Mistral, herself a Nobel winner. Neruda identified himself with the Communist cause and became a member of the Central Committee of the Chilean party. He served in several political capacities, and his politics greatly influenced the direction of his poetry. He was a Chilean Consul in Burma, Ceylon, and Java during the late twenties and early thirties and later at Buenos Aires, Thailand, Cambodia, Annam, and Madrid. He served the embassy in Mexico City from 1939 to 1941. Returning to Chile he was elected to serve as a Communist senator, whereupon he charged President González Videla with selling out to the United States. He lost the court case, traveled on to Italy, France, and Red China, and finally returned to Chile in 1953. He was awarded the Stalin Peace Prize in 1953 and the National Prize of Literature, the highest literary award in Chile. From 1971 until 1973 he served as Ambassador to Paris. He died in Chile only twelve days after the overthrow of the government in September 1973.

Neruda's output has been prodigious, and he has greatly influenced modern Latin American writing. His best known works in America are *Selected Poems: A Bilingual Edition,* 1970, edited by Nathaniel Tarn; *Twenty Poems of Pablo Neruda,* translated by James Wright and Robert Bly; and *The Heights of Macchu Picchu,* translated by Nathaniel Tarn, 1967.

Neruda himself has served as a translator, rendering *Romeo and Juliet* into his native language in 1964.

Work: Tarn's *Selected Poems* contains selections from fourteen of Neruda's works. Not only has he been called the greatest of all Latin American poets, but he has also been labeled the Whitman of Latin America. Actually, because of his vast production, Neruda appears to be many poets fashioned into one.

In "Body of a Woman" from *Veinte poemas de Amor* (1924), he writes of sensual desire. In the representative poems from *Residencia en la tierra, I* (1933), his direction changes as he offers us his personal despair. Still, he affirms an elemental harmony between man and nature. In "Love, America (1400)" from *Canto General* (1950), he shows a close identification with Walt Whitman:

> Before wig and frockcoat
> where the rivers, the arterial rivers,
> the cordilleras, on whose scraped escarpments
> the condor or the snow seemed immobile. . . .

In "The Names" from *Una casa en la arena* (1966), he lists those writers who have influenced him not only as examples but also as companions. Neruda concludes:

> Why did they leave so soon? Their names will not
> slip down from the rafters. Each one of them was
> a victory. Together they were my sum of light.
> Now: a short anthology of my sorrows.

Because Neruda attempts to show us the complete and universal man, anything to him is a fit subject for a poem. As one critic remarked, "What Picasso is to painting, Neruda is to poetry."

Comparative: Neruda admits to the influences of Walt Whitman and Rubén Darío. Their guidance is particularly obvious in the earlier poems, but equally pronounced is the Marxian political influence and a mystical strain akin to William Blake's.

Nguyen, Ngoc Bich, editor. A THOUSAND YEARS OF VIETNAMESE PO-
ETRY. Translated by Nguyen Ngoc Bich with Burton Raffel and W. S.
Merwin. Alfred A. Knopf, 1975. Poems. Vietnamese.

Authors: The two hundred or so poems in this collection were selected from a thousand years of poetic tradition; yet they reflect a distinctive culture, even as that culture has absorbed strains from China and France, even as that culture has been irredeemably modified in the twentieth century by the impact of the Communists and the Americans.

Work: The selections share themes with poems from Japan and China: the influence of Buddhism and Confucianism, war and separation, celebrations of nature, and reflections on birth, age and death. The vigorousness of the folk poetry dispel any notion one might have of a fragile people. The Vietnamese poets speak in such multiple voices that the anthology cannot be characterized in general terms, but all of the poems are direct and accessible. Life for the Vietnamese has seldom held long periods of tranquility, and the war poems written throughout the centuries are of special interest, including those by contemporary poets.

Comparative: Those who wish to make a more thorough study of Vietnamese poetry than these poems allow will enjoy *The Tale of Kieu* by Nguyen Du, translated and annotated by Huynh Sanh Thong. This long narrative poem by the poet-statesman Nguyen Du is a story of romance and sacrifice. It should be read, however, with some reservations about the quality of the translation.

Selections from Nguyen's *A Thousand Years of Vietnamese Poetry* are appropriate in the study of world poetry and world literature, especially when that study is based on a thematic approach: love, war, separation, religion, nature, death. Selections, of course, are also useful in the study of East Asian poetry and literature. For those comparisons see selections in this work under China, Japan, and Korea.

Another work with which this anthology might be compared are *Li Po and Tu Fu,* poems selected and translated with an introduction and notes by Arthur Cooper. (See, in particular, "Ballad of the Army Waggons," a war poem that might be compared with the Vietnamese poem "Lament for a Warrior's Wife.") Also *Mother and Son: The Wartime Correspondence of Isoko and Ichiro Hatano* translated by Margaret Shenfield; *Love Protest: Chinese poems from the Sixth Century B.C. to the Seventeenth Century A.D.,* edited and translated by John Scott; and *Poems from Korea: A Historical Anthology* compiled and translated by Peter H. Lee.

Palacio Valdés, Armando. JOSÉ. 1885. Novel. Spanish.

Author: Palacio Valdés (1853-1938), contemporary of Valera, Pérez Gladós, and Unamuno, reacted against the naturalistic trend of his times, especially the *groseros excesos* of French naturalists like Zola. The characters and scenery of this novel are based on his youthful vacations on the Spanish coast. As seems so often to be true of European literary men, Valdés was a lawyer who turned to writing.

Work: José, a prosperous fisherman from Rodillero and the bastard son of Señora Teresa, loves Elisa, daughter of Señora Isabel, who manages the village store and rules the town with her harsh economics and her harsher tongue. When José asks Señora Isabel for Elisa's hand, the storekeeper is unwilling to make the match. The business she manages is really the inheritance of Elisa, and the shrewish old woman does not want to give it up. Señora Isabel and Señora Teresa have several terrible battles (reminiscent of the hairpulling women in Zola's *L'Assommoir*). Their wedding postponed, José and Elisa grow more and more unhappy.

Señora Isabel tricks the village idiot into cutting the cable of José's fishing boat on a stormy night. This stroke of bad luck and a long winter of poor fishing bankrupt José, and Señora Isabel feels assured that she has made the marriage impossible. The lovers, though separated, meet at night. Finally, acting as a *deus ex machina,* the old, poverty-stricken lord of the village, last of his race, Señor de Meira, sells his family home and gives José the proceeds to finance a new boat. This beneficent aristocrat also contrives to steal Elisa legally away from her mother's guardianship and to establish a separate residence so that the pair may marry. Happy at last, the lovers are saddened when the body of the starved Señor de Meira is discovered, but they set their wedding date.

Comparative: Other works offering sketches of a fisherman's life are Verga's *The House by the Medlar Tree,* Synge's *Riders to the Sea,* Mishima's *The Sound of Waves,* Pierre Loti's *Iceland Fisherman,* Melville's *Moby Dick,* and Hemingway's *The Old Man and the Sea.* The sacristan's wife who places a curse on José, in Palacio Valdés's novel is a stock figure in Spanish literature; see Fernando de Rojas's *Celestina.*

Pasternak, Boris. DOCTOR ZHIVAGO (DOKTOR ZHIVAGO). 1957. Novel. Russian.

Author: Pasternak (1890-1960) was born in Moscow, the son of a distinguished painter and a concert pianist. Despite an early passion for music, he studied philosophy and was graduated from Moscow University. After his first volume of poetry was published in 1914, he became associated with various experimental and symbolist writers, including Blok and Mayakovsky.

These poems and those he wrote until 1932 praised the Revolutionary movement, but Pasternak came increasingly under attack for not conforming to socialist-realist ideology. In 1934 he ceased publishing, devoting himself mainly to translating masterpieces of English and German literature. From 1946 until Stalin's death in 1953 he was again under attack for his ideology and again ceased publishing, but during this period he began serious work on his novel *Doctor Zhivago.* Banned in the Soviet Union, it was published in Italy in 1957. Pasternak was awarded the Nobel Prize in 1958 but was forced to decline it.

Work: Pasternak's claim that his art is a record of the displacement of reality through emotion helps to explain the strange mixture of romanticism and realism in this novel. Although the cataclysmic events of the Russian Revolutions and World War I form its background, the novel's main concern is the personal response and development of its protagonist, Yuri Zhivago—his upbringing among the Moscow intelligentsia, his initial enthusiasm for the Revolution, his gradual rejection of the Revolution's goals, and his growing struggle to preserve his individual personality in the face of Marxist collectivism. Zhivago's refusal to take sides is not a refusal to commit himself but rather a refusal to surrender his individuality to any collective whole.

Believing initially that the Revolution will free the individual personality, Zhivago welcomes the Marxist uprising, only to learn that the new government has replaced one form of slavery with another. Zhivago is thus forced to seek life's meaning in his personal development as a poet and in the expression of an intensely personal communion with the world. It is this desire for personal development that forms the core of his affair with Lara, for with her he feels most intensely his own individuality as well as his relation to the "total design of the universe." She thus plays a role which his wife, Tonya, could not, and Zhivago's struggle to return to Lara comes to symbolize this individual's struggle to develop his full potential and to discover a personal mission within the grand design. Thus Zhivago becomes a Messianic figure, and his poems express this Christ-like role.

Comparative: As a novel concerned with the fate of individuals played out against the backdrop of history, Pasternak's work might be compared with Dicken's *A Tale of Two Cities,* Tolstoi's *War and Peace,* Sholokhov's *The Silent Don,* or the novels of Sir Walter Scott (which Pasternak translated). Pasternak's work, however, differs from that of Tolstoi, Sholokhov, or Scott in that the individual's response to history rather than the history of a nation is his main concern.

Like Mann's *Magic Mountain, Doctor Zhivago* traces the individual's initial seduction by and eventual rejection of collectivist ideologies; like Zamyatin's *We* and Orwell's *1984,* it warns that an attempt to solve humanity's problems through a dehumanizing system is doomed. Like Solzhenitsyn's *One Day in the Life of Ivan Denisovich,* Pasternak's novel insists on the preservation of individual dignity and human brotherhood in the face of such a dehumanizing threat.

Echoes of Goethe's *Faust,* which Pasternak also translated, are found throughout the novel, particularly in its view that one must always err in the struggle to develop, but that only by continuing to strive can one discover true individuality and establish a personal relationship with the universe.

Pérez Galdós, Benito. DOÑA PERFECTA. 1876. Novel. Spanish.

Author: Pérez Galdós (1843–1920) was born in the Canary Islands and went to Spain for his higher education. His life was devoted to the creation of literary sequences something like Balzac's *Comédie humaine,* for Galdós wrote a cycle of forty-six historical novels, *Episodios nacionales,* as well as a long sequence of naturalistic psychological novels, *novelas españolas contemporáneas.* Many consider Galdós to be Spain's greatest novelist after Cervantes.

Work: To Orbajosa, noted for its garlic culture (and that is not the only thing that smells about this town), comes Pepe Rey. He intends to see his inherited lands for the first time, to make a government metallurgical survey, and to claim the hand of his cousin Rosario in marriage. Almost as soon as he is installed in the house of his aunt, Doña Perfecta, he has the ill luck to express his scientific and liberal ideas to the village priest, Padre Inocencio. The priest is scandalized, and Pepe's aunt, a blue-stocking aristocrat and petticoat dictator of the town's society, begins a vicious series of plots to discredit Pepe. Nevertheless, the two young people fall in love, and Rosario is kept locked in her room.

The owners of the land adjacent to Pepe's holdings begin a barrage of legal suits against him, and gossip begins its machinations. Though friendly to Pepe on the surface, Doña Perfecta organizes a cadre against him and is responsible for the loss of his metallurgical appointment. An army commander billeted in the Doña's house agrees to help Pepe win the hand of Rosario and arranges for the conveyance of love letters. Pepe and Rosario arrange to meet in the garden one night but Doña Perfecta discovers the plan and catches Pepe. Her companion, a minor brigand named Caballuco, shoots and kills Pepe at Doña Perfecta's command. In the satiric epilogue, Pepe's death is attributed to suicide, and Rosario loses her mind. Consumed with guilt, Padre Inocencio and even Doña Perfecta herself decline into illness.

The opposing forces in this novel are traditionalism and progress, religious orthodoxy and scientific determinism—and thus the story poses a rather modern conflict.

Comparative: Bazarov, the young intellectual in Turgenev's *Fathers and Sons,* dies as uselessly as Pepe. Dr. Stockman, in Ibsen's *An Enemy of the People,* presents another would-be reformer in conflict with his town. Another outsider who disturbs the conservative peasant world is Charles Grandet in Balzac's *Eugénie Grandet;* and the evenings "at home" of Doña Perfecta and the Grandets are amusingly similar. Pepe also resembles Raskolnikov in Dostoevski's *Crime and Punishment,* and *Fathers and Sons.* The machinating old woman reminds us of the central character of Fernando de Roja's *Celestina.* Doña Perfecta rules her household autocratically, as does the mother in García Lorca's *The House of Bernarda Alba.* The rebellious chieftain and rascal Caballuco is much like the brigands in Mérimée's *Colomba.*

Other small towns that fight the ideas of the outside world are found in Lewis's *Main Street* and Flaubert's *Madame Bovary.* The morally diseased small town is also presented in Sartre's *The Flies,* in Lope de Vega's *Fuenteovejuna,* in Dürrenmatt's *The Visit,* in Giraudoux's *The Enchanted,* in Gerstäcker's *Germelshausen,* and in Mark Twain's *The Man That Corrupted Hadleyburg.*

Petrarch (Francesco Petrarcha). SONNETS. 1374. Poems. Italian.

Author: Petrarch (1304-1374) is generally considered a Florentine, though he was born in Arezzo, where his family lived in political exile from Florence. Petrarch showed signs of intellectual brilliance early and became the first, and greatest, humanist. He diligently searched out old and important manuscripts and had them copied. He was a dedicated scholar of antiquity and a flawless writer in Latin. Indeed, some scholars date the Renaissance from 1341, the year Petrarch was crowned poet laureate in Rome. Ironically, though he set great store by them, Petrarch's Latin works are seldom read today, but his songs and poems in Italian remain popular. Petrarch is regarded as second only to Dante in Italian literature.

Work: The sonnet, a highly disciplined verse form, originated in Italy in the early thirteenth century, and Petrarch brought it to perfection. The Petrarchan (or Italian) sonnet is divided into two sections, the octave and the sestet. The two parts convey a question and an answer, a situation and a result, a cause and an effect; and the interlocked fourteen lines are admirably suited to convey a single idea.

Most of Petrarch's sonnets, and some of his other poetry as well, are written to or about Laura. Laura, whose exact identity cannot be confirmed, was apparently married and somewhat younger than Petrarch. She was beautiful, of course, but his feelings for her reflected a kind of being in love with love. He had no thought of knowing her intimately, but he admired her from afar—and wished the situation to remain that way. His love for Laura was in the tradition of courtly love, and such love conceived of ladies as the gentle tamers of men and paragons of virtue and high-mindedness. They were loved more as ideals and aspirations than as flesh-and-blood people. The lover's adoration for his lady was pure and selfless. Through his uncorrupted love, he elevated himself to a plane of spirituality that could lead to the love of God.

Petrarch's sonnets are tender, sensitive, and individualistic. They are eloquent, subtle, and moving. Largely because of these sonnets, later poets turned to love-sick melancholy as a source for their verses.

Comparative: Petrarch's idealized love for Laura parallels Dante's love for Beatrice and Boccaccio's love for Fiametta, and each wrote sonnets to or about their lady loves. Comparing these highly circumspect love affairs provides a point of entry into the writing and thinking of the three poets. Because Petrarch was largely responsible for motivating the sonnets of Wyatt and Surrey—and Sir Philip Sydney and Shakespeare, among others—a study of their sonnets, in the English form, is appropriate. The theme of courtly love found in Petrarch can also be observed in Mallory's *Morte d'Arthur* and in the tales of courtly love found in *The Decameron* by Boccaccio and *The Canterbury Tales* by Chaucer.

Petronius (Gaius Petronius Arbiter). THE SATYRICON. 1st Century A.D. Novel. Roman.

Author: All the information we possess about Petronius comes from Tacitus. Petronius was an intimate friend of the emperor Nero and seems to have been the Director-in-Chief of Imperial Revels *(arbiter elegantiae)* until treasonous slander forced him to commit suicide in about 66 A.D. Evidence suggests that this Petronius was in fact the author of *The Satyricon.*

Work: Fragments of two books discovered in Dalmatia in 1663 are all that remain of the original work, which was probably twenty books long. *The Satyricon* is a kind of picaresque novel about Encolpius, Asclytus, and Giton, three knavish young men who wander through southern Italy, carousing, clashing with authority, living by their wits. Its longest and best known episode is "Trimalchio's Banquet." Trimalchio is a *nouveau riche* who thinks only of wealth and of displaying his learning, although he often fails to carry off such displays. Roman society is satirized at length: its illiteracy and superstition; its posturing poets, professional rhetoricians, pompous academics, and legacy hunters. All varieties of language are used, from street Latin to the most inflated rhetoric, and dialogue is admirably suited to character. Unfortunately, much of the literary parody and many of the allusions are lost to us now.

Comparative: As the earliest example of a novel, *The Satyricon* is vivid and picaresque in the mode of Le Sage's *Gil Blas* and Smollett's *Roderick*

Random. As a Menippean satire (verse satire with prose interludes, dealing with a range of attitudes), it compares with Boethius' *On the Consolation of Philosophy,* Apuleius' *The Golden Ass,* and works of Rabelais. By contrast with other Roman satire, it is far more comic; neither Horace nor Juvenal is so light-hearted. Even Nabokov's *Lolita,* a recent example of Menippean satire, lacks such gaiety. As a mock-heroic work *The Satyricon* is comparable to Pope's *Dunciad* and Byron's *Don Juan.* Beyond these similarities, *The Satyricon* remains unique in its combination of raunchiness, variety, and comprehensive vision. Its hero, Trimalchio, is a comic creation in his own right, like Don Quixote or Falstaff.

Pindar (Pindaros). ODES. 498–446 B.C. Poems. Greek.

Author: Of this Greek choral poet (518/522–ca. 438 B.C.) we know only certain details: that he was born in a village near Thebes of an aristocratic family, that he was educated in Athens in music and poetry, that he became a professional poet and the friend of kings and aristocrats in a period of considerable political turmoil (the Persian invasion occurred in 480–479 B.C.), that he was employed by various states and princes to write choral odes, and that he was considered the greatest lyric poet in the Greek world.

Work: Forty-five of Pindar's victory odes *(epinicia)* survive, along with fragments of other kinds of choral poems *(paeans, dithyrambs, partheneia)* discovered since 1900 at Oxyrhynchus and Hermopolis. Alexandrian scholars divided his work into seventeen books, of which the victory odes comprise four. These odes celebrated the victories of athletes at various national games; there are fourteen Olympian odes, twelve Pythian, eleven Nemean, and eight Isthmian. Choirs of men or boys sometimes sang these at the scene of victory, sometimes at a celebration in the victor's home. The contest itself is never described; rather, mythical associations with the victor's family or town are used as the thematic focus. In Pythia 1, the mythical allusions are scattered; in Pythia 4, the story of Jason is nearly a self-contained episode. Nemea 6 is exceptional in its exclusion of mythical material and its entirely personal focus. The difficult allusions and mythical material in some odes continue to puzzle scholars (e.g., Olympia 9), but others are limpid, relying directly on chronicle rather than on allusion (e.g., Olympia 10). Sometimes the connection between myth and family or town is no longer clear—as in Olympia 7, which celebrates the famous Diagoras of Rhodes.

The odes vary in length from twenty-four to nearly three hundred lines, averaging about one hundred. They are modeled on the choruses in drama (cf. Aeschylus and others) and have a triadic structure: that is, they are written in series of identical triads in which the first stanza (strophe) is sung with the chorus dancing to the left, the second (antistrophe) with the chorus dancing to the right, and the final one (epode) with the chorus standing still. Generally there is an imposing opening passage. Most of the content (specific myths and allusions) would have been specified by the person commissioning the poem, and Pindar wove his hymns of praise and thanksgiving around those elements. The long Pythia 4 is probably Pindar's masterpiece. From the earliest ode (Pythia 10, 498 B.C.) to the last extant ode (Pythia 8, 446 B.C.), one observes the same depth of religious sentiment, the same brilliant language, the same elevated thought.

Comparative: Pindar has influenced profoundly the course of European literature. His influence on Horace was important, though Horace himself pointed out the dangers of trying to rival Pindar. The Renaissance discovered Pindar after it had discovered Horace, and his influence was consequently more intense. During the mid-sixteenth century, both Italian and French poets attempted to rival Pindar. Ronsard (1524-1585) and his fellow poets of the Pléiade set out to synthesize classical modes and French poetry. Imitations of Pindar also flourished in England. Milton's "On the Morning of Christ's Nativity," written Christmas morning, 1629, is the first Pindaric poem in English. Others include John Dryden's "Alexander's Feast" (1687), set to music by Handel, and Gray's "Progress of Poesy" (1754). Collins and Keats are other descendants. Wordsworth's "Intimations of Immortality" (1802-1804) counts among the world's finest irregular odes. In Germany, Goethe, Schiller, and Hölderlin admired Pindar and wrote Pindaric poems.

The attraction of Pindar's imagery, his sense of occasion, his emotional intensity and eloquence, and the comparative freedom of his form (by contrast with the homostrophic Horatian ode) have inspired both great poems and rubbish. Pindar's control of his material is masterful, if turbulent, and few of his imitators have commanded both his technical control and his emotional force. The twentieth century, it must be acknowledged, finds his spiritual energy appealing but his themes remote, his allusions difficult.

Pirandello, Luigi. SIX CHARACTERS IN SEARCH OF AN AUTHOR (SEI PERSONAGGI IN CERCA D'AUTORE). 1921. Drama. Italian.

Author: Luigi Pirandello (1867-1936), Nobel Prize winner and author of forty-three plays, three hundred short stories, and numerous other writings, was born in Girgenti, Sicily. He studied at Palermo and at the University of Rome and took his doctor's degree at Bonn. He was already writing at eighteen, using ideas and characters drawn from his life. Pirandello's life was often unhappy, for, among other troubles, he had a wife who was mad. In his writing he wrestled with two themes—uncertainty and the nature of reality. His writing, filled with complexities about what is real and what is illusory, teems with intentional ambiguities. Characters are not realistic; instead, they are puppets working out Pirandello's message, which is that all is transitory.

Work: Six Characters in Search of an Author is a profound play that can be read and acted on several levels. It examines life, artistic creation, and the theater. As Pirandello does in so many of his works, he slips back and forth between reality and unreality, and the bemused reader and playgoer are left with many questions.

The play opens with a director and cast rehearsing a play by Pirandello. The rehearsal is going badly when six people walk in and announce themselves as characters in a play abandoned by the author. They are characters, not actors, so obviously they are not real. Or are they? In his stage directions Pirandello avers that they are more real than real people. The characters plead to be allowed to work out their roles, and the director, since his rehearsal is going badly anyway, gives them permission. The characters turn out to be a family group—father, mother, step-daughter, a four-year old son, another daughter, and another son, age twenty-two. Theirs is a bitter, ugly story, seething with strife and anguish. Among other details, the father nearly has physical relations with his step-daughter at the establishment where she works as a whore. Then there is the sordid life the mother has lived with a male secretary and the three illegitimate children she has had by him. At a point in this drama, the actors on stage begin acting out the roles of these characters. Now what is real, and what is unreal? The characters protest that they are not being properly interpreted by the actors and take over the stage again to act out their roles to the dismal end. The director shrugs his shoulders and returns to his rehearsal.

Comparative: Pirandello's manner of blending the real and unreal is peculiarly his own, although Eugene O'Neill in *A Long Day's Journey into Night* treats the same theme, as does Edward Albee in *Who's Afraid of Virginia Woolf?* Friedrich Dürrenmatt was influenced by Pirandello and has in his plays something of the same tragic juxtaposition of real and unreal. His play *The Visit* especially echoes Pirandello.

Plautus, Titus Maccius. THE TWIN MENAECHMAE (MENAECHMI). ca. 190 B.C. Drama. Latin.

Author: Few details are known about the life of Rome's famous writer of comedy. Born about 254 B.C. of humble Umbrian origin, Plautus seems to have gone to Rome where he made sufficient money working in the theater (in an unknown capacity) to establish himself briefly in business before going bankrupt. While poor and working in a flour mill, apparently, he began writing plays, managing to earn for himself both a living and some considerable reputation. He died about 184 B.C.

Of the 130 plays reputedly written by Plautus, twenty-one survive and have been established as genuine. Though scholars do not know enough about Greek New Comedy to determine what Plautus took directly from the Greek plays, he confessed to borrowing plots and situations, freely adapting them to suit his own dramatic purposes. He preserved in his comedies the Greek trappings (dress, names, situations), managing thereby to avoid offending his countrymen with coarse banter and depictions of vice. Where his Greek comic models relied mainly on dialogue, Plautus added song and dance, creating a kind of musical comedy. The audience was abused in direct address, a practice going back to the *parabases* or Aristophanes. Verbally, Plautus was highly inventive, using every variety of wordplay and joke, even inventing new words to supplement his lively colloquial Latin.

Work: The Twin Menaechmae, Plautus' best known comedy, exploits the farcical possibilities of mistaken identity. (The setting throughout is the standard Roman one: a street in front of two houses.) A pair of Sicilian twins had been separated at an early age. Menaechmus had accompanied his father on a business trip and was kidnapped; Sosicles, having remained home, was thereafter called Menaechmus by his grief-stricken parents. Searching for his lost brother, Sosicles-Menaechmus arrives finally at Epidamnus where, unbeknownst to him, Menaechmus has become a substantial citizen. Sosicles-Menaechmus becomes involved in situations where he is confused with his twin by the latter's wife, by the parasite (a stock character in Roman comedy), and by his mistress. The confusion of Sosicles' own slave adds further comical complication. At last, of course, the brothers meet and the mysteries are solved.

Comparative: This play is best known as the source of Shakespeare's *Comedy of Errors,* although Shakespeare added the theme of parental danger as well as further plot complications. Numerous other plays have clearly been based on this and other Plautinian comedies, since they are a veritable storehouse of comic situations and characters. Popular during the late Republic and Empire but ignored during the Middle Ages, the comedies of Plautus were rediscovered and have been continually readapted by major and minor playwrights. His *Pot of Gold* became Molière's *The Miser,* and Pyrogopolynices, his braggart soldier, became a perennial stock character, especially as the braggart captain of the Elizabethan stage. Giraudoux's *Amphitryon 38* may not literally be the thirty-eighth version of Plautus' play in which the myth surrounding the birth of Heracles is travestied, but it ranks alongside the versions of Dryden and Molière.

POEM OF THE CID (CANTAR DEL CID or POEMA DE MIO CID). ca.1140.
     Epic poem. Spanish.

Author: Unknown.

Work: Based on the legendary figure of Rodrigo Díaz de Vivar, the daring and unprincipled soldier who seems to have fought on both sides of the long war between Christians and Moors, this national epic of Spain makes the Cid (a corruption of the arabic word meaning "Lord") an ideal figure of chivalry and Christian honor. The poem, in three parts, deals with his fall from high regard in the court, his exile, his successes as a soldier, his reconciliation with the King, the marriages of his daughters, their mistreatment, his revenge, and their remarriages.

Comparative: Beowulf and the *Song of Roland* are obvious comparisons. Unlike Beowulf, the Cid always remains an exalted hero and does not assume the domesticity of the Anglo-Saxon leader. The movement of this poem is made up of battle after battle, and the hero must hold together what often seems to be a confusing tapestry of medieval warfare. It is interesting to note the emphasis on religion which this epic and the *Song of Roland* share, but which in *Beowulf* is merely superimposed. Thus the French and Spanish chronicles elaborate the concept of the holy war that was to find culmination in the Crusades.

 Poem of the Cid is better matched with the *Iliad* than with the *Odyssey*, since the first two are localized in action and most of their story content is about combat. See also Corneille's treatment in *Le Cid*.

Polo, Marco. THE TRAVELS OF MARCO POLO (IL MILIONE). 1559.
  Travel narrative. Italian.

Author: Marco Polo (ca. 1254–1324), his father, and his uncle were the first Westerners to visit the distant lands of Asia. Setting out from Venice, their home city, they sought the vast domain of the Emperor Kublai Khan. Their purpose was commercial—to open new areas to trade. Arriving at the Khan's palace in 1275, Marco Polo established a warm friendship with that powerful leader and as his representative came to be entrusted with key matters. Though the emperor was unwilling to lose them, Polo's little party returned to Venice after seventeen years in his service. Altogether, the party was away from Venice for twenty-four years. Ironically, Polo was home for only three years when he was captured by the Genoese in a war between them and Venice. While imprisoned, he dictated the book of his travels to a fellow prisoner.

Work: The first printed version of *The Travels* appeared in Italian in 1559. In 1824 the French version, which scholars agree is the best, was published. In it Marco Polo appears as a man of courage, daring, wisdom, and imagination. The incredible dangers he faced, the remarkable events in which he participated, and the scarcely believable things he saw caused readers for centuries to assume the book was fiction.

 Parts of the book still read like fantasy, for some of the areas in Asia and some of the customs are still relatively unknown to Westerners. Indeed, contemporaries of Polo referred to the book as "Marco's Millions," (meaning millions of lies). The subtitle gives a rather good idea of what the book is about: "Journey from Lesser Armenia to the court of the Khan, an account of the fabulous Khan, his court, his government, Japan, Southern India, Coasts of Islands of the Indian Sea, an account of some of the Northern Countries." The book is engaging, sometimes dramatic, and filled with adventure. It is known now that it is highly accurate as well.

Comparative: Hakluyt's *Voyages,* though sometimes fanciful, parallels *The Travels* in many ways. Though Richard Halliburton's style and romanticism are dated, he, too, wrote about the exotic places he visited. Margaret Landon's *Anna and the King of Siam* recounts the trials and pleasures of an English governess working for a king in a land of unfamiliar customs and values, and that relationship can be compared to the friendship between Polo and the Khan.

Premchand, pseudonym of Dhanpat Rai Śrīvāstav. THE GIFT OF A COW (GODĀN). Translated by Gordon C. Roadarmel. Indiana University Press, 1968. 1936. Novel. Indian.

Author: Premchand (1880–1936) was born near Benares. He taught in various schools before being selected for teacher training and appointment as a sub-inspector of schools. At the age of thirty-nine he completed his B.A. and devoted himself to literature and journalism. He rejected government employment during the Gandhian protest against British rule. For Premchand, as for so many Indian writers since the early nineteenth century, social reform was a burning concern.

Work: The Gift of a Cow, a modern Hindu classic, is not only a literary work but a historical and social document as well. Premchand pre-dates Mao Tse-tung in his call for a literature that would portray noble and idealistic aspirations, and he is a kindred spirit of Murasaki in his belief that characters should bring enobling emotions into play.

The economic and social conflict in a North Indian village is graphically portrayed in the story of Hori, a typical Indian farmer, and his struggle for survival and self-respect. Grinding poverty is the Indian farmer's greatest enemy, and Hori fights it to the bitter end of his life. He cherishes the desire to make the gift of a cow to a Brahman at the time of his death, for he believes that this gift will enable him to enter heaven.

Comparative: This novel balances the widely read *Nectar in a Sieve* by Jamal Markandaya, a novel written in English for the Western reader. It might also be read with the novels of R. K. Narayan—for example, *The Financial Expert.*

Narayan is a superior storyteller, who looks with humor and candor on the Indian experience and raises it to the universal. See also *Pather Panchali (Song of the Road),* the Bengali novel by Bibhutibhushan Banerji.

The widely circulated paperback *Godān,* translated by P. Lal, does not include some of the scenes and characters that this translation of G. Roadarmel includes because Premchand wrote more than one version.

Pushkin, Aleksandr Sergeyevich. BORIS GODUNOV. 1831. Drama. Russian.

Author: Pushkin (1799-1837) was born in Moscow and educated at home until the age of twelve, when he became one of the first students at the Lyceum of Tsarskoye Selo, founded by Alexander I to educate gifted children. He was soon recognized as a promising poet with a passionate and liberal temperament. Although never himself a member of revolutionary groups, Pushkin formed many friendships with political radicals and in 1820 was exiled for circulating political poems that were considered revolutionary. In the Caucasus he fell under the spell of Byron's poetry and began writing *Eugene Onegin* and several exotic verse-tales. In 1824 he was transferred to his family estate, where he occupied his time writing and listening to his old nurse retell Russian folktales, tales that were to provide him with materials for much of his prose and folk poetry. He also studied Russian history and wrote *Boris Godunov.*

Following the failure of the Decembrist revolt, Nicholas I allowed Pushkin to return to St. Petersburg and over the next few years he finished *Eugene Onegin,* much poetry, and several short tales, including "The Queen of Spades." In 1831 he married a beautiful but flirtatious woman, and for the next six years his enemies at court spread rumors of her infidelities. In 1837 he was finally provoked into a duel, in which he was killed. Shortly thereafter, an anonymous poem, "The Death of a Poet," was circulated, accusing the tsar's court of complicity in the death of Pushkin and heralding the beginning of the equally short and brilliant career of Mikhail Lermontov.

Work: Before *Boris Godunov,* Russian plays were largely used in the academies to teach Latin and moral lessons or were merely imitations of French classical drama. Pushkin's play, written in imitation of Shakespeare's historical tragedies, freed Russian drama from the strict rules of French classicism and pointed the way toward the realist drama of later generations.

Pushkin's story is taken from history and revolves around the tyrant Boris, who has been chosen tsar following the murder, which he had ordered, of the young tsarovich Dmitri. But Boris is haunted by conscience, and the appearance of a false Dmitri, in reality an escaped monk, produces an ambivalent reaction. On the one hand, Boris sees the pretender as a threat to his dynasty, but Boris is also a guilt-ridden man who is relieved that the false Dmitri's appearance provides him with a chance to expiate his sin, or indeed to believe that the murder was never committed. It is this psychological conflict that forms the real subject of Pushkin's play. Boris dies, believing that his son will now rule without the stain which has overshadowed his own reign. But the young tsar's rule is short, and he is quickly overthrown by the false Dmitri, whose own eventual overthrow is indicated by the sullen masses, reminiscent of Shakespeare's fickle crowds.

The play is one of the finest romantic imitations of Shakespeare. Pushkin wanted realism, not French classical rules: "Verisimilitude must be in situations, and truth in dialogue—there is the real rule of tragedy." The play therefore violates the unities of time, place, and action and abandons the strict verse form of previous Russian drama for a Shakespearean mixture of prose and blank verse. But the play is not mere imitation. Its psychological exploration of the guilt-stricken Boris and its attempts to portray all the primary characters in their psychological completeness are distinctly modern and distinctly Russian.

Comparative: Pushkin was an avid reader, and many of his favorite authors have left their traces in his work. In *Boris Godunov* the most obvious influence is Shakespeare, and Pushkin's play and title character owe much to *Richard III, Henry IV,* and, especially, *Macbeth,* another man torn between ambition and conscience. This conflict later formed the central theme of Pushkin's "The Queen of Spades," and a further comparison may also be made with Dostoevski's *Crime and Punishment.*

In his attempt to create a more realistic drama and his romantic concern for totality of character rather than unity of action, Pushkin may be compared to Goethe *(Götz von Berlichingen* and *Egmont),* Schiller *(Don Carlos),* and Victor Hugo *(Hernani).*

Pushkin's play provided the inspiration for one of the greatest operas ever written, Mussorgski's *Boris Godunov,* an opera which perfectly captures the enormous scope of the original, from the psychological depths of a single figure to the broad portrayal of a nation's history.

Pushkin, Aleksandr Sergeyevich. EUGENE ONEGIN (YVGENI ONEGIN).
Begun in 1823, completed in 1831, published in 1833. Novel. Russian.

Author: See Boris Godunov.

Work: Pushkin's verse novel has often been called the first Russian novel because it is the first extended work that develops a complete and complex portrait of its hero and presents a realistic and serious portrayal of Russian life. The attitude toward the characters is, however, somewhat inconsistent, the result perhaps of Pushkin's changing fortunes during the years in which the work was written.

The novel begins with a rather sympathetic treatment of Onegin, who is largely a mask for the poet himself and provides Pushkin with a vehicle for satirizing Russian society. Onegin escapes from an endless and senseless round of aristocratic parties to a simple and equally boring life in the country. But the tone changes as Onegin becomes less identified with Pushkin and more representative of the Byronic hero and finally of the "superfluous man" so common in nineteenth-century Russian literature, the hero with remarkable capabilities who is stifled by a vain and petty society and becomes a sterile, destructive cynic.

Onegin develops a friendship with Vladimir Lenski, mostly out of amusement with Lenski's naiveté and enthusiasm. The portrait of Lenski, satirized as the misty romantic dreamer, does not reflect ill on Onegin, who is at least realistic; and Onegin's rejection of Tatyana (who like Lenski is a romantic dreamer in love with love), if it does not win our sympathies, it at least does not reduce Onegin to a heartless seducer. But when Onegin, in a fit of pique and boredom, taunts Lenski into challenging him to a duel, and Lenski is killed, the reader is confronted with a hero of considerable abilities whose cynicism has nevertheless killed an innocent man and hurt an innocent girl. We are left with a sense of poetic justice in the final rejection of Onegin by Tatyana, now an intelligent and beautiful princess with a firm understanding of reality.

Comparative: Eugene Onegin was begun during Pushkin's Byronic phase and may well be compared to the poetic tales of the English poet, particularly *Beppo, Don Juan,* and *Childe Harold's Pilgrimage,* all of which combine narrative with a satire of contemporary society. But unlike the work of Byron, Pushkin's work is not primarily satirical; rather, it is realistic, describing modern society and the type of man which that society creates. Among Byron's heroes, Childe Harold is perhaps the closest to Onegin, and parallels may be found in the hero of Goethe's *The Sorrows of Young Werther,* Chateaubriand's *Atala* and *René,* Constant's *Adolphe,* Musset's *Confessions of a Child of the Century,* and, particularly, Lermontov's *A Hero of Our Time,* whose hero was based on Onegin.

The "superfluous man" is evident in Russian literature up to the Revolution, from *Eugene Onegin,* through Dostoevski's *Crime and Punishment* and *Notes from Underground* and Turgenev's *Fathers and Sons,* to many of the heroes of Chekhov's tales. The antithesis of this unproductive hero is found in the revolutionary hero of Chernyshevski's *What Is to Be Done?* or Pasternak's *Doctor Zhivago.*

Pushkin, Aleksandr Sergeyevich. THE QUEEN OF SPADES (PIKOVAYA DAMA). 1834. Story. Russian.

Author: See *Boris Godunov.*

Work: This story, which at the beginning seems to be a romantic tale about young love but which ends in prosaic reality, firmly establishes Pushkin as a founder of the realistic style that was to bear much fruit in later generations of Russian writers. Throughout the tale the author systematically satirizes the romantic elements and emphasizes the elements which point to a rational explanation of events.

The reader is tempted at first to see Hermann, with his German ancestry, as a Byronic hero filled with passion and destined to bring doom to those who love him, and Lizaveta as an innocent girl whose love for Hermann brings about her destruction. In this light, the countess's knowledge of the magical sequence which guarantees success at the card tables, her murder by Hermann in his desire to learn her secret, and the supernatural penalty which her ghost exacts from him are elements in a romantic ghost story of crime and punishment. But the story also points to more prosaic possibilities. Hermann is, after all, not a poet but an engineer, and his love for Lizaveta is more materialistic than idealistic, inspired as it is by Tomski's tale, which now appears as a mere practical joke. Lizaveta, for her part, is perfectly paired with Hermann; however sympathetic her life as a ward makes her, her love for the engineer is as opportunistic as his is materialistic. The story of supernatural revenge thus becomes more psychological than ghostly, the result of an overdose of conscience and vodka. That this is Pushkin's intention is clearly seen in the short concluding section which firmly places each of the characters in the realistic world: Lizaveta is married and will raise a ward much as she had been raised, and Hermann is consigned to the madhouse where the real world exacts its penalty from those who mistake it for a world peopled by ghosts and avenging spirits.

Comparative: The romantic elements of this tale are largely drawn from German romantic tales, particularly those of Ludwig Tieck and E. T. A. Hoffmann, and they may be found in many of the French, English, Russian, or American writers who were influenced by the German romantic movement, for example Mérimée, Nodier, Scott, Byron, Coleridge, Dostoevski, Lermontov, Gogol, Poe, and Hawthorne. Pacts with the devil and revenge from beyond the grave may be found in many of the works by these authors as well as in numerous Gothic novels and horror stories. This romantic side of "The Queen of Spades" also forms the basis for Tchaikovski's opera of the same name.

But comparisons between Pushkin's tale and romantic ghost stories are not nearly so productive as those between it and the realistic tradition it helped engender. Certainly Gogol, in "The Overcoat," uses realistic elements to debunk romantic elements, right down to the supernatural revenge which the author explains away at the very end of the story. Similarly, the "Taman" episode of Lermontov's *A Hero of Our Time* appears romantic until a rational explanation is given.

The murderer tortured by conscience rather than by ghosts is central to Dostoevski's *Crime and Punishment* and several tales by Poe—for example, "The Tell-Tale Heart."

Perhaps most productive of all comparisons, however, is that between "The Queen of Spades" and other works in which realistic characters function in roles and situations formerly reserved for romantic figures—for example, Balzac's *Le Père Goriot*, Flaubert's *Madame Bovary*, Maupassant's *Bel-Ami*, and many of Chekhov's short stories.

Racine, Jean. ANDROMACHE (ANDROMAQUE). 1667. Drama. French.

Author: Racine (1639-1699) was orphaned early and was placed in Port-Royal Jansenist monastery for his education, which was strict, classical, and religious. Later in Paris he made friends with Boileau and Molière and embarked on a literary career that included the writing of twelve plays. Suddenly, at age thirty-seven, he renounced literature and retired to a religious life, marrying, however, on the advice of his confessor. Only twice was he coaxed back from retirement into writing, to create two religious dramas, *Esther* and *Athalie*.

Work: Andromache, a French neoclassical tragedy based on the *Aeneid* and the *Andromache* of Euripides, is a penetrating study of passion and its capacity to engender human weakness. It is "internal" drama, far removed from the more familiar stage action of openly declared conflicts.

Pyrrhus comes back to Epirus bringing as his spoils from the Trojan war Hector's widow Andromache and her son Astyanax. Pyrrhus loves Andromache, though his countrymen forbid the marriage and he is already pledged to Hermione. The Greeks send Orestes to Pyrrhus to ask that he surrender Astyanax to them so that Troy's succession may be wiped out. Orestes, however, is in love with Hermione and hopes that Pyrrhus will refuse to deliver the child so that Orestes may thus bring Hermione back to Greece. At first this turn of events seems likely, but Andromache's devotion to her dead husband angers Pyrrhus and he announces his determination to wed Hermione. Andromache then agrees to marry Pyrrhus to save her son's life, and Hermione, once more abandoned, asks love-crazed Orestes to kill Pyrrhus. This Orestes does as Pyrrhus leads Andromache to the altar. The distraught Hermione now accuses the astonished Orestes of murder and kills herself over the body of Pyrrhus. Orestes, confused and tortured with emotion, goes mad.

To simplify the tense seesaw of this story of overwhelming love and jealousy, we might say that Orestes loves Hermione who loves Pyrrhus who loves Andromache who loves Hector. But these passions all run on one-way streets and can move only from left to right. The key figure to watch in the swaying emotional battle is Hermione, who suffers intensely as Pyrrhus variously succeeds or fails in his bid for Andromache.

Comparative: Euripides' play, an obviously comparable work, is interesting for its different interpretation of the same basic plot. For treatments of women in quite different situations, see the *Medea* of Euripides, the *Antigone* of Sophocles, and the *Lysistrata* of Aristophanes. For the nature of the tragic protagonist and the concept of tragedy, consider representative drama from ancient Greece (e.g., Sophocles' *Oedipus*), from the Romantic movement (e.g., Schiller's *William Tell*), and from realism (e.g., O'Neill's *The Hairy Ape* and Gerhardt Hauptmann's *The Weavers*).

Racine, Jean. PHAEDRA (PHÈDRE). 1677. Drama. French.

Author: See *Andromache.*

Work: As in the *Hippolytus* of Euripides, Phaedra, wife of King Theseus, falls in love with Hippolytus, her stepson. She conceals her love and tries to master her passions until she believes Theseus to be dead. Then, urged on by her nurse, Oenone, she declares her love to Hippolytus. He, however, is in love with Aricia, a captive and the daughter of an enemy king. Phaedra, aghast at herself, discovers that once she has admitted the possibility of declared love to Hippolytus she has lost the power to restrain her passion.

   Theseus now returns, and Oenone takes revenge against Hippolytus for scorning her mistress by accusing him of having made advances to Phaedra. Hippolytus, however, has by now approached Aricia, proposing to rescue and marry her. Interrupted by the approach of Theseus, he leaves, asking her to follow. Theseus denounces Hippolytus and Aricia defends him. Theseus, confused, wants to hear Oenone's version of what has happened, but she has hanged herself. Word then comes of the death of Hippolytus by a raging sea monster. Phaedra takes poison and dies after denouncing Oenone as the source of her own wicked passion. Theseus is left alone to acknowledge that he is "of my own error now too well enlightened." In a last act of contrition he proposes to adopt Aricia as "my own true child."

Comparative: While the plot has essential similarities with the *Hippolytus* of Euripides, Racine's *Phaedra* is quite a different drama, told with a different purpose. It is particularly interesting to note differences in motivation and the greater emphasis on character in Racine's play. Eugene O'Neill's *Desire Under the Elms* uses the same family complications but without the nobility of character emphasized in Racine's treatment. Tennessee Williams's *A Streetcar Named Desire* offers a modern and altogether different treatment of passions run wild.

Ramanujan, A. K., trans. THE INTERIOR LANDSCAPE: LOVE POEMS
FROM A CLASSICAL TAMIL ANTHOLOGY. Indiana University Press,
1967. Poems. Indian.

Author: Fifty-one classical Tamil poets are represented in this anthology
from the first three centuries A.D. They have been translated by the distinguished A. K. Ramanujan (1929-   ), translator of *Speaking of Shiva* and
author of two volumes of poetry. As with the *Rubāiyāt,* these poems will be
remembered for their translator rather than for the fifty-one individual
poets who originally wrote them.

Work: These selections from the Tamil anthology *Kuruntokai* are exquisite
examples of mature classical poetry. In them, as their translator has stated,
"passion is balanced by courtesy, transparency by ironies and nuances of
design, impersonality by vivid detail, sparseness by richness of implication."
A conventional design provides a vocabulary of symbols, and the landscapes
of the Indian countryside become the "interior landscape" of the poems. The
poetry deals with the world of inner experience, with the love of men and
women as its ideal expression. The poems are of meetings and partings,
jealousy and betrayal—the entire cycle of love. The poems can be arranged to
form a drama, and students may wish to select and arrange poems to form
their own dramas in which two or more students might participate.

Although fifty-one poets are represented here, the poems are unified by
theme and form, a form which the translator has brilliantly conveyed through
typographic approximation. The visual shape of the poem on the page becomes a means of communicating the total design. An example is found in
the quiet and dramatic beauty of a poem spoken by "she":

> Only the thief was there, no one else.
> And if he should lie, what can I do?
>   There was only
>   a thin-legged heron standing
>   on legs yellow as millet stems
>   and looking
>   for lampreys
> in running water
>   when he took me.
>
>   *Kapilar*
>   *Kur 25*

Comparative: The Interior Landscape is a rare example of secular Indian
literature. (Much of the source of Indian literature is religious.) It may be
used as an introduction to Indian literature or Indian poetry in general, as
it is most accessible to the student who knows little about Indian culture.

Recommended additional readings are *In Praise of Krishna: Songs from
the Bengali* translated by Edward C. Dimock, Jr. with Denise Levertov;

An Anthology of Sanskrit Court Poetry, translated by Daniel H. H. Ingalls; and *Speaking of Shiva,* translated with an introduction by A. K. Ramanujan.

For other comparisons, see the comparative sections under the *Book of Songs* and *The Penguin Book of Japanese Verse* in this work.

For further Tamil works see *Shilappadikaram* by Prince Illango Adigal, translated by Alain Daniélou. For background on the Tamil landscape see *Landscape and Poetry, A Study of Nature in Classical Tamil Poetry,* by Xavier S. Thani Nayagam.

Remarque, Erich Maria, pseudonym of Erich Paul Remark. ALL QUIET ON THE WESTERN FRONT (IM WESTEN NICHTS NEUES). 1929. Novel. German.

Author: Erich Maria Remarque (1898-1970) was born in Osnabrück. At barely eighteen he served in World War I and was wounded in action several times. Perhaps these experiences helped him to attain the realism that gives *All Quiet on the Western Front* such immediacy. After the war he became a teacher and then an editor of a sports magazine. In 1931 he moved to Switzerland. Two years later when Hitler came to power in Germany, Remarque's books were burned and he was stripped of his German citizenship. In 1937 he went to the United States and was granted citizenship in 1947. He spent the remainder of his life primarily in the United States.

Though Remarque is not recognized as a great author, he is a master of narration and realistic characterization, and his works lose little in translation. *All Quiet on the Western Front,* his major achievement, is the first book in a trilogy which includes *The Way Back* (1931) and *Three Comrades* (1938).

Work: Perhaps the most successful of modern war novels, this book is concerned with the "lost generation" of German youth in the trench warfare of World War I. It follows the fortunes of a typical German soldier, Paul Bäumer, and of Paul's friends—Tjaden, Katczinsky, Kemmerich, Müller, Kropp, and Leer. Age twenty as the novel opens, Paul is killed about a year later on an October day in 1918 when military activity is so minimal that official reports say of it, "All quiet on the western front."

Paul's concern, and that of his friends, is simple: to stay alive if possible. In the trench warfare to which they are subjected, keeping warm and dry and having enough to eat are matters of paramount importance. Their plight is so extreme that when they do have decent food they have mixed emotions: their stomachs appreciate the food but their minds know that improved rations mean an enemy attack is imminent.

The book follows Paul into combat and back from the front several times, through the horrors of trench warfare interspersed with leave and hospital stays as a result of wounds. Along the way Paul loses one friend after another through death or maiming. A number of scenes remain permanently implanted in the mind of the reader, among them the agony of wounded horses, the bombardment of a cemetery, and Paul's feelings at killing a Frenchman in no-man's land.

Two quotes from the book clearly illustrate its anti-war message. At the beginning Remarque observes, "This book is to be neither an accusation nor a confession, and least of all an adventure, for death is not an adventure to those who stand face to face with it. It will try simply to tell of a generation of men who, even though they may have escaped its shells, were destroyed by the war." At the end, describing Paul's corpse, Remarque writes, "He had fallen forward and lay on the earth as though sleeping. Turning him over one saw that he could not have suffered long; his face had an expression of calm, as though almost glad the end had come."

Comparative: Remarque, like Stephen Crane in *The Red Badge of Courage,* presented war through the eyes of a "little man" instead of through those of the hero; see the *Aeneid,* the *Song of Roland,* or other epics, for contrast. For American statements about World War I, see Dos Passos's *Three Soldiers* and Hemingway's *A Farewell to Arms;* in these, one may contrast the psychologies of the victorious and the defeated. For similarly realistic treatments of war, see Sassoon's "Counter Attack" and "A Concert Party" or Rupert Brooke's "The Soldier."

A unit comparing young men's reactions to war as weaponry becomes more efficient and deadly might include *The Red Badge of Courage* (Civil War), *All Quiet on the Western Front* (World War I), and Nicholas Monsarrat's *The Cruel Sea* (World War II). Other excellent books dealing with World War II are John Hersey's *Hiroshima* and Ibuse Masuji's *Black Rain,* both frightening accounts of the attack on Hiroshima; Anatoly Kuznetsov's *Babi Yar,* describing the horrible massacres in Russia (events also treated in Yevgeny Yevtushenko's poem "Babi Yar"); and Heinrich Böll's novella *Within and Without,* which describes another young German soldier's reactions to war and defeat.

Burlesque treatments of the individual in wartime may be found in Voltaire's *Candide* and in Hašek's *Good Soldier Schweik.* Other propaganda efforts against war are Euripedes' *The Trojan Women* and Karel Čapek's *The Life of the Insects.*

Rilke, Rainer Maria. LETTERS TO A YOUNG POET (BRIEFE AN EINEN JUNGEN DICHTER). 1929. Letters. German.

Author: Rainer Maria Rilke (1875-1926) was born in Prague to German-speaking parents. He was subjected to many strains in childhood, for his father was an army officer and his mother a neurotic who dressed him as a girl until he was five. At ten he was enrolled in a military school, for which he was psychologically unfit. He records one unhappy recollection of his years there in the short story "Gym Period." After leaving military school, Rilke attended several universities but did not take a degree.

Rilke began writing at an early age, and his talent encompassed many areas: poetry, fiction, drama, and translation. However, his genius was sporadic, and periods of frustrating barrenness alternated with spurts of almost unbelievable creativity. Rilke himself wrote a monograph on Rodin, for whom he worked as a secretary for about two years and whose philosophy of constant work he attempted to follow, though not always with positive results. Rilke traveled extensively and lived in many areas of Europe, notably Paris, Munich, and Switzerland. While his best works, the *Duino Elegies* and the *Sonnets to Orpheus,* are difficult, *The Book of Hours* and *New Poems* are good and are more accessible to student readers, as is his semi-autobiographical novel, *The Notebooks of Malte Laurids Brigge.*

Work: Occasionally a "different" work of literature comes along, a work that has great appeal, but perhaps to a limited audience. Such is the case with these ten letters written by Rilke over a period of five years to a young man, Franz Xaver Kappus, who had aspirations—unfortunately never realized—of becoming a poet. Rilke never met Kappus, who initiated the correspondence when he accidentally discovered that Rilke had once been a student at the military school he was then attending. As is often the case with aspiring young authors, Kappus sent samples of his writing to Rilke. Responding with great sympathy and consideration, the older man attempted to guide and strengthen the poetic bent of his young correspondent. In doing so, however, Rilke revealed a good deal of himself. Although the letters give few details of Rilke's activities, they do reveal the workings of his mind over many areas suggested by his young friend's correspondence: the need for a poet to develop "solitariness," to work within himself (letter 1 and almost all the others); the affirmation of life and the simple things in life (letter 4); the continuous chain of life from generation to generation (letter 6); the changed roles of the sexes in the world of the future (letter 7).

Comparative: In their expression of poetical theory, the letters may be compared with Aristotle's *Poetics* and Wordsworth's preface to the second (or 1800) edition of the *Lyrical Ballads.* Because they reveal Rilke's underlying philosophy of composition, the letters may also be used in conjunction with his literary works, notably the short story collection *Stories of God,* which embodies elements of Christian existentialism, and the lyric poems, especially "The Panther," which epitomizes his theory that the poet must transform within himself the object of his poem and then present it concretely and vividly to his reader. A longer poem suitable for high school students is "The Lay of the Love and Death of Cornet Christopher Rilke," which describes a young man's experiences in wartime. If this sample of Rilke's letters appeals to students, *The Selected Letters of R. M. Rilke* would be a natural extension.

Rizal, José. THE LOST EDEN (NOLI ME TANGERE). 1887. Novel. Philippino.

Author: José Rizal was born in 1861 in the Philippines. He was an eye doctor, fluent in several languages, who imposed self-exile on himself in much the way that Younghill Kang and Mirok Li of Korea did. During this period the Philippines were reaching the end of five hundred years of subjugation to Spain but had not yet fallen under American domination. Rizal is said to be the soul of the first nationalist revolution in Asia, and his novels are credited with inspiring that revolution, which in turn triggered a string of events that finally resulted in Philippine independence from Western colonialism. Not only did his novels inspire a revolutionary movement, they caused his death. Rizal was executed in public by a firing squad of colonial troops on December 30, 1896.

Work: It would be misleading to think of this novel merely as a political or revolutionary novel, though it did foster the revolution. It also has the characteristics of a nineteenth-century Gothic melodrama, resembles a comedy of manners, and is an irreverent satire on the last years of the Spanish colonial regime.

As James Michener wrote in a Foreword to the Leon Ma. Guerrero translation:

> In its characterizations *Noli Me Tangere* is worthy of being a national monument; the men and women who populate these pages seem to have come from nowhere but the Philippine Islands. The hero is indeed a young man who reveres his Spanish heritage but who also loves his Philippine homeland. The revolutionary Elias foretells the real-life Aguinaldos who were to follow him. Doña Victorina is a real horror of a provincial beldame trying to live down her Tagalog ancestry.
>
> But it seems to me that what marks this novel is its constant gratuitous flashes of benign insight into various aspects of Philippine life. Often these comments are brief, witty pinpricks for pomposity, as applicable now as when they were written: "The Sabbath day is generally kept holy in the Philippines by going to the cockpit in the afternoon, just as in Spain it is kept by going to the bullring."
>
> Or when another periodic massacre of Chinese is supposed to have taken place: "What a pity!" exclaimed Sister Rufa. "All the Chinese dead before Christmas, when they send us such nice gifts. They should have waited for New Year's Day."
>
> Or when a loving father explains to his daughter the Spanish ideal of a perfect husband: "That is why I sought for you a husband who could make you the happy mother of children, who would command, not obey, who would have the power to inflict punishment, not endure it."

Comparative: This novel may be read in the context of the literature of colonialism: Kartini's *Letters of a Javanese Princess,* Younghill Kang's *The Grass Roof,* Mirok Li's *The Yalu Flows,* and Richard Kim's *Lost Names.* It might well be included in any course dealing with the nineteenth-century novel or with classics of world literature. There also seems to be a bond between many of the characters in this novel and those in the novels of Thackeray.

While the novel is not anti-Catholic, it is anti-clerical and can be compared with the Portuguese novel *The Sin of Father Amaro* by Eça de Queiroz. Its portrayal of the clergy could also be compared with those of Willa Cather in *Death Comes to the Archbishop* and Honor Tracy in *The Straight and Narrow Path.*

Rojas, Fernando de. LA CELESTINA. 1499. Novel. Spanish.

Author: This tragicomedy is attributed to Rojas (ca. 1465-1541). Rojas studied in Salamanca but moved to Talavera because of racial discrimination. He later became mayor of Talavera. His Jewish parents had converted under force, and some critics hold that his novel is a *roman-à-clef* on the Spanish conversions. *La Celestina* is generally considered to be the most significant literary work produced in Spain during the fifteenth century.

Work: Critics of Spanish literature generally rank this "novel in twenty-one acts" second only to *Don Quixote.* Certainly it presents one of the most lively and realistic pictures we have of Renaissance Spain, with sharply sketched and credible characters. Dialogues range from those spoken in high-flown courtly Spanish to those delivered as racy repartee, and they are spiced with proverbs and wit. This is a novel of intrigue, sorcery, and skulduggery enacted by the unforgettable old priestess of love, Celestina, who goes muttering through glaring daylit streets and misty passionate nights, always working evil.

Calisto falls in love with the haughty Melibea. About to die from love's fever, he heeds the suggestion of his servant Sempronio and hires the old crone Celestina to further his affair. Sempronio and Pármeno, his other servant, now plan to benefit financially at their master's expense as Celestina also plays both ends against the middle. Celestina slyly achieves a slight favor from Melibea for Calisto and shrewdly uses this incident as a psychological wedge to begin the spiritual degeneration of the proud maiden. Meanwhile, Sempronio and Pármeno, angry with the witch for appropriating the profits from this affair, wait at her house and murder her. The murderers are in turn set upon by Elicia and Areusa, servant and friend of Celestina, who summon a crowd that kills the murderers. Calisto dies in a fall from a ladder while making a tryst with Melibea. Melibea, ruined and grief-stricken, ascends a tower, nobly addresses her father below, and plunges to her death.

Almost every character in *La Celestina* shows a degree of mendacity in a vulture world where everyone is out to feed and fatten himself.

Comparative: Hardly a tragedy (for all the characters are touched with dishonor), this work has few descendants; however, Dürrenmatt's *The Visit* shows the same type of vulture world, as does Fellini's film, *La Dolce Vita.* The theme of the lovers' double death can be compared with that in Chikamatsu's *The Love Suicides at Sonezaki.* The machinations of Celestina resemble those of the old woman in Pérez Galdós's *Doña Perfecta,* and the malevolence she shows is similar to that of the raconteur in Lagerkvist's *The Dwarf,* which contains other psychological parallels.

Rostand, Edmond. CYRANO DE BERGERAC. 1897. Drama. French.

Author: Rostand (1868-1918) was born in Marseilles, France. He admired Goethe and Shakespeare, and both writers influenced him against the rigidities of French neoclassicism. Rostand wrote much verse—in addition to *Cyrano de Bergerac* and other plays including *Chanticleer,* a satirical beast-fable drama; *L'Aiglon (The Eagler),* a historical drama based on the life of Napoleon's son; and *Les Romanesques (The Romantics),* later to appear on Broadway as *The Fantasticks.*

Work: Cyrano de Bergerac, author of science fiction and philosophical fantasies, including *A Voyage to the Moon* which preceded Jules Verne's better known story, lived in seventeenth-century France. He was studious, a free-thinker, a soldier, and noted for his grotesque appearance.

In Rostand's play, Cyrano enjoys two distinctions in Paris—he is the deadliest of all swordsmen and he has the longest nose in all of France. Sensitive about this nose, Cyrano will duel with anyone he fancies has insulted his appearance.

Cyrano falls in love with his cousin Roxane but hesitates to reveal his love because of his ludicrous appeance. Instead, he agrees to help a slow-witted but handsome fellow guardsman, Christian, court Roxane. Under her balcony Cyrano whispers the words which Christian repeats to win her love. Cyrano writes love letters signed with Christian's name. This illusion, adding splendor to Christian's name and leading Roxane to agree to become his wife, is maintained until Christian has died in battle and both Cyrano and Roxane have grown old. At the play's end, Cyrano's nobility of character and ardor are accidentally revealed in a touching scene; now Roxane knows that the words and the soul she had loved were really those of Cyrano.

Cyrano de Bergerac represents a resurgence of Romanticism in France (in Germany it never quite died), where naturalism, realism, and other movements had come to dominate the literary scene under the influence of Antoine's *Théâtre Libre.* Rostand depicted a lively hero, and the play abounds in humor, heroics, and swordplay. It offers more fun and pathos than most theater-goers can resist.

Comparative: For other swashbuckling heroes, see Dumas's *The Three Muske-teers* and its sequels, Pushkin's *The Captain's Daughter* with its Russianized Gascon-type hero, or the books of P. C. Wren, especially *Beau Geste.* Molière's *Les Précieuses ridicules* presents infatuated females that may in some ways be compared to Roxane.

Rutt, Richard, ed. and trans. THE BAMBOO GROVE: AN INTRODUCTION TO SIJO. 1971. Poems. Korean.

Author: The great *sijo* poets from the fourteenth century to the present are included in this anthology. Among the most famous are Chŏng Mong-ju (1337-1392) and Chŏng Ch'ŏl (1536-1593), who wrote under the penname of Songgang.

Work: The *sijo* is a distinctive Korean verse form (as the *haiku* is Japanese and the *ghazal* Urdu) ordinarily composed to be sung. Originally the music and words formed a single unit, but it is within the Korean tradition to gather these *sijo* together in an anthology. The *sijo* in this collection have been arranged according to themes such as history, politics, loyalty, love, solitude, music, morality, nature, retirement, and the rustic life. Modern *sijo* form a separate section.

Richard Rutt, editor and translator, lived among the Korean people for more than twenty years and has written an excellent introduction, including information on the history, language, and form of the *sijo.*

While there is a distinctive Korean sensibility particularly evident in the folk art and music of Korea, the influence of Chinese poetry (indeed, some-times the imitation of its ideas and images) is more evident in these Korean *sijo* than in the poems from Vietnam and Japan, countries which also were influenced by China.

Comparative: The selections in this book provide an excellent introduction to the Korean sensibility, which should add to the appreciation of other Korean works included in this guide.

To compare the approach to *sijo* of another translator, consider Rutt's work along with *Poems from Korea* by Peter Lee.

For those who wish to examine the themes of Buddhism and Confucianism in East Asian poetry, these *sijo* may be compared with selections listed under

China, Japan, and Vietnam in this guide. A concept such as loyalty in East Asian thought might be examined through these same sources along with *The Arts of Korea, An Illustrated History* by Evelyn McCune.

Saint-Exupéry, Antoine de. NIGHT FLIGHT (VOL DE NUIT). 1931. Novel. French.

Author: Saint-Exupéry was born in Lyons in 1900. He rebelled against his Jesuit education, failed his naval academy exams, and found at last a satisfactory career in flying. He flew as an officer in Morocco and in 1926 became a commercial pilot. He visited the United States in 1943 and here published *The Little Prince,* a beautiful children's fairytale and allegory for adults. That year he went back to North Africa as a flight instructor. He was reported missing as a reconnaissance pilot over southern France in 1944.

Work: Objectively the story recounts Fabien's night flight towards Buenos Aires. Suddenly caught up in a cyclone, he runs low on fuel and is unable to make radio contact because of the lightning. He struggles to reach a landing field but disappears. Subjectively, the story still concerns Fabien, his courage and his emotions, but others enter: Fabien's wife, who awaits news of him with diminishing hope and gradually comes to face the truth; Robineau, the airport inspector; and especially Rivière, chief of the airmail service and ultimate hero of the novel. Rivière's duty is to stifle emotions, to insist on absolute obedience, to be feared and respected rather than liked, so that the mail service may be established. Conflicting emotions beset him as he accepts sovereign duty but feels the call of sympathy for Fabien's wife, for Fabien, and for the veteran mechanic who must be dismissed after years of service because of one mistake. The airmail service is a machine that moves and keeps on moving because of men like Rivière; personal tragedies happen and are forgotten.

Night Flight is a novel one does not quickly forget. Saint-Exupéry relies on the technique of understatement, allowing tragedy to exist without overt notice by emphasizing slight events which become significant to Rivière and hence to the whole service and by portraying an antiheroism which in itself becomes a measure of one's capacity to endure. The quality of Saint-Exupéry's prose in this as in his other works merits special mention. It combines a sensitivity that is poetic and almost delicate with a strength that lends epic quality to what many have come to think of as commonplace. It raises unassuming, unsung individuals to heroic stature.

Comparative: Hemingway's *The Old Man and the Sea* is another work which raises the commonplace to the heroic. The ocean and the old man's aloneness upon it in Hemingway's work is closely akin to Saint-Exupéry's lone pilot in a universe of air and stars. One is also reminded of Fate as dramatized by

Cocteau in *The Infernal Machine.* The characters of Saint-Exupéry are men with missions, comparable in this respect to the captin in Conrad's *Youth* and to Ch'en in Malraux's *Man's Fate.* The technique of building a novel from slight events suggests Jules Romain's *Death of a Nobody.* The courageous decisions of Rivière, alone in a thankless job, recall the role of king as Creon sees it in Anouilh's *Antigone* and in Sophocles' *Oedipus Rex.* The description of the growing storm, and the anxious people who watch it, suggest George R. Stewart's short novel, *Storm.*

Sappho. THE POEMS OF SAPPHO. Translated by S. Q. Groden. Bobbs Merrill, 1966. 6th Century B.C. Poems. Greek.

Author: Apart from knowing that Sappho (ca. 630–570 B.C.) was the first lyric poetess in the West, we know only that she was born on the island of Lesbos, apparently of an aristocratic family, that she married and named her daughter Cleïs after her mother, and that she lived in Mytilene at the center of a group of young women forming a cult, almost a kind of finishing school, dedicated to poetry and Aphrodite. As a young woman, Sappho apparently spent a few years in Sicily due to political turmoil in Lesbos at that time. Her reputation rests on some 200 fragments of poems—at most 700 lines— many of which were discovered as recently as 1900 in Oxyrynchus, Egypt. Perhaps because of the very paucity of real information about Sappho, many unreliable tales about her have grown up to give her a lively biography. Her poems even in ancient times were revered and imitated.

Work: The "Ode to Aphrodite" is the only poem that survives in its entirety. "To Anaktoria" is nearly complete. Problems of translation, of course, are insuperable when so little context exists for mere scraps of poems; yet what survives is brilliant. Sappho wrote of her personal world, of her family and friends, of her emotional and religious experiences. The Alexandrian scholars arranged her poems into seven books, the last being epithalamia (wedding songs). Most of the poems are monodies—songs for the single unaccompanied voice. Sappho's intensity, the range of her imagination, and her feeling for beauty are couched in simple, almost conversational diction. Even in these fragments, snatches of detail convey to the reader a heightened sense of reality. Because they are fragments, the reader sometimes has the feeling of overhearing an emotionally charged conversation. No résumé can substitute for even the briefest excursion through this vivid, unforgettable work.

Comparative: Sappho's influence on Greek and Latin poets was enormous. Horace and Catullus deliberately imitated her meter and style. In *The Greek Anthology,* a couplet attributed to Plato speaks of Sappho as the tenth muse. Through Horace and Catullus, Sappho's influence filtered throughout European poetry. Rainer Maria Rilke, for example, wrote some Sappho poems in

Neue Gedichtc (New Poems). Hilda Doolittle ("H.D."), like Sappho, emphasized implication and brevity. The universality of the themes in Sappho's poems makes comparison possible with much lyric poetry. Recent attention to women writers now places her at the wellspring not only of lyric poetry but of the feminine imagination.

Sartre, Jean-Paul. THE FLIES (LES MOUCHES). 1943. Drama. French.

Author: Sartre (1905-1980) was graduated in philosophy from the École Normale Supérieure and traveled in Europe until 1939, when he entered the French army. Taken prisoner in 1940, he escaped to Paris where he re-entered teaching, became an important writer, and edited the underground resistance paper *Combat*. In 1964 Sartre was awarded the Nobel Prize, but he refused it, saying he did not want to be "transformed into an institution." He has also refused the Legion of Honor.

Work: This drama in three acts, based on the *Electra* of Sophocles and the *Oresteia* of Aeschylus demonstrates the continued vitality of the Greek legends as well as Sartre's contemporary philosophy of existentialism.

Existentialism (in paraphrase) is said to define existence as "a hole in Nothingness." Orestes, in *The Flies*, states as a corollary the self-determinism of this movement's beliefs: "I, Zeus, am a man, and every man must find his own way." This statement explains Orestes' philosophical rejection of old religions and old social habits that free him from the revenge slayings of the tyrant Aegisthus and of his mother, Clytemnestra. (Consult the *Electra* of Sophocles for a more complete background summary.)

The significant changes in the play that reflect Sartre's philosophical stance may be briefly noted. The village of Argos shares in the complicity of Agamemnon's murder; thus all of society partakes of individual guilt. Religion is based on fear, and the populace wallows in guilt and enjoys the ritual of it. The people worship the dead and delight in the grief and guilt that thinking about them engenders. Orestes, the one person who *acts,* is thus able to assume penitence for all of society's guilt. The *Oresteia* is compressed almost entirely into Sartre's single drama: here are the Harpies, and here also is the expression of Orestes' "freedom" from them, the freedom of acceptance. Zeus himself is on stage, a decadent symbol of punishment and death who delights in both. The tense, hate-ridden Electra that we knew in Sophocles and Aeschylus (or in Mérimée's *Colomba*) is here a girl who outwardly is courageous enough to offer garbage on the altar of Zeus and to scream for revenge, yet who weakly collapses when she learns the price of guilt. Although the Harpies, those symbols of the gods' vengeance or of humanity's own curse, are present, they are not nearly so pervasive and effective as the household flies that fill the air, symbolic of the corruption which fills Argos and which makes punishment an everyday and familiar thing.

Comparative: The Aeschylean and Sophoclean comparisons have already been noted. The theme of the morally diseased small town is found in many works, among them Lope de Vega's *Fuenteovejuna,* Pérez Galdós's *Doña Perfecta,* Dürrenmatt's *The Visit,* Giraudoux's *The Enchanted,* Gerstäcker's *Germelshausen,* Ibsen's *An Enemy of the People,* and Twain's *The Man That Corrupted Hadleyburg.*

Sartre, Jean-Paul. THE WALL (LE MUR). 1939. Story. French.

Author: See *The Flies.*

Work: In Spain during the civil war in 1936, Tom, Juan, and the narrator are captured, interrogated, and put into a coal cellar to wait out the night before their execution. Two guards and a medical doctor are with them. The doctor is there to observe their psychological behavior. Fear and common feeling bring the three imprisoned men together for brief contacts, but these feelings also separate them as individuals. "I didn't see why, just because we were going to die together, I should like him any better," the narrator thinks. He begins to feel that everything that has ever happened to him, everything his body has done or stood for, was false and separate; not love or comradeship or nature or wine counted in the least: "I was alone." The only solid fact is the wall against which they are to die the next morning.

At dawn, Tom and Juan are taken out and shot. The narrator is interrogated further about the hiding place of Ramon Gris. He refuses to tell, not because he cares any longer; everyone is going to die anyway, and who cares whether Ramon is important to Spain? Who cares about anything? To put off his questioners, he tells them to look for Ramon in a cemetery. Our narrator is freed in detention. Later a fellow prisoner brings him news that Ramon was found in the cemetery (he had suddenly changed his hiding place) and was shot. The narrator concludes his tale: "I laughed so hard the tears came to my eyes."

Comparative: The imprisoned Meursault in Camus's *The Stranger* wrestles with the same problem of human identity. Like Sartre, Ernest Hemingway looks at fate operating within the Spanish Civil War in *For Whom the Bell Tolls.* Other thematic references may be found in Koestler's *Darkness at Noon* and Malraux's *Man's Fate.*

SAVITRI, an episode from the MAHABHARATA. Poem. Indian.

Work: "Savitri" is an episode in verse from the *Mahabharata* (*maha* meaning great and *Bharata,* a family of the governing caste), a collection about eight times as long as the combined *Iliad* and *Odyssey*. It consists of stories and Hindu lore, including the *Bhagavadgita.*

Savitri, a Hindu model of the perfect wife, has made her choice of a husband only to learn that he is to die in exactly one year. Still, "once a maiden's troth is given it may never be denied," and they are married. In India, as in many cultures, a son's first duty is to his father. As a wife, Savitri's first duty, like her husband's, will be to his father.

On the day fated for her husband's death Savitri follows him into the forest. When Yama, God of Death, comes to take her husband's *purusha,* the spark of life "no bigger than the human thumb," she gains three successive wishes, designed to help her father-in-law fulfill his "dharma" or duty as a ruler. Through these carefully chosen wishes she regains her husband, restored to life. She is clever, but more important to the Indian reader she is true to the duties of a wife and daughter-in-law. Her triumph is less one of trickery than one of dutiful correctness.

Comparative: Other Hindu models of womanly perfection include Sita in the other great Indian epic, the *Ramayana,* and Shakuntala from Kalidasa's fifth-century drama *Shakuntala.* Chaucer's Wife of Bath, offers a striking contrast in female motivation, and Edith Wharton's *Ethan Frome* suggests quite a different view of married life. Rómulo Gallegos's *Doña Bárbara* gives us a Latin American view of an exceptional frontier woman, and Mérimée's *Colomba* presents a woman against a relatively primitive background. There are, of course, innumerable others, such as Shakespeare's Portia *(Merchant of Venice),* Hawthorne's Hester *(The Scarlet Letter),* and Tolstoi's *Anna Karenina.*

Schreiner, Olive. THE STORY OF AN AFRICAN FARM. 1883. Novel. South African.

Author: Schreiner (1855-1920) was born in Basutoland, South Africa, a daughter in a German missionary family of twelve children. Entirely self-educated, she made her living as a governess. She wrote this novel in her twenties and brought it to England for publication. George Meredith discovered it. After eight homesick years in England, Schreiner returned to Africa, married Samuel Cronwright, a farmer, lawyer, and member of the Cape Colony Parliament. Mr. Cronwright later gave up his own career to serve as his wife's literary assistant and finally as her literary executor.

Work: In its time a sensational examination of women's rights, *The Story of an African Farm* is a beautiful, serious study of human loneliness.

A strange family lives on a desert farm in South Africa: Waldo and his German father, Otto, the overseer for Tant' Sannie's farm; Tant' Sannie, a fat Boer woman whose second husband has died and left her to rear his English daughter, Lyndall; and Em, Lyndall's orphan cousin. The three children are sensitive and ingrown and filled with the terror of primitive Christianity. A sinister adventurer named Napoleon Bonaparte Blenkins comes to the farm and insinuates himself into the family through the kindness of the old German and the weakness of Tant' Sannie. By courting the Boer woman, Napoleon's position is made unassailable, and he drives out Waldo's father and cruelly abuses young Waldo. But he is discovered making love to a niece of Tant' Sannie's and is sent packing.

In Book II, Waldo meets a stranger who tells him an allegory of life (Chapter 15), which is crucial to an understanding of the novel. A new English overseer, the feminist Gregory, courts Em and wins her consent. Chapter 18 recounts the hilarious courting of Tant' Sannie by little Piet Vander Walt. Lyndall, disillusioned with what she has learned about life, comes back from her city school, captures Gregory away from her good friend Em, and proposes marriage to him. But impulsively Lyndall sends for a friend from the city and asks him to take her away with him. Waldo also goes out into the world to seek not fortune but himself, and Gregory, driven by grief over Lyndall, goes to look for her. After a long search, he finally finds Lyndall, her baby dead, and she herself abandoned and ill. Dressed as a female nurse, Gregory takes care of her until she dies. The last scenes are of Waldo's return with his eyes unhappily opened. Gregory too returns to tell Lyndall's story. Greg and Em, reconciled, once more agree to marry.

The story is compounded of many elements: the tremendous loneliness and wild beauty of the open country, the polyglot mixture of racial characters, the biblical mood, and the tale itself of children and their exquisite sadness—children who, even as adults, keep both innocence and sadness.

Comparative: For the African locale, compare Paton's *Cry, The Beloved Country,* written more than half a century later. The powerful descriptions of the wild beauty of the country can also be compared to those of Thomas Hardy. The character of Napoleon Blenkins strongly resembles Mr. Jingle in Dickens's *Pickwick Papers;* Otto is a pathetic character also out of Dickens, and the other adults are caricatured in the manner of Dickens. The delightful and complex heroine searches for and recognizes truth as Giraudoux's young girls do; rebels against convention like Ibsen's Nora or Synge's Nora; and ends tragically like Madame Bovary or Anna Karenina. Tant' Sannie is almost a Wife of Bath.

Selormey, Francis. THE NARROW PATH. 1966. Novel. Ghanaian.

Author: Francis Selormey, born in 1927, was educated in Roman Catholic schools and at St. Augustine's Training College, Cape Coast. After studying physical education in Ghana and Germany, he directed physical education at

St. Francis Teacher Training College, Hohoe, and served as Senior Regional Sports Organizer for the Ghana Central Organization of Sports. He has worked for Ghana television and written scripts for two films: *Towards a United Africa* and *The Great Lake.*

Work: *The Narrow Path* is an absorbing fictional autobiography filled with morbidity, despondency and desperation. It is the life story of Kofi, an African youth who dared to make a place in life for himself. Both his father, Nani, and his mother, Edsi, are teachers. Steadfastly religious, Kofi is brought up in strict adherence to African customs such as praying to the family god before the birth of a child, pouring libations on ceremonious occasions, and performing rituals before fishing trips.

The Catholic Church Mission sends Nani to various villages to teach and direct school programs. Finally, having given up home after home, he is reduced to the house of reeds. Thus Kofi's life is a maze of obstacles and filled with adversity. He is his father's example for any misconduct in each new school and on occasion is severely punished. As he gets older, Kofi is forced to live with other families in order to attend school. The ultimate end of these extreme hardships is the disintegration of the family, with Nani returning to his family and Edsi to hers.

Throughout the story one marvels that Kofi has survived to tell his story, but social pressures keep Kofi on the narrow path and enable him to receive the School Leaving Certificate and finally to depart for college—200 miles away.

Comparative: Kofi's sorrow-filled life typifies that of other African youths as may be seen in Achebe's *No Longer at Ease,* where we experience Okonkwo's tragedy; in Ekwensi's *Jagua Nana,* where we see Freddie fall victim to social ills while he seeks the "Golden Fleece of knowledge and leadership"; and in Armah's *The Beautiful Ones Are Not Yet Born,* where "The Man" recalls a childhood that is impoverished, desperate, disillusioning, and dehumanizing.

Similar hardships may be seen in Johnson's *Autobiography of an Ex-Colored Man* and in Washington's *Up from Slavery,* although these works are larger in stature.

**Solzhenitsyn, Aleksandr Isaevich. ONE DAY IN THE LIFE OF IVAN DE-
NISOVICH (ODEN DEN' IVANA DENISOVICHA). 1962. Novel.
Russian.**

Author: Solzhenitsyn was born in Rostov in 1918 and was graduated with a degree in physics from Rostov in 1941. During the war he served as an artillery officer but was arrested in 1945 for anti-Stalinist remarks and spent the next eleven years in labor camps and in exile. He taught mathematics and physics until 1962 when *One Day in the Life of Ivan Denisovich* was published with Nikita Krushchev's permission. In 1963 several short stories appeared which were critical of the Russian bureaucracy. Since then Solzhenitsyn's writings have not appeared in Russia, although his novels were widely published in the West and he was awarded the Nobel Prize for Literature in 1970, particularly for *The First Circle* (1968) and *Cancer Ward* (1968). His most recent works have been studies of Russian history, most notably *The Gulag Archipelago*, a study of the Soviet penal system. He was forced into exile in 1975 and now lives in Vermont.

Work: This short novel traces the life of Ivan Denisovich Shukhov, a prisoner in a forced labor camp in Siberia, from reveille to lights-out on a single day. It is a picture of men treated like beasts, subjected to arbitrary imprisonment and punishment, nearly endless starvation, cold, and brutality. It is a world Solzhenitsyn knew well. For vastly differing crimes—some religious and some political, some real but most merely trumped up, reflecting the reactions of a paranoid government—a group of men of various backgrounds and intellectual capabilities have been thrown together and have learned to survive. But the story is more than a depiction of the prisoners' brutal and brutalizing life; it is the story of their stubborn refusal to lose their humanity, to become like beasts. A few, such as the scavenger Fetyukov, succumb and are described in ways suggesting animals (the name for one of the guards is derived from the Russian word for wolf). But the majority of the characters maintain their dignity as human beings and manage to find fulfillment.

At the close of the day Shukhov feels quite satisfied. Although he has had little to eat but mush, soup, and bread, he is not hungry; although he has been forced into labor, he has taken pride in his work; although it is bitter cold, he has kept warm with labor and fellowship. And if he is in prison, life is not much different on the outside. The guards have it little better than the prisoners, and the fact that the prisoners are building a town which "free" men will inhabit, men who will be exposed to most of the same hardships, underscores the point that life is much the same inside or outside the camp and that it remains for the individual to find satisfaction for himself in a threatening and unjust world.

Comparative: Many Russian authors have written about the penal camps in Siberia. Like Solzhenitsyn, Dostoevski was a prisoner in one of these camps and described his experiences in *The House of the Dead*. Chekhov, though not himself a prisoner, visited and described the convict settlement at Sakhalin. Both of these earlier authors also wrote elsewhere of the necessity for people to oppose an environment which turns them into animals. Chekhov's short stories, such as "Peasants" or "Ward Six," are not far removed from Solzhenitsyn's novel, and different as the two characters are, Shukhov's insistence on defending his humanity would be supported by the protagonist of Dostoevski's *Notes from Underground*.

Numerous other works have described the police state—for example, Koestler's *Darkness at Noon,* Huxley's *Brave New World,* Orwell's *1984,* Andreyev's *The Seven Who Were Hanged,* and Bulgakov's *Master and Margarita.*

Also rewarding are comparisons with works which see all of humanity, whether in or out of prison, as forced to find fulfillment in the little victories of daily life and in the face of a sometimes hostile, sometimes unjust, and always inexplicable universe. Like many of the prisoners in Solzhenitsyn's novel, Josef K. in Kafka's *The Trial* doesn't understand what his crime is, and the heroes of Camus's *The Stranger* and Sartre's *The Wall* also learn through imprisonment about the human condition. Finally, in their refusal to give in to a brutalizing system, MacMurphy in Kesey's *One Flew Over the Cuckoo's Nest* and Yossarian in Heller's *Catch-22* insist on the dignity of humanity and the sanctity of life, the central theme in Solzhenitsyn's work.

SONG OF ROLAND (LA CHANSON DE ROLAND). ca. 1100. Epic poem. French.

Author: Unknown.

Work: In 778, the Basques slaughtered a small French force in the Pyrenees, among them "Roland, Duke of the Marches of Brittany." From historical fact to legend and epic, however, the tale emerges like this: Charlemagne enters Spain to wipe out the Moors who menace Christianity. His mission successful, he takes his army back to France, leaving Roland in charge of the rear guard. Roland's stepfather, Ganelon, tells Masillon, King of the Moors, that he may safely attack this small force, the cream of the French Army. Thus the whole might of the Saracen army falls on Roland's troops at Roncevaux.

With Roland are two knights who help to make the triumvirate memorable —Archbishop Turpin, as mighty with the sword as the chasuble, and Oliver, Roland's best friend. "Roland is fierce, but Oliver is wise," says the poem, and it is Oliver who wishes that Roland would blow his horn, the famous Oliphant (elephant), and summon aid from Charlemagne. From pride in the charge that has been given him, Roland refuses.

The slaughter is terrible, and Roland witnesses the deaths of friend after friend. At last, alone on the field of battle, he blows his horn for help, attempts to break his sword Durendal to prevent the enemy's having it, holds up his glove to Heaven, and dies facing the enemy. St. Gabriel himself comes down to receive Roland's soul.

So ends Roland's story (through *Laisse* [stanza] 176); the remaining 15 *laisses* are concerned with Charlemagne's revenge against the Moors, his return to France, the death from grief of Roland's beloved, and the trial and dreadful punishment of Ganelon the traitor.

The characters are brilliantly delineated; the action, a series of single combats, is sustained. The conflicts range through treachery versus loyalty, Christianity versus paganism, "la doulce France" versus the Moors, "le sage Olivier" versus single-minded Roland, and glory in battle versus Roland's grief at the death of his friends.

Comparative: France's epic poem in 291 *laisses* in dignified and restrained verse is a direct statement of man's courage and devotion to country, leader, and religion. It has many distinguished peers among the world's literature, such as *Poem of the Cid, Beowulf,* and the *Nibelungenlied,* for the rise of an epic hero has often signaled the birth of a nation and a national language.

See also the *Ramayana* and *Gilgamesh,* the latter being similar to the *Song of Roland* in its thoughtfulness and expression of comrade love. See also Homer's *Odyssey* and Virgil's *Aeneid.*

Sophocles. ANTIGONE. ca. 441 B.C. Drama. Greek.

Author: After an excellent education in music, gymnastics, and dancing, Sophocles (ca. 495–406 B.C.) won his first prize as a tragic poet at the age of twenty-seven, victorious over Aeschylus, who was thirty years his senior. Thereafter he won first prize some twenty times. Though not a politician, he held several military and civic offices. A prolific poet, one hundred of his approximately one hundred and thirty plays are known to us either by title or fragment; seven have survived complete. He also wrote paeans, elegies, and epigrams. Sophocles increased the importance of dialogue by introducing a third actor; he made each play a separate unity built around one character, abandoning the Aeschylean practice of writing trilogies; he diminished the importance of the chorus; and he showed surpassing skill with dramatic irony. Even in his own time, he was considered the most perfect tragedian.

Work: As the play opens, Antigone and Ismene, the daughters of Oedipus, discuss King Creon's edict that one of their brothers, Eteocles, shall be buried with honors while the other, Polynices, shall remain unburied as a traitor. Disobedience to this decree will bring death by stoning. Polynices has been decreed a traitor for leading an expedition against Thebes to seize the throne of his brother, and the brothers have killed each other in a duel. Antigone informs Ismene that she intends to defy the decree and bury Polynices, whatever the cost; divine law and family duty demand this act, she maintains. Ismene holds back and is unable to dissuade her.

A guard announces that Polynices has been ceremonially buried, that is, dust has been strewn upon him. Antigone, admitting both guilt and premeditation, glorys in her deed and praises divine law as higher than Creon's. Creon, believing obedience is essential to civic harmony, summarily condemns her to death. Though Antigone is engaged to Creon's son, Haemon, Creon nevertheless persists in his decision. He orders that Antigone be entombed alive so that her blood will not be on his hands.

The seer Tiresias enters, announcing that the gods are angry and that the city is polluted because Polynices lies unburied. Creon accuses Tiresias of accepting bribes, but Tiresias retorts that Creon will soon pay for his folly by death in his own house. This announcement spurs Creon to action, but he is too late. Antigone has hanged herself in the cave, and Haemon, determined to die with her, commits suicide embracing her, having first attempted to kill Creon. Even as Creon admits his guilt, a messenger arrives with the news that his wife, Eurydice, has killed herself in grief, cursing him.

Conflict in the play springs from Antigone's contact with outside forces— first Ismene, then the chorus, finally the king. Creon stubbornly sees in Antigone only disobedience, wickedness, and madness. Only Tiresias can frighten him into recognizing the error of his logical decision, even though it is based on experience and tradition. Antigone's tragedy comes swiftly; the impact of the play then grows from Creon's tragedy which develops before our eyes. Built on a multiple foundation, the play demonstrates a clash of irreconcilable opposites with irremediable consequences.

Comparative: The clash of civil versus religious duty, of individual conscience versus community standards, occurs often enough in literature. Rarely, however, is it presented with such force, clarity and dignity. Anouilh's *Antigone* concerns itself more directly with the predicament into which Antigone forces a peace-loving administrator; Creon is seen in a more compassionate light and Antigone's decision seems mere willfulness. Shaw's *Major Barbara* and *Saint Joan* are women who share a similar determination to carry out a singular mission in life.

Sophocles. ELECTRA (ELEKTRA). ca. 410 B.C. Drama. Greek.

Author: See *Antigone.*

Work: In this play Sophocles retells the story of Agamemnon's children, Electra and Orestes, following the basic outline provided by earlier versions (see Aeschylus, *The Libation Bearers*). But the main interest of Sophocles is not in the unfolding of the plot, although he is a master at building tension. His chief concern is with human character, and, therefore, the role of Fate and the gods is minimized; the characters, although sometimes idealized or relatively one-dimensional, always remain motivated by human desires. Thus Orestes, who had been sent away by Electra to protect him from Clytemnestra and Aegisthus, is urged to avenge his father's death by his sister, his tutor, and his conscience, not by the gods, who merely help to devise a plan. Clytemnestra has murdered her husband not to avenge his murder of their daughter Iphigenia, as she claims, but out of love for Aegisthus and a desire for power.

And Aegisthus is merely an arrogant tyrant who killed Agamemnon to gain his crown and his wife, not to avenge the murder of his brothers.

As the title suggests, however, Sophocles is most interested in the character of Electra. In his version she is motivated completely by a sense of moral duty and a desire to see justice done, at whatever cost to herself or others. She refuses to compromise her principles in exchange for a life of comfort, the path chosen by her sister Chrysothemis, a character added by Sophocles to highlight Electra's noble and principled character. Even when threatened with imprisonment she will not yield, and when she hears the false report of Orestes' death she vows to kill Aegisthus herself. When Orestes reveals himself and murders his mother and her lover, Electra feels neither remorse nor sorrow.

The emphasis on human character and the absence of divine intervention is evident throughout the play. There is no indication at the end that further vengeance or divine justification is necessary. Electra and Orestes are offered to us as symbols of the tragedy of human life, which we must meet with bravery and suffer with dignity.

Comparative: The art of Sophocles as a dramatist can be demonstrated by comparing this play with *The Libation Bearers* by Aeschylus. The latter's concern with religious and moral questions led him to produce a stately drama with an emphasis on plot; characters merely act out the will of the gods or Fate. Sophocles, on the other hand, presents us with characters who are often idealized but who are nonetheless subject to the tragedy of human life. It was primarily in the dramas of Sophocles that Aristotle found his examples of the subject matter of tragedy: the actions and emotions of elevated human beings.

The *Electra* of Sophocles might have been written in response to the *Electra* of Euripides, and the two plays make an interesting contrast. Sophocles presents us with a noble Electra and a completely villainous Clytemnestra and Aegisthus; Euripides portrays a heroine motivated by an exaggerated egotism, by sexual frustration, and by jealousy; and his Clytemnestra is a much more motherly and sympathetic figure.

The vision of a woman as a symbol of implacable justice is also found in Mérimée's heroine in *Colomba,* although her manipulative and vengeful nature remind us at times of the less than noble Euripidean Electra. In O'Neill's *Mourning Becomes Electra,* Vinnie is at first a Euripidean heroine, motivated by sexual frustration and jealousy, but in the end she becomes more like the implacable heroine of Sophocles in her demands for justice, even if it must be exacted from herself. Giraudoux's *Electra* and Sartre's *The Flies* present Sophoclean heroines who refuse to compromise principles for political expediency, although Sartre humanizes the character considerably.

Sophocles presents us with other figures who must choose between a life of easy compromise or a difficult life lived according to one's principles, most notably in *Antigone,* where Ismene acts, like Chrysothemis, as a dramatic foil. The same difficult choice between compromise and principle is made in Anouilh's *Becket* and *Antigone* and in Camus's *The Stranger.*

Sophocles. OEDIPUS, THE KING (OIDIPOUS TYRANNOS). ca. 430 B.C. Drama. Greek.

Author: See *Antigone.*

Work: Based upon the prophecy that Oedipus will kill his father and marry his mother, this play deals with the gradual discovery by Oedipus of what he has done. King Oedipus believes that through the power of his intelligence he can solve the mystery of the plague in Thebes. The audience, represented by the chorus, senses long before he does that something terrible will be revealed. The blind prophet, Tiresias, warns about the unveiling of truth, but Oedipus treats him arrogantly and persists in his quest. He accuses various persons of plots against him. Toward the end of the play Jocasta, his queen, grasps the truth that she is mother to Oedipus as well as his wife and the mother of his children, and she kills herself. Oedipus sees the truth about himself at last; recognizing that he is the cause of the plague, he puts out his eyes and condemns himself to exile. Though Oedipus was unaware of his parentage, he is nevertheless responsible for his actions and guilty of believing that human intelligence—especially his own—is the highest good. He learns that the mysterious will of the gods is superior to human intelligence and that humans must gain insight into the limits of their nature. Images of sight and blindness within the play illuminate the ironies.

Comparative: The myth of Oedipus, particularly as it was given to us by Sophocles, is a significant theme in many works—especially in modern times because of Freud's theory of the "Oedipus complex" in psychoanalysis. See, for example, Cocteau's *Infernal Machine* for a discussion of a modern version of the story and its differences.

Soyinka, Wole. THE STRONG BREED. 1964. Drama. Nigerian.

Author: Wole Soyinka (1934-   ), poet, actor, and playwright, was educated at the universities of Ibadan and Leeds. He has contributed poems to such literary journals as *Encounter* and *The Times Literary Supplement.* Versatile though he is, it is for his plays that he is best known. Among these, in addition to *The Strong Breed,* are *A Dance of the Forests* (1960), *The Trials of Brother Jero* (1964), and *The Lion and the Jewel* (1964).

Work: The Strong Breed, a one-act play, examines traditional African beliefs and customs—circumcision, ridding the village of evil at the year's end, and the deep respect for the strong breed.

Eman, a schoolteacher and the only stranger in the village, lives with Sunma, daughter of Jaguna. Living with them is Ifada, a malformed idiot whom Sunma has come to despise and wants to send away. Meanwhile, Ifada plays with a girl whom Eman has allowed to come in bringing her "carrier." The reader understands at once that she foreshadows the evil soon to befall Eman, for it is he who permits her to stay, even though she is unwell.

The girl has Ifada hang her "carrier" in a tree to which she later "sets fire." At midnight, then, she will once more be well. Again, an apprehensive note is struck as Eman and Sunma vacillate between staying in and going out while the New Year's Eve festivities are carried on in the village.

Sunma tells Eman, "Even if you lived here for a lifetime, you would remain a stranger." "But," Eman replies, "There is peace in being a stranger." Later, two men arrive, "sack up" Ifada, and carry him away to serve as village scapegoat. He escapes, returns, and Eman lets him in despite Sunma's pleas.

According to African lore, "Anyone who doesn't guard his door when the carrier goes by has himself to blame. A contaminated house should be burnt down." Thus Eman breaks a strong taboo and becomes the sacrifice. He is captured, severely beaten, and afterwards meets with an Old Man (his father) who is wearing white trousers, white cap, and two white rings and "who is going on the boat down the river—his last journey." Now the Old Man enlightens Eman: "Ours is a strong breed ... No woman survives the bearing of the strong ones [for just as Eman's mother had died at his birth, so had Omae, once Eman's betrothed, died while bearing his child]. Son, it is not the mouth of the boaster that says he belongs to the strong breed. It is the tongue that is red with pain and black with sorrow." Later, when Omae appears to Eman (for the African believes that one may commune with the spirits of the dead), he expresses contentment with his lot: "For the first time, I understand that I have a life to fulfill."

Finally, after brief dialogue with a priest, Eman falls into Jaguna's trap and he follows the Old Man to the river. Thus Eman, through misconception and misinformation, is consumed by the forces of tradition. Jaguna remarks, "I am sick to the heart of the cowardice I have seen tonight." A villager responds, "That is the nature of men." Jaguna concludes, "Then it is a sorry world we live in."

Comparative: The ritual of ridding a community of evil at the end of a year finds a close parallel in Shirley Jackson's *The Lottery.* Another interesting comparison may be found in the Old Testament story of *Abraham and Isaac,* which may be a source of Soyinka's play.

Soyinka, Wole. IDANRE AND OTHER POEMS. 1967. Poems. Nigerian.

Author: See *The Strong Breed.*

Work: Two poems may stand as representative. In "I Think It Rains" the poet establishes a pattern of circling greyness that attracts the reader's attention at once. As the speaker reflects on "strange despairs," he perceives "the purity of sadness." The African values pain and sorrow, for they identify him as one of the Strong Breed. Here the reader may also be reminded of Shelley's "To a Skylark": "Our sweetest songs are those that tell of saddest thought."

Rain, a generative phenomenon, may effect a release, the cleansing of a man's "dark desires." Thus the "cruel baptisms" may be the beginning of a new and stronger life.

The poem illustrates, among other things, the African's love for and "conjugation" with nature. Its tone is reminiscent of that in "Dream Deferred" by Langston Hughes.

In "Prisoner" (possibly written while Soyinka was in prison) the speaker again refers to the "grey essence." His years of confinement have bred "wise grey temples." This speaker too experiences intimations, not of life, but of "sudden seizure." Like a potsherd, his life is broken. Like the lichen, he is "rootless," for while he is imprisoned his life remains suspended.

Comparative: Wordsworthian echoes may be found in Soyinka's poems. He draws his symbols from nature and reflects on an intimate harmony between man and nature. His "flowers," however, are the cactus, beautiful but thorny, and the lichen, abundant but rootless—a strong contrast to the daffodils, pansies, and violets in Wordsworth.

Stendhal, pseudonym of Henri Beyle. THE RED AND THE BLACK (LE ROUGE ET LE NOIR). 1830. Novel. French.

Author: Stendhal (1783-1842) was born and educated at Grenoble. His life spanned the Romantic movement from its infancy to its peak of productivity in France, Germany, and England. Like other Romantics, Stendhal was centrally concerned with the experiential (as opposed to the conceptual) nature of the meaning of life and the responsibility of each individual to achieve a genuine meaning for life. A consciousness of psychological factors, of actions which conflict with one's own nature, of one's responsibility to be or become oneself rather than to fit the mold which society casts or seems to cast are of ultimate importance. Aside from *The Red and the Black,* Stendhal's best-known novel is *The Charterhouse of Parma.* Stendhal also wrote essays, memoirs, and criticism.

Work: *The Red and the Black* is set in France just before the July Revolution of 1830, a period in which ambition, fear, and intrigue prevailed. Julien Sorel, the hero, is a young *petit-bourgeois* of remarkable intelligence and of high ambitions. He contemplates two careers: one in which he would rise to a position of great importance through the church (black is the color of the clergy), and the other in which he would rise to wealth and influence in the secular world (the red of aristocratic clothing and perhaps also the red of blood).

His brief career involves him in two love affairs, one with Mme de Renâl the mother of the children he is hired to tutor, the other with Mathilde, a girl of a rich and noble family. His initial impulses in the first affair are ambition and the desire to prove to himself that he can manage a conquest such as those men of the upper classes engage in. The second affair is initiated by the young lady, whom Sorel sometimes thinks he loves. He fathers the child of Mathilde, a marriage is planned, and wealth and position are assured. But his first love, Mme de Renâl, writes a letter denouncing him as a man who employs seduction to obtain advancement. He returns to see her and shoots her, intending to kill her. Sorel is imprisoned. Mme de Renâl, recovering from her wound, tries to save him, as does Mathilde. Jurors are bought off in his behalf, but Sorel speaks at his trial and condemns himself to conviction and death.

The love plots are, however, secondary in this novel, which is remarkable for its depiction of the mores of the period and the character of its hero. In the end it is Julien Sorel, the convicted criminal, who emerges as the genuinely moral character. The novel admirably portrays the Romantics' quest for the real self and the difficulty of achieving it in a corrupt society. Both the red and the black stand condemned—at least as guilty as the individual they send to the guillotine. Sorel's judgment upon himself ("I am nothing but a *Perhaps*") contrasts with his judgment upon society: "I have loved truth. . . . Where is it? Everywhere hypocrisy, or at least charlatanism, even among the most virtuous, even among the greatest."

Comparative: The intrigues of love and quest for power among the aristocracy suggest Mme de Lafayette's *The Princess of Clèves.* The hero's interrogation of and judgment upon himself and others suggest Dostoevski's *Notes from Underground.* Hugo's *The Hunchback of Notre Dame* also offers comparisons in the characters of Quasimodo and Julien and in the quality of the societies portrayed.

Strindberg, August. THE FATHER (FADREN). 1887. Drama. Swedish.

Author: Strindberg (1849-1912) has been called the Swedish Shakespeare. As a youth in Sweden he served as teacher, tutor, actor, and journalist, and he has left several conflicting autobiographies. His unfortunate experiences with and mistrust of women served as material for *The Father.*

Work: As current as today's newspaper and almost a psychological thriller, Strindberg's play was ahead of its time and has not dated. As a study of the age-old natural forces that victimize humanity and as an examination of the competitive environment of marriage, this play is a good introduction to naturalism.

Laura, wife of the Captain, is engaged in a fight with her husband for control of their daughter Bertha. She wages, therefore, a campaign to convince the world first and then her husband that he is losing his mind. She sows doubt as to Bertha's paternity, intercepts her husband's mail, supplants a loyal doctor, and uses for her own purposes the few supporters the Captain has. The strong male, helpless though knowing his innocence, goes down in defeat in a struggle that is made to seem unequal because a man may not fight a woman.

In addition to the problem of female dominance, as Strindberg sees it, there is the modern note on "cerebral marriage." The Captain comments in Act III: "In the old days one married a wife. Now one goes into partnership with a businesswoman or sets up house with a friend. What becomes of love, the healthy love of the senses? It dies of neglect."

Comparative: The nineteenth century began a reexamination of the position of women in society. See, for example, Mlle Vatnaz in Flaubert's *Sentimental Education,* Nora in Ibsen's *A Doll's House,* Hedda in Ibsen's *Hedda Gabler,* and Eudoxie in Turgenev's *Fathers and Sons.*

A general comparison with the Strindberg play may be found in the *Agamemnon* of Aeschylus. Here Clytemnestra outmaneuvers her husband as Laura does the Captain. The situation of Hippolytus, helpless against Phaedra, offers another comparison. For another man-hater such as Laura, consider the mother in *The House of Bernarda Alba* by García Lorca. In the Victorian period, George Meredith wrote a sonnet cycle, *Modern Love,* that told of a "cerebral" relationship between man and wife. For more recent and more amusing examples of the battle of the sexes, see the plays of Courteline or James Thurber's delightful "The Secret Life of Walter Mitty" and "The Catbird Seat."

Sutherland, Efua T. EDUFA. 1968. Drama. Ghanaian.

Author: Efua T. Sutherland, born in 1924, was educated in Ghana, in England at Homerton College, Cambridge, and at the University of London School of Oriental and African Studies. Mrs. Sutherland is the founder of the Ghana Drama Studio and the Writers' Workshop in the Institute of African Studies at the University of Ghana, Legon.

Recognized as one of Ghana's foremost authors, she has written poetry and plays. Outstanding among her dramas, in addition to *Edufa,* are *Odasani* (a Ghanaian interpretation of *Everyman*), *Foriwa* (a three-act community play), and *Nyamekye* (a musical drama). Mrs. Sutherland's plays for children include, among others, *Ananse and the Dwarf Brigade* and *Two Rhythm Plays.*

Work: This drama in three acts opens with a prologue of sadness as Abena, Edufa's sister, sings as she cares for the dew water which she has caught in the black pot. There is also stream water, and both are spiritual agencies used to bring blessings. Edufa, the protagonist, is a pious, wealthy man and a respected sovereign in the village. His wife, Ampoma, is seriously ill. Edufa orders the house matron, Mother Seguwa, to prepare his and Ampona's baths: "Pour first the dew water and then the stream water over the herbs in the bathroom. Quickly. Then bring out the incense."

Outside the chorus (having come early in the morning) chants a death-song "as if clamouring for a soul." Seguwa doubts that the dew water, the stream water, and the incense will bring relief for Ampoma, but she keeps the latter burning. The chorus, now inside the courtyard, continues singing, for they have come to "smack the spirits of calamity . . . for calamity is for all mankind and none is free from woe." The chorus moves rhythmically through the courtyard, ceremoniously chanting: "One's death is the death of all mankind." Ampoma apparently feels somewhat better and talks, though randomly, of her concern for her children when she is gone. She exacts a promise from Edufa that he "will keep them from harm." The chorus now performs several rituals, including one to the health of Edufa, his wife, and his household. According to African tradition, the chorus leaves before noon.

As the chorus leaves, Senchi, poet and song-writer, comes in. In his battered leather case he has, "songs for everything: for goodness, for badness, for strength, for weakness." He observes, however: "I never make songs about ugliness, because I simply think it should not exist." Sincere and philosophically optimistic, it is Senchi who entertains the court, obviously a foil for Edufa.

At this point, Sam, an idiot servant, appears bringing a tin box and an owl. Seguwa is horrified, but Edufa has been anxiously waiting for Sam's return, for this box suggests what may be the climax of the drama. It contains three stones, a ball of red stuff which Sam uses to draw "a ray of the sun on the riser of the first step," and an old leather pouch. The latter Edufa himself is to burn and to bury its ashes.

The final act shows Edufa deeply troubled as he confronts what may be Ampoma's death. He is giving a party, celebrating what he hopes is improved health for Ampoma. The chorus enters, and Senchi leads them in a colorful ceremony to the delight of Ampoma. Edufa proposes a toast to her health, Ampoma is gracious, though serious, as she welcomes the guests. She talks to them of her approaching death and, in a moving show of affection for Edufa, re-declares their marriage vows. On returning to her room, however, Ampoma dies amid the hooting of owls. Edufa swears, "Death, I will lie closely at the grave again, and when you come gloating with your spoil, I'll grab you, unlock her from your grip, and bring her safely home to my bed. . . . I will do it; I am conqueror."

The chorus leaves singing a funeral song, "Make a river of sorrow, for Ampoma is dead."

Comparative: In *Edufa* the author probes the African's love of money, the attraction to sovereignty, the nature of the African personality, and dependence on folklore, myths, and a deity. The story itself is the subject of the

Alcestis of Euripides. Its theme—human fear of and desire to conquer death— is similar to that in *The Palm-Wine Drinkard* by Amos Tutuola. Chaucer also treats this theme in *The Pardoner's Tale* and it may also be found in the epic *Gilgamesh*. The role of the chorus may be compared to that of the chorus in Greek drama. Another point worth discussion is the playwright's skill at combining standard and pidgin English to portray character and to lend color to the whole play.

Tagore, Rabindranath. **A TAGORE READER.** Translated in part from Bengali by Amiya Chakravarty. Macmillan, 1961. Originally written in English. Poems, essays, stories, dramas. Indian.

Author: Rabindranath Tagore (1861-1941) was born in Calcutta and studied law in England. He founded an international university (Visva-Bharati) in Santiniketan, where he hoped to combine the best in the Indian and Western traditions. In 1913 he was awarded the Nobel Prize for Literature, and he is known for his novels, short stories, plays, poetry, and miscellaneous prose. He sometimes wrote in English, but usually in his native Bengali. Tagore also composed music for more than three thousand songs and was well known as a painter. He was recognized during his lifetime as the embodiment of Indian culture and its greatest spokesman; his fame has spread throughout the literary world.

Work: Tagore's work is available in English primarily in collections. The short stories, plays, and poems are especially suitable for comparative studies, both because they are readily understood by Western students and because they portray Indian culture in a modern light without, however, neglecting its ancient traditions.

Of his poetry, the poems included in the *Reader* from the *Gitanjali* (literally "handful of song") are among the best.

Of his short stories, "The Cabuliwallah" (the fruit-seller from Kabul) is representative. A fruit-seller from far away Kabul becomes acquainted with Mini, a young girl who reminds him of his daughter. He is imprisoned for many years, and after his release returns with such gifts as he used to give her. When he sees her arrayed for her wedding, he suddenly realizes that his own daughter, too, has grown into something quite different from the image he carries in his heart. Time has rolled on, though memory had seemed to hold it motionless.

Among Tagore's plays, *Sacrifice* is characteristic. In it Kali, a goddess to whom blood sacrifices have traditionally been made, is again to receive the blood of a human. The king, Govinda, recognizes the savage cruelty of the custom and declares an end to it; no more blood, human or animal, is to be shed for Kali. Gunavati, his wife, commands as queen that the sacrifices continue and, in order to appease the goddess, plots to have the king's own life taken and his blood sacrificed. The various characters take sides, and the plot against the king develops as Gunavati insists that royal blood must appease Kali. Jaising, himself of royal blood and a servant of the temple, promises to do as Gunavati asks, but in the end he sacrifices himself. Those who have demanded royal blood are appalled at this product of their own savagery. The stone goddess is cast out, the blood sacrifice ended.

Comparative: The poems from Tagore's *Gitanjali* have a quality which at times touches that of the biblical psalms; they may also be compared to Blake's *Songs of Innocence.* "The Cabuliwallah" is perhaps best compared with other stories and plays by Tagore, for he has a quality all his own. Comparison, however, also suggests contrast, and it is interesting to read Mérimée's "Mateo Falcone," the story of an altogether different relationship between a man and a child, in conjunction with Tagore's story. The play *Sacrifice* may be directly compared to Racine's *Athalie,* a play in which a temple and a tradition are subject to rebellion. Here both comparison and contrast are pointed. Again, however, other Tagore stories and plays offer the most enriching reading, especially for their underlying sensitivity and for their revelation of one of the major cultures of the world.

Tolstoi, Lev Nikolaevich. ANNA KARENINA. 1878. Novel. Russian.

Author: Tolstoi (1828-1910) was a novelist, dramatist, social reformer, and mystic. He served in the Crimean War, commanding forces at Sevastopol, and retired to the country to write. There he evolved a mystical approach to Christianity that eventually separated him from the Orthodox church. In 1861 he freed his serfs and instituted land reforms. Tolstoi was an important force in Russia as it emerged from feudalism.

Work: This psychological love story is set against a sociological examination of nineteenth-century aristocratic Russia; in it a man and a woman defy the institution of marriage but find in passion no substitute.

Anna Karenina comes to Moscow to patch up a quarrel between her brother, Stepan Oblonski, and his wife, Dolly, a quarrel that threatens to end in divorce. Anna's peacemaking provides a fine irony, for it is here that she meets the cavalry officer, Count Vronski, a meeting that will lead to an affair. Unable to secure a divorce from her husband, the ambitious, cold, remote Alexei Karenin, Anna and Vronski go off to Italy after she has borne Vronski's child.

Paralleling the domestic rupture between Stepan and Dolly is the relationship between Karenin and Anna; contrasting with these affairs is the story of the bumbling, honest Levin, the foil to Vronski, and his patient courtship of Kitty, Dolly's sister.

After a grand tour, Anna and Vronski return to Russia and try to find happiness in rebuilding Vronski's country estate. Again a strong contrast, for what Vronski attempts in a lordly manner, the conscientious Levin, the vehicle for Tolstoi's social beliefs, accomplishes humbly. Tension grows between Anna and Vronski, who are confronted with the unyielding self-righteousness of Karenin, everywhere regarded as a saint for his tolerance. Gradually the lovers sense their growing need for the sanctions of society. When events reach a desperate pitch, Anna, remembering a railroad accident on the day she met Vronski, throws herself under an approaching train and is killed. The carefully nurtured love and marriage between Levin and Kitty continues in happiness for both.

Comparative: An equally famous story of passion is Flaubert's *Madame Bovary;* however, Emma aspires to the social glory that Anna at first spurns, throwing away everything for love. Another love triangle that ends fatally is found in Goethe's *The Sorrows of Young Werther,* a romantically passionate story without the desperate realism of Tolstoi's lovers. The inflexible Karenin is the typical Russian bureaucrat; see Tolstoi's *The Death of Ivan Ilyich* and Gogol's "The Overcoat" for other examples. Vronski seems to follow the prototype of Pechorin in Lermontov's *A Hero of Our Time.* More light on Tolstoi's views about marriage may be gained from his *Kreutzer Sonata,* a bad-tempered exposé.

Tolstoi, Lev Nikolaevich. THE DEATH OF IVAN ILYICH (SMERT' IVANA ILYICHA). 1886. Novella. Russian.

Author: See *Anna Karenina.*

Work: In his early novella *Family Happiness* (1859) Tolstoi wrote: "The only certain happiness in life is to live for others." That statement might serve as an epigraph for this later tale about a man who tried and failed to find happiness, not in living for others but in living for their approval.

Ivan Ilyich Golovin, since adolescence, has lived a proper, pleasant, decorous life. A shallow man, he has always acted out of a sense of propriety and to advance his career. Only through a freak accident that leads to a slow and painful death does he come to recognize the deceit of his own life and its utter waste. As his body decays, he examines his past actions and, though at first he refuses to admit the possibility, comes to realize that his whole life has been cut off from meaningful human contact or emotion. Only a few incidents in his childhood appear to have been truly happy. Even now his only truly human contact is with his servant Gerasin, whose patient and simple devotion to his master show Ivan how life should be lived, in contrast to the coldness and deceit of those who surround the dying man and pretend to care about his comfort. But Tolstoi ends this story on a note of optimism, and Ivan re-establishes contact with his family immediately before his death. Instead of the darkness which he feared, there is light and joy. Although the beginning of the tale, which describes events after his death, indicates that his death has had little impact on his wife and friends, the sincere sorrow of his son is proof that Ivan Ilyich has not lived in vain.

Comparative: The idea of finding happiness in living for others is found throughout Tolstoi's work, particularly in *Anna Karenina* and in the novellas *Family Happiness* and *Master and Man.* This theme appears in numerous works of literature by other authors, including Coleridge's *Rime of the Ancient Mariner,* Dostoevski's *The Dream of a Ridiculous Man, Crime and Punishment* and *Notes from Underground,* Hesse's *Steppenwolf,* and Camus's *The Plague.* Chekhov's "A Dreary Story" also contains the reminiscence of a man who dies realizing he has led a spiritually bankrupt life; Chekhov, however, does not offer us Tolstoi's optimistic ending.

The importance of living according to principles gained from a meticulous and thoroughly honest appraisal of one's self and one's society is a chief concern of numerous existential authors, although not all of them have Tolstoi's spirituality. The characters in Sartre's *No Exit* realize too late that their lives have been total deceptions, and the hero of his *Nausea* viciously attacks the arrogant bourgeois who remind us of Ivan Ilyich before his self-examination.

Turgenev, Ivan Sergeyevich. FATHERS AND SONS (OTTSY I DETI). 1862.
    Novel. Russian.

Author: Ivan Turgenev (1818–1883) was born in Russia and educated in Petersburg, Moscow, and Berlin. His works are concerned with the social problems of Russia and ultimately were important in effecting changes in Russian ideology. His earliest work to receive public acclaim was *A Sportsman's Sketches,* published in 1852. His most popular novel, *Fathers and Sons,* caused a furor among critics and resulted in his leaving Russia and living until his death in France, an expatriate. Among his other novels are *Smoke, On the Eve, Virgin Soil,* and *Clara Milich.*

Work: In this novel we have a realistic treatment of social problems existing in mid-nineteenth century Russia. Bazarov, nihilist son of Vassily Ivanovich, and Arkadi, son of Nikolai Petrovich, are recent graduates of the University at Petersburg. The long ride home from the university provides occasion for the young men to see the countryside and to sense the necessity for social reforms as they observe the almost barren landscape, the small villages of "low hovels under dark and often tumble-down roofs," and the peasants themselves, appearing in bold relief "like beggars along the roadside." Both

Arkadi and Bazarov are warmly welcomed home, but each lacks a completely satisfying contact with his father, especially Bazarov, whom Arkadi idolizes and who is the more radical in his thinking.

Here the reader sees the influence of the new theory of science which caused much concern regarding humanity's place in and relation to the universe. Bazarov is the exponent of the new scientific theory of Nature, and his arrogant, negative attitude toward Russian romanticism becomes intolerable, especially to Pavel, Arkadi's uncle. Arkadi describes his friend "as a man who does not bow down before any authority, who does not take any principle on faith, whatever reverence that principle may be enshrined in."

The reader also sees a direct contrast between the misery of peasant life and the luxury of aristocracy as Bazarov and Arkadi enjoy a visit with Madame Odintsov and her sister, Katya. Attractive and educated, Madame Odintsov proves an ideal match for the nihilistic Bazarov. Arkadi, meanwhile, is charmed by Katya.

There is an outright confrontation between the old aristocracy and its romantic ideas and the new generation as we breathlessly watch Bazarov engage in a duel with Pavel (at Pavel's suggestion). And just as Pavel is only slightly wounded, so does Bazarov make only small gains toward reforming the traditional Russian culture. Consistently pursuing his interest in physics and science, Bazarov does not accept Madame Odintsov. In medical practice with his father, he becomes infected with typhus, and "the lamp" of the times goes out while Madame Odintsov stands by affectionately.

Finally, Arkadi's father marries his mistress and Arkadi marries Katya, and father and son work harmoniously to implement significant reforms in the Russian social structure.

Both fathers have been made aware of the impact and inevitability of change. Speaking of Bazarov, Vassili explains to his wife, "A son is a separate piece cut off. He's like the falcon that flies home and flies away at his pleasure. While you and I are like funguses in the hollow of a tree, we sit side by side, and don't move from our place. Only I am left for you unchanged forever as you for me."

Comparative: The conflict between the old and the new is central to Chekhov's *The Cherry Orchard,* to Gerhart Hauptmann's *The Weavers,* and to Zola's novel *Germinal.* Relationships between fathers and sons are also seen in Thomas Mann's *Buddenbrooks,* in Homer's *Odyssey,* and in Mérimée's short story "Mateo Falcone," to suggest only a few.

Tutuola, Amos. MY LIFE IN THE BUSH OF GHOSTS. 1954. Novel. Nigerian.

Author: Amos Tutuola (1920–   ), a young Yoruban writer of Nigeria, lacks the formal training of many of his contemporaries, but he is one of the most prominent of African writers. He received only six years of schooling, and his unsophisticated use of English has been both praised and condemned by critics. His best works include, in addition to the above novel, *The Palm-Wine Drinkard* (1952), *Simbi and the Satyr of the Dark Jungle* (1955), and *The Brave African Hunters* (1958).

Work: My Life in the Bush of Ghosts recounts the traumatic and terrifying experiences of a seven-year-old boy, but it is on a deeper level a study of West African life and culture, incorporating myths, folktales, and proverbs with the deep religious conviction with which the African is born.

Because of the hatred of their father's wives and their daughters, two brothers, ages seven and eleven, are forced to leave home. Neither knows the meaning of *bad* and *good.* The seven-year-old, our hero, is abandoned by his brother under a fruit tree which he calls "The Future Sign." As an army of slave-traders comes near, the boy dodges unknowingly into the Bush of Ghosts.

Relying upon a stream-of-consciousness technique, the author now presents the boy on an imaginary journey filled with horror. He ventures from one ghost town to another, becoming variously a dead man, a teacher of ghosts, and finally a magician. Through his magic powers, the boy becomes a person again. After many death-defying episodes, he meets the Television-handed Ghost whom he cures of her two-hundred-year-old sores. In return, she gives him a view into her palm "exactly as a television" where he sees his home town, his family, and his friends. A second look at her palm reveals that he is already back under the fruit tree from where his journey began. Thus, after twenty-four years of wandering in a kind of inferno, the boy, now a learned man and a Christian, is once again reunited with his family. Having eaten from the fruit of the tree, he emerges with full knowledge of *good* and *bad.*

The boy embodies the African's natural "sorrows,"—pain and suffering; but he also represents the African's hopes,—social, economic, and political aspirations.

Comparative: The story contains many biblical allusions. The tree of The Future Sign parallels the tree of knowledge in Eden, and snakes have a prominent role in the novel as does the serpent in the story of Adam and Eve. The boy's experiences are similar to Dante's in the *Inferno* and in some respects to those of Gulliver in Swift's *Gulliver's Travels.* His innocence and youth may bring to mind experiences in Carroll's *Alice in Wonderland.* The "Super Lady," his second wife in the Bush of Ghosts, exerts the same power over him that Circe wields over Odysseus in Homer's *Odyssey.*

Undset, Sigrid. KRISTIN LAVRANSDATTER. 1920–1922. Novel. Norwegian.

Author: The daughter of a well-known archaeologist, Sigrid Undset (1882–1949) had a life-long interest in history; indeed, much of her prolific writing consists of historical novels. She won the Nobel Prize in 1928. She was also deeply concerned with the role of women and gave that concern a large place in her writing. Her first novel, *Marthe Oulie*, was published in 1907 when she was twenty-five. This, *Vigaljot and Vigdie* (1909) and *Jenny* (1920, her first really successful novel) may be regarded as preparation for her magnum opus, the trilogy, *Kristin Lavransdatter*. Women, history, and saints are prominent in her writing. Undset died in the loghouse she had built in Lillehammer, a home that was almost a copy of the typical Norwegian home of the fourteenth century.

Work: Kristin Lavransdatter consists of three novels: *Kransen* or *The Bridal Wreath* (1920), *Husfrue* or *The Mistress of Husaby* (1921), and *Korset* or *The Cross* (1922). The trilogy presents the life, first, of a young woman torn between the Christian morality of her home and her love for a dashing young man, Erlend, who is far more pagan than Christian. They marry, and the conflict grows as she alternates between joyful love and pangs of conscience. As a mother she finds that she must become manager of the household and agricultural estate while her husband pursues adventure. The story is deeply moving, as Kristin is forced either to bow to unfavorable circumstances or to grow, as she does, to remarkable stature.

The work combines psychological insight with historical penetration, and the reader learns what it is to live in a period of transition, to confront the pull of a tradition which does not want to die and the force of a new era struggling to become established. The story is set in the fourteenth century, when Norway was moving from a deeply rooted Nordic faith to Christianity, from a society based on hunting, fishing, and adventure to one built on a fixed agricultural economy. The superstitious and the physically strong tend to cling to the old ways; the aged, the crippled, the weak, those who are unfit for the physical struggle, gradually turn to the gentler Christian tradition, supported by the priests and by the few of great spiritual strength. This period of transition is brought to us with great force in *Kristin Lavransdatter,* a work that stands among the best historical fiction.

Comparative: Sir Walter Scott's *Quentin Durward,* a historical novel of fifteenth-century France, offers a fine comparison, both for its strong, central character and for its background of Medieval-Renaissance transition. *Lydia Bailey* by Kenneth Roberts gives us another heroine in a historical setting, the native uprisings in Haiti under Toussaint L'Ouverture.

Valmiki. RAMAYANA. 300 B.C. Epic. Indian.

Author: Valmiki, traditionally believed to be the author of the *Ramayana,* includes himself in the action as a minor character. It is generally held that the poet brought together material from the oral tradition in order to compose a court epic. Little is known of him other than what he has chosen to record within his own work.

Work: This Indian epic is read both for its story (swiftly moving in English abridged translations) and for its religious meaning to the Hindu, who hold it in reverence as Christians do the New Testament. Dasaratha's eldest son, Rama, by bending a heroic bow, wins the hand of Sita, princess of a neighboring kingdom. Dasaratha identifies Rama as his successor; however, Kaikeyi, one of Dasaratha's wives, desires the throne for her own son, Bharata, and exacts fulfillment of an old promise (much like the promise of aid that Theseus had from Poseidon in Euripides' *Hippolytus*). Rama is exiled for fourteen years. He accepts the banishment, and with Sita and Laksmana, his brother, goes into the wilderness.

    After many adventures, Laksmana is one day desired by the princess Surpa-Nakha. He spurns her, and in a rage she compromises Laksmana to her brother Ravana, king of the Raksasas—half-beastlike, half-godlike people who inhabit Ceylon (note a similar implication in Phaedra's accusation of Hippolytus). Ravana lures Laksmana and Rama away on a hunt and takes the beautiful Sita prisoner. Rama makes an alliance with the monkey-people and begins a war for the recovery of his wife.

    The battle, fierce and long, is described in the conventional detail of epic warfare. Both Ravana and Rama are aided by supernatural powers, but Rama has Shiva on his side and is able to slay the brave but ungodly Ravana. Sita is freed from captivity and proves that she has maintained her virtue. The heroes Rama and Laksmana return to their kingdom and to peace and honor. In an epilogue, Laksmana is later condemned to death by Rama for a breach of faith, and Sita is exiled.

Comparative: There are obvious parallels with the *Iliad:* The siege of Ceylon is similar to that of Ilium; the "rape" of Sita compares with that of Helen; and gods and goddesses enter into the action. The *Ramayana* perhaps shows a greater sensitivity to nature than do Western epics, and the heroic figures of Indian legend are gentle sages as well as fierce warriors. The *Nibelungenlied* is also a strikingly comparable epic, not only in its scenes of war and of travel, but in its young, heroic Siegfried (like Rama, a too-perfect hero) and in the young Kriemhild, who bears some resemblance to Sita. The tests of loyalty, essential in both epics, differ greatly, however, and the characters in the *Nibelungenlied* are portrayed with greater depth.

Vega Carpio, Lope de. FUENTEOVEJUNA. ca. 1619. Drama. Spanish.

Author: Lope de Vega (1562–1635) founded Spanish national drama. Born in Madrid, he was banished from Spain at the age of twenty-two as a result of a duel. He served in the Spanish Armada, became secretary to the Duke of Alba, and at thirty-four returned to Spain. He was ordained a priest after the death of his wife and finally became a doctor of theology. He is reputedly the author of over 1,500 plays, of which 431 survived.

Work: In this three-act comedy a small town, Fuenteovejuna, revolts against the injustices of its military commandant, who has incited a young nobleman to engage in a war against Isabella and Ferdinand and has then returned to Fuenteovejuna, where he rules with an iron hand—particularly the women of the town. Among the maidens who strike his fancy is Laurencia, but her lover, Frondoso, threatens the Commander with his own crossbow. The Commander is more successful with Jancinate, in spite of Mengo's courage in standing up to the Commander's henchmen. When the Commander leaves Fuentoeovejuna to fight another battle, Laurencia and Frondoso plan a wedding festival, but the Commander returns in the midst of it, arrests the bold Frondoso, and drags Laurencia to his castle to be beaten and tortured.

When Laurencia is released, her taunts drive the villagers to rebellion. The men are joined by the women in a successful assault on the Commander's castle. King Ferdinand, notified of this uprising, sends a judge and a military unit to investigate. Even under torture the villagers refuse to implicate one another, testifying only that "Fuenteovejuna did it." Brought before the King himself, the villagers tell of the Commander's injustices, and Ferdinand pardons the town.

Comparative: The play was not meant to tell the story of a town's rebellion against injustice, as it seems; rather, Lope de Vega intended that the play document the King's mercy and honor. A twentieth-century reader not indoctrinated with classical Spanish doctrines of honor will, however, discover commonalities with the peasants' revolt in Hauptmann's *The Weavers,* with that of the miners in Zola's *Germinal,* and with a similar revolt in Corrado Alvaro's *Revolt in Aspromonte.* As a compulsive lover the Commander resembles Molière's Don Juan; like Almaviva in Beaumarchais's *The Marriage of Figaro,* he exercises certain seigneurial privileges toward women. The descriptions of medieval armor, panoply, war, and procession given by Flores in Act I shows a closeness to epic models; see *Poem of the Cid,* the *Song of Roland,* and the *Aeneid.* The notion of the morally diseased small town is found in Sartre's *The Flies,* in Pérez Galdós's *Doña Perfecta,* in Dürrenmatt's *The Visit,* in Giraudoux's *The Enchanted,* in Gerstäcker's *Germelshausen,* in Ibsen's *An Enemy of the People,* and in Mark Twain's *The Man That Corrupted Hadleyburg.*

Verne, Jules. JOURNEY TO THE CENTER OF THE EARTH (VOYAGE AU CENTRE DE LA TERRE). 1864. Novel. French.

Author: Jules Verne (1828-1905) was born at Nantes. After studying law in Paris, he wrote librettos for two operas and then divided his time between the stock exchange and literature. Verne had a vivid imagination and a gift for popularizing science. His early successes were short stories, and novels followed rapidly—*Five Weeks in a Balloon, 20,000 Leagues under the Sea,* and *Around the World in Eighty Days*—all written with verve and all prophetic.

Work: This novel is considered by many to be the grandfather of all science fiction. Professor Hardwigg discovers an old Icelandic manuscript that tells him and his nephew, Harry, how to climb down an extinct volcano and reach the bowels of the earth. With the help of taciturn, capable, and loyal Hans, an Icelandic guide, they descent into Mt. Sneffels. They are injured, lost, and starved; they suffer incredible frights (an electrical storm over a monstrous subterrestrial sea, a battle between antediluvian creatures, a boiling stream); and they make amazing discoveries (primitive man, alive and well near the center of the earth) before they are finally cast out on the slopes of Stromboli by the good graces of an erupting volcano.

Comparative: Verne's lively style derives from Dumas. Comparatives in the genre of travel-science fiction include H. Rider Haggard's novels and Edgar Rice Burrough's *Pellucidar* or *At The Earth's Core.* Science fiction often takes a philosophical and social turn, and one might compare Verne's work with *Gulliver's Travels,* emphasizing Swift's allegorical handling of an impossible travel story and Verne's relatively trivial manner.

Villon, François, pseudonym of François de Montcorbier. THE COMPLETE WORKS: LE LAIS, LE TESTAMENT, POÉSIES DIVERSES, AND LE JARGON ET JOBELIN. Edited by Andre Lanly. French and European Pubns., 1969. Written from 1456 to 1463. Lyric poems. French.

Author: François Villon was born in Paris in 1431. Little accurate biographical data is available. The name Villon he adopted from his patron. Villon received his Master of Arts degree in 1452 from the Sorbonne, and his life as a student and afterwards is notable for association with the *demi-monde.* In 1455 Villon killed a young priest, presumably over a young woman. While awaiting a pardon for his crime, he composed *Le Lais* or *Petit Testament.* Soon afterwards he was involved in the robbery of the College of Navarre and quit Paris to avoid police inquiry. Thus Villon began four and a half years of self-imposed exile. Much of the material in *Poésies Diverses* was written during this period. By 1461 he was imprisoned for an unknown crime but released. Returning to the outskirts of Paris, he spent the winter of 1461–1462 hiding out and composing his masterpiece, *Le Testament,* a poem of some two thousand lines. In 1463 he was again involved in an ugly street crime involving a papal functionary. Exasperated by Villon's criminal record, the authorities had him tortured and sentenced to be "strangled and hanged on the gallows of Paris." However, Villon appealed to Parliament, which annulled the sentence but banished him from Paris for ten years "in view of his bad character." Villon left Paris in January of 1463, never to be heard of again.

Work: In *Le Lais* or *Petit Testament* (1456), translated as *Bequests* or *The Legacy,* Villon employs a recognized medieval form composed of forty stanzas of eight octosyllabic lines on three rhymes. The work is satirical and allegorical, a half-mocking, half-serious farewell to his Parisian friends. The various bequests suggest the legatee's weaknesses as well as those of the poet, who bequeaths his "poor, pale, and piteous heart" to his mistress.

Le Testament (1461), Villon's principal work—186 stanzas similar to those of *Bequests* interspersed with "showpiece" *ballades.* Here a saddened Villon jests with life's pathos and mixes the sublime with the sordid. "Ballade des dames du temps jadis" ("Ballade of the Ladies of Bygone Times") laments the passing of youth and beauty and the inevitability of death and includes the famous refrain: "But where are the snows of yesteryear?" Tennessee Williams uses this refrain in *The Glass Menagerie.* "Ballade pour prier Nostre Dame" ("Ballade as a Prayer to Our Lady") has Villon's old mother voicing the tender and passionately devout faith of a humble, illiterate woman. This piece reflects a serious religious theme which colors but does not motivate much of his poetry. "Ballade de la Grosse Margot" ("Ballade for Fat Margot") is a realistic, frank, and sordid picture of his entanglements in a brothel, with a fatalistic recognition of his shame, defiance, and self-loathing: "We both love filth, and filth pursues us; We flee from honor, honor flees from us." The Lament of the Belle Heaulmiére for her lost beauty parallels that of Chaucer's Wife of Bath and the advice Heaulmiére gives to beautiful women ("Love while you are able, spare no man/Take all the profit you can get") sounds as modern as the words of Lorelei Lee in *Gentlemen Prefer Blondes.*

Miscellaneous Poems (Poésies Diverses) is often called *The Codicil.* This collection of 693 lines is composed mainly of ballades. Ballade XIV, "L'Épitaphe Villon" or "Ballade of the Hanged," combines several of Villon's themes which spring from intensely personal sensations. Brotherhood, religious faith, vice, and suffering humanity are echoed in the famous epitaph of the gibbeted corpse, lines 21-30. Here Villon, the subjective realist, imagines his own death by hanging and calls on God to "absolve us all."

Poems in Slang (Le Jargon et Jobelin, 1463) total 189 lines. These six poems rely on the slang of Villon's *demi-monde* and can not be translated with accuracy. Jobelin is taken from the Patriarch Job, the patron of beggars.

Comparative: The poetry of Villon is troublesome in its allusive nature; however, it is also the poetry of personal experience, unembarrassed by self-revelation. As such, it has much in common with the works of St. Augustine, Byron, Baudelaire, and Verlaine. Oscar Wilde's *Ballad of Reading Goal,* Jean Genet's *The Thief's Journal* and *Our Lady of the Flowers,* Brendan Behan's *Borstal Boy,* and A. E. Houseman's *A Shropshire Lad* possess similarities to

Villon's poetry in emotional impact, in the quality of personal revelation, and in subject matter.

Virgil (Publius Vergilius Maro). AENEID. 30-19 B.C. Epic poem. Roman.

Author: Virgil (70 B.C.-19 B.C.) was born near Mantua and educated at Cremona and Milan. Weak health prevented him from following a military career, and in 53 B.C. he went to Rome to study rhetoric and philosophy. In 43 B.C. he published the first of his ten *Eclogues;* these imitations of the idylls of Theocritus were immediately successful. Later he lived in Naples, supported by the generosity of friends, especially Maecenas, political advisor to Augustus. Here Virgil devoted himself to study, and in 30 B.C. he published the *Georgics,* a book on agriculture which celebrates in verse the importance of the farmer's life. He now began the *Aeneid,* which he had already promised to Augustus. After eleven years of work, he decided to travel to Greece and to the Middle East while he worked on the revision, but he died abruptly after visiting Athens. At Augustus's command, two friends edited and published the national epic, which was received enthusiastically.

Work: The Trojan prince, Aeneas, son of Anchises and Venus, is hounded by the angry goddess Juno as the epic opens; shipwrecked near Carthage, he and his men are welcomed by Queen Dido. Following a banquet, Aeneas tells of the fall of Troy, how he bade the shade of his dead wife farewell, how he shouldered his old father (who in turn carried the Trojan household goods) and led his son Iulus out of the burning city. The tale of his subsequent wanderings for seven years stirs Dido's admiration and love, and soon their love affair obscures both her queenly duties and his mission (twice he has been told that his destiny is to search for the land of his earliest ancestors and to establish a new Troy). Jupiter now sends Mercury to remind Aeneas of his duty, and Aeneas secretly prepares to depart. Dido finds out, however. Unable to dissuade him, she decides to kill herself. Aeneas and his followers see from their northward bound ship the blaze of her funeral pyre. Aeneas and his men seek out the Cumaen sibyl (an ancient prophetess) who predicts the future of Aeneas and guides him into the Underworld where he meets Dido's shade, many former heroes, and his father, who reveals to him the souls of his illustrious descendants. Reaching Latium (an Italian kingdom at the mouth of the Tiber), Aeneas is befriended by King Latinus, who offers Aeneas the hand of his only daughter Lavinia. Turnus, king of the neighboring Rutulians and Lavinia's former suitor, mobilizes his people against the Trojans and a long war ensues, during which Turnus is killed. No obstacles remain to the founding of the Roman Empire by Aeneas.

Comparative: Comparison with Homer is both instructive and indispensable. In his desire to do for Rome what Homer had done for Greece, Virgil explicitly uses Homeric incidents—the descent to the Underworld, the post-banquet recital, the anger and interventions of the gods. Further, he uses invocations, catalogues, elaborate similes, prophecies, and other devices which have become the conventions of the literary epic.

Insofar as this is a literary rather than an oral or folk epic, its intention is clear: to celebrate great issues and representative individuals. Odysseus is a hero in his own right, and Aeneas knows he must embody the Roman virtues. Similarly, Milton's Adam will later represent the human race. Learned associations indicate Virgil's assimilation of his own literary and historical tradition, and echoes of Catullus, Theocritus, and Apollonius of Rhodes, as well as of Homer, can be heard. After Virgil, many epics echoed his.

Because Virgil was assumed to be prophesying the coming of Christ in the fourth *Eclogue,* he was acceptable to the Christian world and from the earliest middle ages was considered the world's greatest poet. Translated into Gaelic before 1400, and into French, English, Scottish, and German before the mid-sixteenth century, Virgil remained a major influence on European letters. Dante paid him perhaps the greatest homage by making him his guide through the *Inferno* and *Purgatorio* sections of *The Divine Comedy.* Milton, Tasso, and Camões each wrote epics with the explicit intention of rivaling Virgil, doing for their countries what Virgil had done for his.

Romance is yet another descendant of the *Aeneid.* During the late Middle Ages and Renaissance, fabulous adventure and marital prowess provided entire plots without concern for heroic ideals. Fancy was admired for itself: Boiardo and Ariosto *(Orlando furioso)* wrote in this tradition.

Wu, Ch'eng-en. **RECORD OF A JOURNEY TO THE WEST (HSI YÜ CHI).** 16th Century. Novel. Chinese.

Author: Wu Ch'eng-en (ca. 1500-1582) is reputed to be the author of this work, although at least one critic argues that he was the most important author, suggesting that others had a hand in the work. Inconsistency of style would seem to verify this. Wu apparently was a man of leisure, for he found the time to write this very long novel as well as a volume of classical poetry, and prose. Contrary to the literati of his time who called for a classical revival, Wu wrote in the vulgar tongue, the language of the people. For this reason, so it is said, his name was not initially associated with the work. Indeed, the anonymity of the book was so complete that, according to one critic, it was erroneously attributed to a travel writer for over three centuries. The book has been partially translated by Arthur Waley under the title *Monkey.*

Work: This rollicking, robust, episodic novel describes the adventurous pilgrimage to India of the priest Hsüan-tsang in search of the scriptures.

While Hsüan-tsang occupies the pivotal position in the action of the novel, Monkey, a supernatural rogue who accompanies him, is the true protagonist. They are joined by Pigsy and Sandy. If one reads this novel as allegory, Monkey can be seen to represent the restless energies of the imaginative and creative spirit; Pigsy, brute strength and the physical appetites; and Sandy, *ch'eng,* sincerity or wholeheartedness. The novel can also be read as a political satire on bureaucracy, which exists in heaven just as it does on earth. The novel, however, can be enjoyed without looking for hidden meanings or taking it as seriously as some Buddhist, Taoist, or Marxist commentators have taken it. It is above all a high-spirited novel which provokes laughter at ourselves and a recognition that human foibles are perennial and universal. In a translation of the novel, Arthur Waley observes, *"Monkey* is unique in its combination of beauty with absurdity, of profundity with nonsense. Folklore, allegory, religion, history, anti-bureaucratic satire and pure poetry—such are the singularly diverse elements out of which the book is compounded."

One critic, Yi'tse Mai Feuerwerker, has noted that the novel gave the author an opportunity to set forth his views of human nature, without bitterness or regret. People in the quest for salvation, encounter innumerable obstacles and unknown dangers. Bewildered, blundering, rash, absurd, they are unable to understand fully the implications of the journey or, perhaps, to be worthy of salvation, yet are nevertheless pretty tough, resourceful, and above all likable. This novel should be read for the contact it provides with a state of mind.

Comparative: Bunyan's *Pilgrim's Progress* and Cervantes' *Don Quixote* are commonly cited as Western counterparts; however, *The Sot-weed Factor* by the contemporary writer John Barth comes closer to the tone and irreverence of *Monkey.* The novel's use of the supernatural can also be compared to that in some science fiction works. Monkey often reminds the reader of the comic book hero Superman.

Zola, Émile. GERMINAL. 1885. Novel. French.

Author: Born in Aix-en-Provence, son of a French mother and an Italian father, Émile Zola (1840-1902) had an impoverished youth. He became, however, a prolific, successful, and wealthy writer.

Work: Germinal, generally considered one of Zola's masterpieces, effectively depicts the life of French miners in the mid to late nineteenth century. The hero, a socialist who leads a strike against the managers of the mine because of low wages and desperate working conditions, is nevertheless more moderate than some of the miners he leads. At last the miners, starving and feeling that they have nothing to lose, riot. A number of miners are killed and our hero is deported. The conditions in the mine grow worse than ever.

A dedicated Naturalist, Zola conceived of his characters as victims of heredity and environment. The effects he attributed to environment are usually more acceptable to modern readers than are those he granted to heredity. Zola's attempts at scientific observation leave a good deal to be desired, but his descriptions of the seamier side of life in France in his time earn him a secure place in literary history.

Comparative: For similar depictions of society, see Chekhov, Dickens, and Dostoevski. American writers in the naturalistic mode include Theodore Dreiser and James T. Farrell.

Selected Bibliographies

Anthologies

General World Literature

Anderson, George K. and Robert Warnock, eds. *The World in Literature.* 2d rev. ed. Glenview, Illinois: Scott, Foresman & Co., 1967.

Barnstone, Willis, ed. *Modern European Poetry.* New York: Bantam Books, Inc., 1966.

Bentley, Eric, ed. *The Classic Theatre* (Vol. I Six Italian Plays; Vol. II Five German Plays; Vol. III Six Spanish Plays; Vol. IV Six French Plays). New York: Doubleday Anchor, 1959.

Giamatti, A. Bartlett. *Western Literature.* New York: Harcourt Brace Jovanovich, 1971.

Haydn, Hiram and John Cournos, eds. *A World of Great Stories.* New York: Crown Pubs., Inc., 1947.

Junkins, Donald, ed. *The Contemporary World Poets.* New York: Harcourt Brace Jovanovich, 1976.

Mack, Maynard, et al., eds. *World Masterpieces.* 3d ed., 2 vols. New York: W. W. Norton, 1973.

Martin, Michael Rheta, ed. *The World's Love Poetry.* New York: Bantam Books, Inc., 1960.

McDonnell, Helen M. *Nobel Parade: Selections by Winners of the Award for Literature.* Glenview, Illinois: Scott, Foresman & Co., 1975.

Classical Literature

Fitts, Dudley, trans. *Poems from the Greek Anthology.* New York: New Directions, 1956.

Guinagh, Kevin and Alfred P. Dorjahn, eds. *Latin Literature in Translation.* New York: Longman, Green and Company, Ltd., 1942.

Grene, David and Richmond Lattimore, eds. *The Complete Greek Tragedies.* Chicago: University of Chicago Press, 1959.

Harsh, Philip W., ed. *An Anthology of Roman Drama.* New York: Holt Rinehart Winston, 1960.

Murray, Gilbert. *The Classical Tradition in Greek Poetry.* New York: Vintage Press, 1957.

African Literature

Cartey, Wilfred G., ed. *Whispers From a Continent.* New York: Vintage Books, 1969.

Hughes, Langston, ed. *An African Treasury: Articles, Essays, Stories, Poems by Black Africans.* New York: Crown Pubs., Inc., 1960.

Komey, Ellis Ayitey and Ezekiel Mphahlele, eds. *Modern African Stories.* London: Faber and Faber, 1964.

Litto, Fredric M., ed. *Plays from Black Africa.* New York: Hill and Wang, 1968.

Moore, Clark D. and Ann Dunbar, eds. *Africa Yesterday and Today.* New York: Praeger Pubs., 1969.

Moore, Gerald and Ulli Beier, eds. *Modern Poetry from Africa.* Baltimore: Penguin Books, 1963.

Mphahlele, Ezekiel, ed. *African Writing Today.* Penguin Books, 1970.

Okpaku, Joseph, ed. *New African Literature and the Arts, Volumes I & II.* New York: Thomas Y. Crowell Company, 1970.

Parsons, Donald St. John, ed. *Our Poets Speak.* London: University of London Press, Ltd., 1966.

Rive, Richard, ed. *Quartet: New Voices from South Africa.* New York: Humanities Press, Inc., 1963.

Rutherfoord, Peggy, ed. *African Voices: An Anthology of Native African Writing.* New York: Grossett & Dunlap, 1970.

Shelton, Austin J., Jr., ed. *African Assertion: A Critical Anthology of African Literature.* New York: Odyssey Press, 1968.

Tibble, Anne, ed. *African English Literature.* New York: October House, 1969.

French Literature

Bermel, Albert, ed. *The Genius of the French Theater.* New York: New American Library, 1961.

Bree, Germaine, ed. *Great French Short Stories.* New York: Dell, 1964.

Bree, Germaine, ed. *19th Century French Short Stories in the Original French.* New York: Dell, 1966.

Comfort, Andrew, ed. *Seven Short Novel Masterpieces.* New York: Popular Library, Inc., 1965.

Condor, Alan, comp. and tr. *A Treasury of French Poetry.* New York: Harper, 1951.

Fowlie, Wallace, ed. and tr. *Classical French Drama.* New York: Bantam Books, Inc., 1962.

Geist, Stanley, ed. *French Stories and Tales.* New York: Washington Square Press, 1961.

MacIntyre, C. F., tr. *French Symbolist Poetry.* Berkeley: University of California Press, 1961.

German Literature

Lange, Victor, ed. *Great German Short Novels and Stories.* New York: Modern Library, Inc., 1952.

Schwebell, Gertrude Clorius, ed. and tr. *Contemporary German Poetry, An Anthology.* New York: New Directions, 1964.

Spender, Stephen. *Great German Short Stories.* New York: Dell, 1960.

Middleton, Christopher, ed. *German Writing Today.* Baltimore: Penguin Books, Inc., 1967.

Peck, Robert, ed. *German Stories and Tales.* New York: Washington Square Press, 1955.

Lustig, Theodore H., tr. *Classical German Drama.* New York: Bantam Books, Inc., 1963.

Irish Literature

Barnet, Sylvan, Morton Berman, and William Burto, eds. *The Genius of the Irish Theater.* New York: Mentor Books, 1960.

Garrity, Devin A., ed. *Irish Stories and Tales.* New York: Washington Square Press, 1961.

O'Connor, Frank. *A Short History of Irish Literature.* New York: Capricorn Books, 1968.

Italian Literature

Bentley, Eric, ed. *The Genius of the Italian Theater.* New York: New American Library, 1964.

Golino, Carlo L., *Contemporary Italian Poetry: An Anthology.* Berkeley and Los Angeles: University of California Press, 1962.

Johnson, Bed., ed. *Stories of Modern Italy.* New York: The Modern Library Inc., 1960.

Lind, L. R. *Lyric Poetry of the Italian Renaissance: An Anthology with Verse Translations.* New Haven: Yale, 1954.

Latin American Literature

Cohen, J. M., ed. *Latin American Writing Today.* Baltimore: Penguin Books, Inc., 1967.

deOnis, Harriet. *Spanish Stories and Tales.* Repr. of 1954 ed. Darby, Pennsylvania: Darby Books.

Flores, Angel, ed. *Great Spanish Short Stories.* New York: Dell, 1962.

Nist, John A., ed. *Modern Brazilian Poetry: An Anthology.* Repr. of 1962 ed. New York: Kraus Reprints, 1968.

Paz, Octavio, ed. *Anthology of Mexican Poetry.* Translated by Samuel Beckett. Bloomington: Indiana University Press, 1958.

Torres-Rioseco, Arturo, ed. *Short Stories of Latin America.* New York: Las Americas Publishing Company, 1963.

Oriental Literature

Anderson, G. L., ed. *The Genius of the Oriental Theater.* New York: Mentor Books, 1966.

Barondes, R. deRohan. *China: Lore, Legend and Lyrics.* New York: Philosophical Library, 1960.

Blocker, Joel, ed. *Israeli Stories: A Selection of the Best Contemporary Hebrew Writing.* New York: Schocken Books, Inc., 1965.

Casper, Leonard. *New Writing from the Philippines: A Critique.* Syracuse: Syracuse University Press, 1966.

Chai, Ch'u and Winberg Chai, eds. and trs. *The Humanist Way in Ancient China: Essential Works of Confucianism.* New York: Bantam Books, Inc., 1965.

Embree, Ainslie T., ed. *The Hindu Tradition.* New York: Random House, Inc., 1972.

Gibbs, Hamilton A. *Arabic Literature,* 2d ed. New York: Oxford University Press, 1974.

Giles, Herbert A., ed. and tr. *Gems of Chinese Literature.* New York: Paragon Book Reprint Corporation, 1965.

Gluck, Jay, ed. *Ukiyo: Stories of "the Floating World" of Postwar Japan.* New York: Vanguard Press, Inc., 1964.

Grossman, William L., ed. *Modern Brazilian Short Stories.* Berkeley: University of California Press, 1974.

Hanrahan, Gene Z., ed. *50 Great Oriental Stories.* New York: Bantam Books, Inc., 1965.

Henderson, Harold G. *Haiku in English.* Rutland, Vermont: Charles E. Tuttle, 1967.

Henderson, Harold G., ed. *Introduction to Haiku, Anthology of Poems and Poets from Basho to Shiki.* New York: Doubleday Anchor, 1958.

Keene, Donald, ed. *Anthology of Japanese Literature: Earliest Era to Mid-Nineteenth Century.* New York: Grove Press, Inc., 1955.

Khouri, Mounah A. and Hamid Algar, eds. *An Anthology of Modern Arabic Poetry.* Berkeley: University of California Press, 1974.

Kritzeck, James, ed. *Anthology of Islamic Literature: From the Rise of Islam to Modern Times.* New York: Mentor Books, 1966.

Narayan, Rasipuram Krishnaswami. *Gods, Demons, and Others.* New York: Viking Press, Inc., 1964.

Payne, Robert, ed. *The White Pony: An Anthology of Chinese Poetry.* New York: John Day Co., Inc., 1947.

Shimer, Dorothy Blair, ed. *The Mentor Book of Modern Asian Literature.* New York: New American Library, 1969.

So-Un, Kim. *The Story Bag: A Collection of Korean Folk Tales.* Translated by Setsu Higoshi. Rutland, Vermont: Charles E. Tuttle, 1955.

Yutang, Lin. *Famous Chinese Short Stories.* Repr. of 1953 ed. Darby, Pennsylvania: Darby Books.

Russian and East European Literature

Blake, Patricia and Max Hayward, eds. *Dissonant Voices in Soviet Literature.* Repr. of 1962 ed. Westport, Connecticut: Greenwood Press, Inc., 1975.

Blake, Patricia and Max Hayward, eds. *Half-way to the Moon: New Writing from Russia.* New York: Doubleday, 1965.

Dodson, Daniel B., ed. *Eight Great Russian Short Stories.* New York: Fawcett Book Group.

Ehrhard, Marcelle. *Russian Literature.* Translated by Philip Minto. New York: Walker and Company, 1963.

Garnett, Constance and Nathan Haskell Dale, trs. *Four Great Russian Short Novels.* New York: Dell, 1959.

Hamalian, Leo and Vera Von Wiren-Garczynski, eds. *Seven Russian Short Novel Masterpieces.* New York: Popular Library, 1967.

Houghton, Norris, ed. *Great Russian Plays.* New York: Dell, 1966.

Houghton, Norris, ed. *Great Russian Short Stories.* New York: Dell, 1958.

Ivanov, Y., ed. *A Treasury of Russian and Soviet Short Stories.* New York: Fawcett Book Group, 1971.

MacAndrew, Andrew R., ed. *Great Russian Short Novels.* New York: Bantam Books, Inc., 1969.

Reavey, George, ed. and tr. *Modern Soviet Short Stories.* New York: Grossett & Dunlap, Inc., 1961.

Reeve, Franklin D., ed. *Great Soviet Short Stories.* New York: Dell, 1962.

Selver, Paul, tr. *Anthology of Czechoslovak Literature.* Repr. of 1929 ed. New York: Kraus Reprint Co.

Scandinavian Literature

Billeskov-Jansen, F. J. and P. M. Mitchell, eds. *Anthology of Danish Literature,* new edition. Carbondale, Illinois: Southern Illinois University Press, 1971.

Sprinchorn, Evert, ed. *The Genius of the Scandinavian Theater.* New York: New American Library, 1964.

Yurka, Blanche, ed. *Three Scandinavian Plays.* New York: Washington Square Press, 1962.

Spanish Literature

Alpern, Hyman, ed. *Three Classic Spanish Plays.* New York: Washington Square Press, 1963.

Bernan, Gerald. *The Literature of the Spanish People.* 2d ed. Cambridge: Cambridge University Press, 1953.

deOnis, Harriet. *Spanish Stories and Tales.* Repr. of 1954 ed. Darby, Pennsylvania: Darby Books.

Flores, Angel, ed. *An Anthology of Spanish Poetry from Garcilaso to García Lorca.* Garden City, New York: Anchor, 1961.

Flores, Angel, ed. *Great Spanish Short Stories.* New York: Dell, 1962.

Literary History and Criticism

General World Literature

Benet, William Rose. *Reader's Encyclopedia.* 2d ed. (Illus.). 2 vols. New York: Thomas Y. Crowell Company, 1965.

Grigson, Geoffrey, ed. *The Concise Encyclopedia of Modern World Literature.* New York: Hawthorn Books, 1963.

Hornstein, Lillian H., et al., eds. *The Reader's Companion to World Literature.* rev. ed. New York: New American Library, 1973.

Ivask, Ivar and Gero van Wilpert, eds. *World Literature Since 1945: Critical Surveys of the Contemporary Literature of Europe and the Americas.* New York: Ungar, Frederick, Publishing Co., Inc., 1973.

Kostelanetz, Richard, ed. *On Contemporary Literature: An Anthology of Critical Essays on the Major Movements & Writings of Contemporary Literature.* Repr. of 1964 ed. New York: Arno Press.

Macy, John. *Story of the World's Literature.* New York: Liveright Publishing Corp.

Remenyi, Joseph, et al., eds. *World Literatures: Arabic, Chinese, Czechoslovak, French, German, Greek, Hungarian, Italian, Lithuanian, Norwegian, Polish, Romanian, Russian, Scottish, Swedish, and Yugoslav.* Repr. of 1956 ed. New York: Arno Press, 1968.

Classical Literature

Hadas, Moses. *History of Latin Literature.* New York: Columbia University Press, 1952.

Kitto, Humphrey D. *Greek Tragedy: A Literary Study.* 3d rev. ed. New York: Methuen Inc., 1961.

African Literature

Beier, Ulli, ed. *Introduction to African Literature.* 2d ed. London: Longman, Green & Company, Ltd., 1979.

Bohannan, Paul and Philip Curtin. *Africa and Africans.* rev. ed. New York: The Natural History Press, 1971.

Dathorne, O. R. and Willfried Feuser. *Africa in Prose.* Baltimore: Penguin Books, 1969.

Finnegan, Ruth. *Oral Literature in Africa.* Oxford: The Clarendon Press, 1970.

Jahn, Janheinz. *Neo-African Literature: A History of Black Writing.* New York: Grove Press, Inc., 1969.

Jones, Eldred, ed. *African Literature Today,* Issues 1–4. New York: Holmes & Meier Pubs., Inc., 1972.

Mbiti, John S. *African Religions and Philosophy.* New York: Doubleday and Co. Inc., 1970.

Mphahlele, Ezekiel. *The African Image.* 2d ed. Salem, New Hampshire: Merrimack Book Service, Inc., 1972.

Moore, Clark D. and Ann Dunbar. *Africa Yesterday and Today.* New York: Bantam Books, Inc., Pathfinder Editions, 1968.

Oliver, Roland and J. D. Fage, eds. *A Short History of Africa.* 3rd ed. England: Penguin Books, 1962.

Pieterse, Cosmo and Donald Munro, eds. *Protest and Conflict in African Literature.* New York: Holmes and Meier Pubs., Inc., 1969.

Tufuo, J. W. and C. E. Donkor. *Ashantis of Ghana. People with a Soul.* Accra, Ghana: Anowuo Educational Publications, 1969.

Wauthier, Claude. *The Literature and Thought of Modern Africa.* Repr. of 1967 ed. Westport, Connecticut: Greenwood Press, Inc.

French Literature

Bree, Germaine and Margaret Guiton. *The French Novel from Gide to Camus.* New York: Harcourt, Brace and World, 1962.

Cazamian, Louis. *History of French Literature.* Oxford: Oxford University Press, 1955.

Moore, Harry T. *Twentieth-Century French Literature.* Carbondale, Illinois: Southern Illinois University Press, 1966.

Turnell, Martin. *The Novel in France: Mme De Lafayette, Laclos, Constant, Stendhal, Balzac, Flaubert, Proust.* Repr. of 1951 ed. New York: Arno Press.

German Literature

Boesch, Bruno, ed. *German Literature.* London: Metheun Inc., 1971.

Friederich, Werner P. *An Outline-History of German Literature.* New York: Barnes and Noble, 1948.

Hatfield, Henry. *Modern German Literature: The Major Figures in Context.* Bloomington: Indiana University Press, 1968.

Italian Literature

Rimanelli, Giose and Kenneth J. Atchity, eds. *Italian Literature: Roots and Branches*. New Haven: Yale University Press, 1976.
Symonds, John A. *Italian Literature*. New York: G. P. Putnam's Sons, 1964.

Latin American Literature

Anderson-Imbert, Enrique. *Spanish American Literature: A History*. 2 vols. Detroit: Wayne State University Press.
Brushwood, John S. *The Spanish American Novel: A Twentieth-Century Survey*. Austin: University of Texas Press, 1975.
Torres-Rioseco, Arturo. *The Epic of Latin American Literature*. Berkeley: University of California Press, 1964.

Oriental Literature

Barondes, R. deRohan. *China: Lore, Legend, and Lyrics*. New York: Philosophical Library, 1960.
Keene, Donald. *Japanese Literature: An Introduction for Western Readers*. New York: Grove Press, 1955.
Liu, James Y. *Art of Chinese Poetry*. Chicago: University of Chicago Press, 1966.
Ming, Lai. *A History of Chinese Literature*. New York: Capricorn Books, 1966.
Pound, Ezra and Ernest Fenollosa. *The Classic Noh Theatre of Japan*. Repr. of 1959 ed. Westport, Connecticut: Greenwood Press Inc., 1977.
Scott, A. C. *The Kabuki Theatre of Japan*. New York: Collier, 1966.

Russian and East European Literature

Brewster, Dorothy. *East-West Passage: A Study in Literary Relationships*. London: George Allen and Unwin, Ltd., 1954.
Brown, Edward J., ed. *Russian Literature Since the Revolution*. rev. ed. New York: Macmillan Publishing Co., Inc., 1969.
Gifford, Henry. *The Novel in Russia: From Pushkin to Pasternak*. London: Hutchinson University Library, 1964.
Hayward, Max and Edward L. Crowley, eds. *Soviet Literature in the Sixties: An International Symposium*. New York: Frederick A. Praeger, 1964.
Mirsky, Dimitry S. *History of Russian Literature: From Its Beginnings to 1900*. Edited by Francis J. Whitfield. New York: Random House, Inc., 1958.

Muchnic, Helen. *An Introduction to Russian Literature.* rev. ed. New York: E. P. Dutton & Co., 1964.

Simmons, Ernest J. *Introduction to Russian Realism: Pushkin, Gogol, Dostoevski, Tolstoi, Chekhov, Sholokhov.* Bloomington: Indiana University Press, 1965.

Simmons, Ernest J. *Through the Glass of Soviet Literature.* New York: Columbia University Press, 1963.

Slonim, Marc. *The Epic of Russian Literature: From Its Origins Through Tolstoy.* New York: Oxford University Press, 1964.

Slonim, Marc. *From Chekhov to the Revolution: Russian Literature 1900–1917.* New York: Oxford University Press, 1962.

Slonim, Marc. *An Outline of Russian Literature.* New York: Oxford University Press, 1958.

Slonim, Marc. *Soviet Russian Literature: Writers and Problems, 1917–1977.* 2d ed. New York: Oxford University Press, 1977.

Scandinavian Literature

Marker, Frederick and Lise-Lone Marker. *The Scandinavian Theater: A Short History.* Rowman & Littlefield, Inc., 1975.

Spanish Literature

Stamm, James R. *A Short History of Spanish Literature.* New York: Doubleday, 1967.

Title Index

Editors

Warren Carrier, Professor of English and Chancellor at the University of Wisconsin—Platteville, received his doctorate in comparative literature from Occidental College and the Intercollegiate Program of Graduate Studies. He was founder and original editor of the *Quarterly Review of Literature*, is the author of several books, and has published numerous articles, translations, poems, reviews, and stories in a variety of scholarly and literary journals.

Kenneth A. Oliver is Professor Emeritus at Occidental College. After receiving his doctorate in comparative literature from the University of Wisconsin, he taught at Occidental College, where he established a comparative literature major, and served as head of the English department for sixteen years. Oliver's publications include *Our Living Language, Words Every College Student Should Know, A Sound Curriculum in English Grammar: Guidelines for Teachers and Parents,* and many articles in various literary journals.